ICTS 177 Reading Teacher
Teacher Certification Exam

By: Sharon Wynne, M.S
Southern Connecticut State University

"And, while there's no reason yet to panic, I think it's only prudent that we make preparations to panic."

XAMonline, INC.
Boston

To obtain permission(s) to use the material from this work for any purpose including workshops or seminars, please submit a written request to:

XAMonline, Inc.
21 Orient Ave.
Melrose, MA 02176
Toll Free 1-800-509-4128
Email: info@xamonline.com
Web www.xamonline.com
Fax: 1-781-662-9268

Library of Congress Cataloging-in-Publication Data

Wynne, Sharon A.
   Reading Teacher 177: Teacher Certification / Sharon A. Wynne. -2nd ed.
   ISBN 978-1-58197-993-0
   1. Reading Teacher 177.   2. Study Guides.   3. ICTS
   4. Teachers' Certification & Licensure.   5. Careers

Disclaimer:

The opinions expressed in this publication are the sole works of XAMonline and were created independently from the National Education Association, Educational Testing Service, or any State Department of Education, National Evaluation Systems or other testing affiliates.

Between the time of publication and printing, state specific standards as well as testing formats and website information may change that is not included in part or in whole within this product. Sample test questions are developed by XAMonline and reflect similar content as on real tests; however, they are not former tests. XAMonline assembles content that aligns with state standards but makes no claims nor guarantees teacher candidates a passing score. Numerical scores are determined by testing companies such as NES or ETS and then are compared with individual state standards. A passing score varies from state to state.

Printed in the United States of America   œ-1

ICTS: Reading Teacher 177
ISBN: 978-1-58197-993-0

TEACHER CERTIFICATION STUDY GUIDE

Table of Contents

Great Study and Testing Tips!

What to study in order to prepare for the subject assessments is the focus of this study guide but equally important is *how* you study.

You can increase your chances of truly mastering the information by taking some simple, but effective steps.

Study Tips:

1. <u>**Some foods aid the learning process**</u>. Foods such as milk, nuts, seeds, rice, and oats help your study efforts by releasing natural memory enhancers called CCKs (*cholecystokinin*) composed of *tryptopha*n, *choline*, and *phenylalanine*. All of these chemicals enhance the neurotransmitters associated with memory. Before studying, try a light, protein-rich meal of eggs, turkey, and fish. All of these foods release the memory enhancing chemicals. The better the connections, the more you comprehend.

Likewise, before you take a test, stick to a light snack of energy boosting and relaxing foods. A glass of milk, a piece of fruit, or some peanuts all release various memory-boosting chemicals and help you to relax and focus on the subject at hand.

2. <u>**Learn to take great notes**</u>. A by-product of our modern culture is that we have grown accustomed to getting our information in short doses (i.e. TV news sound bites or USA Today style newspaper articles.)

Consequently, we've subconsciously trained ourselves to assimilate information better in <u>neat little packages</u>. If your notes are scrawled all over the paper, it fragments the flow of the information. Strive for clarity. Newspapers use a standard format to achieve clarity. Your notes can be much clearer through use of proper formatting. A very effective format is called the <u>*"Cornell Method."*</u>

Take a sheet of loose-leaf lined notebook paper and draw a line all the way down the paper about 1-2" from the left-hand edge.

Draw another line across the width of the paper about 1-2" up from the bottom. Repeat this process on the reverse side of the page.

Look at the highly effective result. You have ample room for notes, a left hand margin for special emphasis items or inserting supplementary data from the textbook, a large area at the bottom for a brief summary, and a little rectangular space for just about anything you want.

3. Get the concept then the details. Too often we focus on the details and don't gather an understanding of the concept. However, if you simply memorize only dates, places, or names, you may well miss the whole point of the subject.

A key way to understand things is to put them in your own words. If you are working from a textbook, automatically summarize each paragraph in your mind. If you are outlining text, don't simply copy the author's words.

Rephrase them in your own words. You remember your own thoughts and words much better than someone else's, and subconsciously tend to associate the important details to the core concepts.

4. Ask Why? Pull apart written material paragraph by paragraph and don't forget the captions under the illustrations.

Example: If the heading is "Stream Erosion", flip it around to read "Why do streams erode?" Then answer the questions.

If you train your mind to think in a series of questions and answers, not only will you learn more, but it also helps to lessen the test anxiety because you are used to answering questions.

5. Read for reinforcement and future needs. Even if you only have 10 minutes, put your notes or a book in your hand. Your mind is similar to a computer; you have to input data in order to have it processed. *By reading, you are creating the neural connections for future retrieval.* The more times you read something, the more you reinforce the learning of ideas.

Even if you don't fully understand something on the first pass, *your mind stores much of the material for later recall.*

6. Relax to learn so go into exile. Our bodies respond to an inner clock called biorhythms. Burning the midnight oil works well for some people, but not everyone.

If possible, set aside a particular place to study that is free of distractions. Shut off the television, cell phone, pager and exile your friends and family during your study period.

If you really are bothered by silence, try background music. Light classical music at a low volume has been shown to aid in concentration over other types. Music that evokes pleasant emotions without lyrics are highly suggested. Try just about anything by Mozart. It relaxes you.

7. <u>**Use arrows not highlighters.**</u> At best, it's difficult to read a page full of yellow, pink, blue, and green streaks. Try staring at a neon sign for a while and you'll soon see that the horde of colors obscure the message.

A quick note, a brief dash of color, an underline, and an arrow pointing to a particular passage is much clearer than a horde of highlighted words.

8. <u>**Budget your study time.**</u> Although you shouldn't ignore any of the material, *allocate your available study time in the same ratio that topics may appear on the test.*

Testing Tips:

1. Get smart, play dumb. Don't read anything into the question. Don't make an assumption that the test writer is looking for something else than what is asked. Stick to the question as written and don't read extra things into it.

2. Read the question and all the choices _twice_ before answering the question. You may miss something by not carefully reading, and then re-reading both the question and the answers.

If you really don't have a clue as to the right answer, leave it blank on the first time through. Go on to the other questions, as they may provide a clue as to how to answer the skipped questions.

If later on, you still can't answer the skipped ones . . . _**Guess.**_ The only penalty for guessing is that you _might_ get it wrong. Only one thing is certain; if you don't put anything down, you will get it wrong!

3. Turn the question into a statement. Look at the way the questions are worded. The syntax of the question usually provides a clue. Does it seem more familiar as a statement rather than as a question? Does it sound strange?

By turning a question into a statement, you may be able to spot if an answer sounds right, and it may also trigger memories of material you have read.

4. Look for hidden clues. It's actually very difficult to compose multiple-foil (choice) questions without giving away part of the answer in the options presented.

In most multiple-choice questions you can often readily eliminate one or two of the potential answers. This leaves you with only two real possibilities and automatically your odds go to Fifty-Fifty for very little work.

5. Trust your instincts. For every fact that you have read, you subconsciously retain something of that knowledge. On questions that you aren't really certain about, go with your basic instincts. **Your first impression on how to answer a question is usually correct.**

6. Mark your answers directly on the test booklet. Don't bother trying to fill in the optical scan sheet on the first pass through the test.

Just be very careful not to miss-mark your answers when you eventually transcribe them to the scan sheet.

7. Watch the clock! You have a set amount of time to answer the questions. Don't get bogged down trying to answer a single question at the expense of 10 questions you can more readily answer.

Foundations of Reading

"Any child, who doesn't learn how to read early and well, will not easily master other skills and knowledge and is unlikely to ever flourish in school or in life."
Reading is Rocket Science, American Federation of Teachers

"If our teaching of reading is to be an art, we need to draw from all we know, think and believe in order to create something beautiful."
Lucy Calkins

This guide was developed to serve the needs of test takers on the PreK-6 level who are preparing for the Foundations of Reading certification test. The quotes which introduce this work point to the crucial nature and significance of effective teaching of reading for our children and our nation's future.

The competencies and skills shared in this guide are also intended to support the educator new to reading certification, in ongoing teaching and learning in Reading. Therefore, sample strategies, web resources, student trade books, picture book citations, and explanations of ready-to-use practices are included.

This guide had a specified page limit and is designed for immediate use. The web resources and bibliographies provided will allow the reader to keep up with new research or investigate a particular strategy, referenced theorist, or term in a deeper, more detailed fashion. In addition, there is in the Appendix, a dictionary of words and terms essential to one's knowledge base as a reading teacher. Yet another study guide is a directory of key reading theorists included for your use as well.

It is my hope that this study guide will merit placement in your home or on your classroom professional library shelf for use as you begin your teaching career. Enjoy and share with your colleagues and parents, as we work together to nurture lifelong readers and writers.

Please let XAMonline know how you are able to use this guide to help you in your teacher certification experience and in your ongoing or future teaching and learning.

THIS PAGE BLANK

SUBAREA I.   **LANGUAGE, READING, AND LITERACY**

COMPETENCY 1.0   UNDERSTAND THE NATURE OF LANGUAGE AND LANGUAGE DEVELOPMENT.

Skill 1.1   Recognize that written language is a symbolic system.

Throughout history, stories have been passed through generations using oral language. For centuries, this was the not only the only form of communication; it was the only method for recording events. As time passed, stories changed and it became important to society that information be recorded in another manner.

To this end, written language was born. Written language is a symbolic system of communication. It ties oral words to a concept (letter/word) and is then recorded in some way (e.g., on paper). Each language has its own method of recording information. Some languages use a symbol system in which one item on the paper may represent an entire sentence or concept.

This is not the case in English. In the English language, sounds, which comprise oral language, are transcribed into letters and letter combinations. As these letters are connected together, they form individual words. Words are then combined into sentences, ideas, and paragraphs.

With this symbolic system there is continuity among all users of the language. All English speakers can convey and share their thoughts and ideas with other English-speaking people. The same can be said for all other languages.

Skill 1.2   Demonstrate knowledge of major theories of language development, cognition, and learning.

Over the years, theorists of language development have disagreed on many levels. One major disagreement can be traced to the 1950's when two predominant theories emerged.

Proponents of behaviorism believed that language learning was the direct result of situations experienced by the child. Children were thought to learn language largely because of environmental influences.
On the other hand, nativist theorists believed that language was most influenced by biology or innate characteristics. They believed that the ability to learn and generate language was intrinsic to being human. They placed less emphasis on outside factors which might influence the language development process.

Eventually, these two opposing viewpoints merged to form the interactionist position. This stance indicates that children learn language as a result of inherent predetermined skills and influences from the surrounding environment.

It is this combination approach that is most accepted in today's society. In relation to reading, it is important to understand the fact that reading is language-based. Children who struggle in language developmental will almost certainly have difficulty obtaining a solid foundation in reading skills.

As language develops, children begin to understand how sounds blend together to form words, how words go together to form sentences, and how sentences go together to form stories. It is through these stories and sentences that meaning is conveyed from one party to another. Children's language learning, however, is rarely as sequential and tidy as this description implies.

If a child is unable to convey meaning or draw conclusions from the message that someone else is sending, they miss a key component of communication. With this skill missing, the natural progression that text conveys meaning is also flawed. Since the ultimate goal of reading is comprehension or understanding, one can see the significant deficit these children experience.

Speech pathologists who specialize in language development can therefore be an essential component to helping children with language disorders. In this way, these trained specialists can also help in preventing and remediating language issues, which will help reading skills.

In summary, language development is crucial to the progress students will experience in reading. Language and reading go hand in hand and this fact should be remembered when bringing in professionals with expertise to help work with children who are struggling.

Cognitive Development

Children go through patterns of learning beginning with pre-operational thought processes and move to concrete operational thoughts. Eventually they begin to acquire the mental ability to think about and solve problems in their head because they can manipulate objects symbolically. Children of most ages can use symbols such as words and numbers to represent objects and relations, but they need concrete reference points. It is essential children be encouraged to use and develop the thinking skills that they possess in solving problems that interest them. The content of the curriculum must be relevant, engaging, and meaningful to the students.

The teacher of special needs students must have a general knowledge of cognitive development. Although children with special needs may develop cognitively at a rate different from other children, a teacher needs to be aware of some of the activities appropriate for each stage to determine what should be taught and when it should be taught.

The following information about cognitive development was taken from the Cincinnati Children's Hospital Medical Center at www.cincinattichildrens.org

Some common features in a progression from simple to more complex cognitive development are as follows:

Childhood (ages 6-12)

Children begin to develop the ability to think in concrete ways. Concrete operations are thinking operations performed in the presence of the object and events that are to be used. Examples include how to combine (addition), separate (subtract or divide), order (alphabetize and sort/categorize), and transform (change things such as 25 pennies=1 quarter) objects and actions.

Adolescence (ages 12-18)

Adolescence marks the development of more complex thinking skills, including abstract thinking, the ability to reason from known principles (e.g., to form own new ideas or questions), the ability to consider many points of view according to varying criteria (e.g., to compare or debate ideas or opinions), and the ability to think about the process of thinking.

What cognitive developmental changes occur during adolescence?

During adolescence (between 12 and 18 years of age), the developing teenager acquires the ability to think systematically about logical relationships within a problem. The transition from concrete thinking to formal logical operations occurs over time. Every adolescent progresses at varying rates in developing his/her ability to think in more complex ways. Each adolescent develops his/her own view of the world. Some adolescents may be able to apply logical operations to school work long before they are able to apply them to personal dilemmas. When emotional issues arise, they often interfere with an adolescent's ability to think in more complex ways. The ability to consider possibilities, as well as facts, may influence decision making, in either positive or negative ways.
Some common features indicating a progression from simple to more complex cognitive development include the following:

Early adolescence

During early adolescence, the use of more complex thinking is focused on personal decision making in school and home environments, including the following:

-Begins to demonstrate use of formal logical operations in schoolwork.

-Begins to question authority and the standards of society.
-Begins to form and verbalize his/her own thoughts and views on a variety of topics, usually more related to his/her own life, such as:
- which sports are better to play.
- which groups are better to be included in.
- what personal appearances are desirable or attractive.
- what parental rules should be changed.

Middle adolescence

With some experience in using more complex thinking processes, the focus of middle adolescence often expands to include more philosophical and futuristic concerns, including the following:

Often questions and analyzes more extensively.
Thinks about and begins to form his / her own code of ethics.
Thinks about different possibilities and begins to develop own identity.
Thinks about and begins to systematically consider possible future goals
Thinks about and begins to make his/her own plans.
Begins to think long term.
Use of systematic thinking begins to influence relationships with others.

Late adolescence

During late adolescence, complex thinking processes are used to focus on less self-centered concepts as well as personal decision making, including the following:
Increased thoughts about more global concepts such as justice, history, politics, and patriotism.

Develops idealistic views on specific topics or concerns.
Debates and develops intolerance of opposing views.
Begins to focus thinking on making career decisions.
Begins to focus thinking on emerging role in adult society.

What encourages healthy cognitive development during adolescence?

The following suggestions will help to encourage positive and healthy cognitive development in the adolescent:

Include adolescents in discussions about a variety of topics, issues, and current events.

Encourage adolescents to share ideas and thoughts with adults.
Encourage adolescents to think independently and develop their own ideas.
Assist adolescents in setting their own goals.
Stimulate adolescents to think about possibilities of the future.
Compliment and praise adolescents for well thought-out decisions.
Assist adolescents in re-evaluating poorly-made decisions for themselves.

Normality in child behavior is influenced by social attitudes and cultural beliefs about what is normal for children (e.g., the motto for the Victorian era was "Children should be seen and not heard"). However, criteria for what is "normal" involves consideration of these questions:

- **Is the behavior age appropriate?** An occasional tantrum may be expected for a toddler, but is not typical for a high school student.
- **Is the behavior pathological in itself?** Drug or alcohol use would be harmful to children, regardless of how many engage in it.
- **How persistent is the problem?** A kindergarten student initially may be afraid to go to school. However, if the fear persisted into first or second grade, then the problem would be considered persistent.
- **How severe is the behavior?** –Self-injurious, cruel, and extremely destructive behaviors, would be examples that require intervention.
- **How often does the behavior occur?** –An occasional tantrum in a young child or a brief mood of depression in an adolescent would not be considered problematic. However, if the behaviors occur frequently, that behavior would not be characteristic of normal child development.
- **Do several problem behaviors occur as a group?** – Clusters of behaviors, especially severe behaviors that occur together, ,may be indicative of a serious problem, such as schizophrenia.
- **Is the behavior sex-appropriate?** Cultural and societal attitudes towards gender change over time. While attitudes towards younger boys playing with dolls or girls preferring sports to dolls have relaxed, children eventually are expected as adults to conform to the expected behaviors for males and females.

Certain stages of child development have their own sets of challenges, and it should be kept in mind that short-term undesirable behaviors can and will occur over these stages. Child development is also a continuum, and children may manifest these problem behaviors somewhat earlier or later than their peers.

About 15-20% of the school-aged population between 6 and 17 years old receive special education services. The categories of learning disabilities and emotional disturbance are the most prevalent. Exceptional students are very much like their peers without disabilities. The main difference is that they have an intellectual, emotional, behavioral, or physical deficit that significantly interferes with their ability to benefit from education.

Skill 1.3   Demonstrate knowledge of the principles of new language acquisition.

There are several different factors that influence early literacy and language acquisition. They include:

1 The intellectual, social and emotional development of the child
2 The culture of the family
3 Socio economic circumstances
4 The support the child receives in reading development in the home – presence of print, books and the reading level of the parents
5 Prior experience with printed materials
6 Parental attitudes toward reading
7 Attendance in a pre-school setting

Skill 1.4   Demonstrate an understanding of the phonemic, morphemic, semantic, syntactic, and pragmatic systems of language and their relation to the reading and writing processes.

The phonemic language system involves the understanding of the sounds in words. It encompasses things such as rhyming, beginning and ending sounds, and how many syllables are in a word. A phoneme is the smallest unit of sound in a language. In English there are generally forty-four sounds, which are represented by the 26 letters of the alphabet.

The morphemic language system refers to meaning.. A morpheme is the smallest unit of meaning in the language. In the word "cats," there are two morphemes: cat and s. An unbound morpheme is one which stands alone, such as cat. A bound morpheme must be attached to something to make sense. The "s" plural marker is a bound morpheme in this example.

Semantics. Semantics refers to the meaning of words and the manner in which they are put together to convey meaning. Semantics can vary by changing one or more words in a sentence. Even if the main nouns and verbs are not changed and simply conjunctions or modifiers are changed, the meaning of the sentence can be significantly altered.

In reality, instruction and modeling in both semantics and syntax are equally important. They are interdependent for both oral and written language. Students who have difficulty grasping the understanding of these skills may require more explicit teaching in this area.

For students for whom English is not their primary language, this may also be a concern. The semantics and syntax of each language varies and applying the rules for one language to another can result in misunderstanding

Syntax. Syntax by definition involves the way words are put together to form a language, or its grammar. It includes the idea of nouns, verbs, adjectives, adverbs and all of the other labels given to specific categories of words. There are bodies of research on polar opposite ends of the spectrum when it comes to the direct teaching of traditional grammar. One camp believes that it is important for students to be given specific instruction in this area. They believe that explicit and specific instruction provides the foundation students need to later develop appropriate skills. Some strategies used include diagramming sentences, word sorts, and categorizing groups of words. The other camp asserts that the identification of words by these labels is pointless. They believe that through practice and modeling of appropriate language with correct syntax, students will develop these skills naturally. Generally, they think that students will be able to use nouns and adjectives correctly whether or not they can identify and name the specific words as either nouns or adjectives.

Pragmatics. The pragmatic language system involves appropriate language use in social situations. This includes knowing when it is acceptable to use informal language or slang to when more formal language is called for (e.g. compare how one might talk to a peer as opposed to a principal). It involves recognizing colloquial phrases as well as other social cues necessary to participate in general daily life activities.

COMPETENCY 2.0   UNDERSTAND THE DEVELOPMENT OF LITERACY.

Skill 2.1   Recognize the importance of literacy for personal and social growth.

It is important for literacy to be a part of every individual's lifelong learning. As the reading specialist, it is important to encourage literacy development within both school and home. Many incentive programs and parenting workshops are provided in schools to help with this process.

Reading Is Fundamental© (RIF) is one such program for low-income families. This program encourages reading and helps to take literacy into the homes by providing students with free books. Typically, there is a theme and other social events involved with RIF as well.

While incentive programs are certainly worth the effort, it is equally important to share with students and parents the need for continued literacy skills in life. Educating the parents to use books as a tool to increase their own personal skills helps them to serve as models for their children. Working in conjunction with the librarian, the schools can provide a collection of parenting books that can help parents and grandparents better support their children's literacy. Having parent education nights where parenting ideas are shared can be useful for more than just improving literacy skills.

Additionally, some teachers have found it beneficial to have social gatherings around the theme of reading. Family reading nights, where the entire family comes into the school to hear books being read or to read together, are a great way to capitalize on the social aspects of literacy. Book groups are another strategy some schools have implemented including parents, other teachers, and students in the mix. In this approach, all parties read the same book and then come together to share and have a discussion around the topic. It is a relaxed, non-threatening atmosphere and provides everyone a chance to enjoy literacy and good literature.

Skill 2.2 **Demonstrate knowledge of the interrelation of language and literacy acquisition.**

Children learn more readily at an early age. This is why teaching the basic skills of reading at an early age is so important in reading development. Many children enter school with a deficiency in prior knowledge because they haven't been read to at home. In Kindergarten, teachers need to surround the children with print, read to them at every opportunity, and balance the reading with instruction about letters and sounds.

The stages of literacy development are:

0 to 4 years
- Enjoys having an adult read to them
- Likes to "pretend read" books
- Reads pictures of familiar books
- Recognizes some of the letters of the alphabet
- Practices printing their own name
- Starts to sound out letters

Beginning Literacy – 5 – 7 years
- Starts to develop phonemic awareness
- Uses invented spelling when writing
- Can associate letters with sounds
- Starts to sound out words
- Can recognize some sight words
- Uses picture clues
- Starts to use context clues when reading

Literacy – 9 – 12 years
- Reads fluently
- Comprehends what is read
- Has an expanded vocabulary
- Writes for various purposes
- Can use a dictionary for help with spelling
- Can express personal tastes in reading

The typical variation in literacy backgrounds that children bring to reading can make teaching more challenging. Often a teacher has to choose between focusing on the learning needs of a few students at the expense of the group or focusing on the group at the risk of leaving some students behind academically. This situation is particularly critical for children with gaps in their literacy knowledge who may be at risk in subsequent grades for becoming "struggling readers."

Phonological awareness means the ability of the reader to recognize the sounds of spoken language. This recognition includes how these sounds can be blended together, segmented (divided up), and manipulated (switched around). This awareness then leads to phonics, a method for teaching children to read. It helps them "sound out words."

Development of phonological skills begins during the pre-K years. Indeed by the age of 5, a child who has been exposed to rhyme can recognize a rhyme. Such a child can demonstrate phonological awareness by filling in the missing rhyming word in a familiar rhyme or rhymed picture book.. We teach children phonological awareness when we teach them the sounds made by the letters, the sounds made by various combinations of letters and to recognize individual sounds in words.

Phonological Awareness Skills include:

I. Rhyming and syllabification
2. Blending sounds into words—such as pic-tur-bo-k
3. Identifying the beginning or starting sounds of words and the ending or closing sounds of words
4. Breaking words down into sounds-also called "segmenting" words
5. Recognizing other smaller words in the big word, by removing starting sounds, "hear" to ear

On a continuum the stages of literacy development are defined as:

1. Role Play Reading
2. Experiential Reading
3. Early Reading
4. Transitional Reading
5. Independent Reading

When students some to school they are at varying stages of the first three levels depending on their experience with reading in the home. The key indicators of each stage are:

1. Role Play – students can imitate reading behaviors, such as holding the book upright, reading the pictures to tell a story, and understanding stories they listen to. During this time, students also start to develop a favorite list of books that they like to hear again and again.
2. Experiential – students realize that print carries meaning. During this phase they are more concerned with getting the meaning of the words rather than reading the words correctly. They also use prior knowledge to predict which words come next.
3. Early reading – students are beginning to reread familiar texts with ease and recognize different forms of writing, such as a letter, a story, and a recipe. . They can talk about the illustrations in a book and can retell a story in their own words, giving details about the setting, characters, and plot.
4. Transitional reading – students can integrate many of the features of the text to construct meaning. They can recognize stereotyping and prejudice in a text and can select different reading material to suit different purposes.
5. Independent reading – students can recognize various forms of writing and express their response in writing. They can comprehend abstract topics and can make connections between sections of the text.

Skill 2.3   **Recognize that students need opportunities to integrate their use of literacy through reading, writing, listening, speaking, viewing, and representing visually.**

Reading. As they read widely, students are exposed to grammar, spelling, and other conventions on a regular basis. As the teacher, it is important to take time to point out these areas to the students who may otherwise pass them by without a second thought. One important strategy for helping in this area is the Directed Reading Thinking Activity(DRTA). This strategy developed by Russell Stauffer (1969) allows the teacher to guide the thinking of the student usually in making predictions and improving comprehension. An adaptation to this strategy would allow the teacher to guide the thinking of the students to recognize and identify the conventions of language.

Writing. Since writing is a more formal skill than oral language, the conventions will be slightly different. Many times students will write the same way they speak which is usually unacceptable for written language. The editing process is probably the most effective method for helping students achieve improved use of grammar, spelling, syntax and semantics. Peer editing and teacher editing provide excellent tools for students.

Listening. Listening is an art. Many times it is obvious that students are hearing what the speaker is saying, but are not truly listening. Setting the purpose for an oral presentation and providing graphic organizers are strategies that help structure listening activities. Having a purpose for listening with a graphic organizer, allows the students to better filter out irrelevant information. Demonstration of correct and incorrect language conventions would provide the students with the opportunity to discriminate the difference.

Speaking. When orally presenting information, it is important the student realize the necessity of using appropriate language conventions. Having the students practice presentations out loud into a tape recorder is a technique that allows them to critique themselves or others and provide valuable feedback.

Skill 2.4 **Demonstrate knowledge of the importance of giving students learning opportunities in all aspects of literacy (e.g., as readers, writers, thinkers, interpreters, reactors, or responders).**

The Language Arts curriculum involves the experiences, study, and appreciation of how language is used for communication through listening, speaking, reading and writing. All four components work together to help develop language abilities. When the various processes are integrated and used within meaningful contexts, this facilitates learning the facets of language.

In the reading classroom, the teacher engages the students in a wide range of experiences and texts so that they can develop an increasing command over the English language. They learn to use and respond to language effectively and understand that literacy is of utmost importance in their lives. The principles that underlie the teaching of reading are:

1 Language is the most powerful tool that students will have for communicating with others through listening, speaking, reading and writing. It is the way by which they will be able to make sense of the world, express their experiences and thoughts and develop ideas.
2 Language is an active process of making meaning by drawing on all sources and ways of knowing.
3 The way students use the components of language is personal and is tied to their individual learning styles and circumstances.
4 Cultural identity is explicitly expressed through language.
5 The prior knowledge and background experiences students bring to learning language directly impact language learning.
6 Language is developmental as students develop sight words, fluency and accuracy in reading over time.
7 The concepts of language are best taught as a whole rather than in isolation.

8   The experiences teachers provide to students should be meaningful and built around experiences that help stimulate ideas.

9   Students need to be aware of the strategies and processes they use to construct meaning.

10 Frequent opportunities must be provided for students to assess their own learning, and they need feedback about their performance.

11 Both formative and summative assessment will help the teacher assess students' language learning.

In order to become fluent readers, students need to have phonemic and graphophonic awareness. This is provided through instruction in the classroom and by practicing the strategies for reading. Listening skills are important for students to hear the individual letter sounds and they need to speak clearly in order to pronounce them. These aspects of language learning are the foci of teachers in the early grades to about Grade 3.

COMPETENCY 3.0   UNDERSTAND THE HISTORY, THEORETICAL MODELS, AND PHILOSOPHIES OF READING EDUCATION.

Skill 3.1   Demonstrate familiarity with research related to and philosophies and theoretical models of reading education and their relevance to instruction.

In reading, there has been no greater debate than the approach to teaching reading. Educators speak of the great pendulum in education where strategies and methods seem to swing from side to side like a giant pendulum. In reading instruction, this great swing has swung between three major philosophies: literature-based, phonics, and whole language.

Literature-Based- In this method, teachers deliver reading instruction through true literature pieces in their entirety. Using trade books, poetry, or other forms of literature, the students are exposed to and taught all of the necessary skills to be successful readers.

Phonics- The phonics instructional approach involves teaching phonics skills explicitly and sequentially that children need to be readers. In this approach, the children read controlled texts, which revolve around the current phonics skill being introduced and practiced. These controlled texts provide numerous repetitions of the skills.

Whole Language- Whole language instruction revolves around a readers' workshop approach. In this manner, the students have assigned tasks to complete that take them through reading skills. The teacher works with the children to guide them through the necessary tasks, but does not sequentially teach skills until they come up in context. It is though through the process of reading many different texts students will learn the necessary skills to become readers.

Currently, the most widespread method of teaching reading is a **balanced literacy** approach. It combines the best from the three approaches described above. Perhaps the greatest fallacy in educational circles is that there is "one right way" to teach reading. Teachers need to have an arsenal of theoretical and practical knowledge to drawn upon when faced with students' differing problems in reading. They must be able to drawn from a variety of approaches to best meet their students' needs.

Skill 3.2 **Demonstrate knowledge of the history of reading education and the contributions of past and present literacy leaders to current theory and practice and the knowledge base.**

Knowledge of the Significant Theories, Approaches, Practices and Programs for Developing Reading Skills and Reading Comprehension

Decoding

In the late 1960's and the 1970's, many reading specialists, most prominently Fries (1962), believed that successful decoding resulted in reading comprehension. This meant that if children could sound out the words, they would then automatically be able to comprehend the words. Many teachers of reading and many reading texts still subscribe to this theory.

Asking questions

Another theory or approach to the teaching of reading that gained currency in the late sixties and the early seventies was the importance of asking inferential and critical thinking questions of the reader which would challenge and engage children with the text. This approach to reading went beyond the literal level of what was stated in the text to an inferential level of using text clues to make predictions and to a critical level of involving the child in evaluating the text. While asking engaging and thought-provoking questions is still viewed as part of the teaching of reading, it is only viewed currently as a component of the teaching of reading.

Comprehension Skills

As various reading theories, practices, and approaches percolated during the 1970's and 1980's, many educators and researchers in the field came to believe that the teacher of reading had to teach a set of discrete "Comprehension Skills" (Otto et al, 1977). Therefore the reading teacher became the teacher of each individual comprehension skill. Children in such classrooms came away with: main idea, sequence, cause and effect, and other concepts that were supposed to make them better comprehenders. However, did it make them lifelong readers?

Transactional Approach

During the late 1970's and early 1980's, researchers in the field of education, psychology and linguistics, began to examine how the reader comprehends. Among them was Louise Rosenblatt who posited that reading is a transaction between the reader and the text. It is Rosenblatt (1978) who explained successful reading as the reader constructing a meaning from the text that reflected both the reader and the text.

She described two general purposes for reading: *efferent* and *aesthetic*. Efferent reading is looking for and remembering information to use functionally. Examples would be filling out a job application, reading a story in preparation for a test, or reading a newspaper article to find out who won the state basketball championship. Aesthetic reading is done to connect one's own life to the text, to be swept away by the beauty of a poem, or to respond emotionally to a book such as *Bridge to Terabithia*.

These differing purposes call for somewhat different reading strategies: one might skim the newspaper article for basketball information but read a poem closely ten times and create mental images of different passages. Lastly, when children are asked to read all fiction differently (What's the setting? What's the main conflict in the plot? There will be a test on this on Thursday!), it can thwart a child's joy in the written word and work against the student's desire to be a lifelong reader.

Bottom-up, Top-down, Interactional Theories of Reading

Bottom-up theories of reading assume that children learn from part-to-whole starting with the smallest segments possible. Instruction begins with a strong phonics approach, learning letter-sound relationships and often using basal readers or *decodable books*. Decodable books are vocabulary-controlled using language from word families with high predictability. Thus we get sentences like "Nan has a tan fan." Reading is seen as skills-based, and the skills are taught one at a time.

Top-down theories of reading suggest that reading begins with the reader's knowledge, not the print. Children are seen as having a drive to construct meaning. This stance views reading as moving from the whole to the parts. An early top-down theory was the *whole word* approach. Children memorized high-frequency words to assist them in reading the Dick and Jane books of the 30s. Then teachers helped children discover letter-sound correspondences in what they read. A more recent top-down theory is the *whole language* approach. This approach was influenced by research on how young children learned language. It was thought that children could learn to read as naturally as they learned to talk. Children were surrounded by print in their classrooms, using quality literature often printed in Big Books and were viewed as writers from the start. Hence journals kept by kindergarten children. Advocates of whole language viewed the "skill'em-drill'em-and kill'em" approach based on bottom-up theories as a deadly dull introduction to the world of reading.

Interactive theories of reading combine the strengths of both bottom-up and top-down approaches. Teachers need to be able to teach decoding, vocabulary, and comprehension skills to support children's drive for meaning and desire for a stimulating exchange with high-quality literary texts from their earliest days in school. Strategies include shared, guided, and independent reading, Big Books, reading and writing workshops, and the like. Today this approach is called the *balanced literacy approach.* It is considered to be a synthesis of the best from bottom-up and top-down methods.

Literacy and Literacy Learning

To be literate in the 21st century world means more than being able to read and write. To live well and happily in today's society an individual has to be able to read not only newspapers and books, but emails, blogs, directions for how to use one's cell phone, and the like. There has evolved a "disconnect" between the isolated reading comprehension skills the schools were teaching and the literacy skills including listening and speaking that are crucial for employment and personal and academic success. Thornburg (1992, 2003) has also noted that technology capacities and the ability to communicate online are now integral parts of our sense of literacy.

Cooper (2004) views literacy as reading, writing, thinking, listening, viewing, and discussing. These are not viewed as separate activities or components of instruction, but rather as developing and being nurtured simultaneously and interactively. Children learn these abilities by engaging in authentic explorations, readings, projects and experiences.

Just as in learning how to ride a bike, the learner goes through various approximations before learning how to actually ride the bike, so too does the reader with the scaffold (support) of the teacher go through various approximations before developing his/her own independent literacy skills and capacities.

Emergent Literacy: This is the concept that young children are emerging into reading and writing with no real beginning or ending point. Children are introduced into the word of print as soon as their parents read board books to them at the age of one or two. When children scribble write or use invented spelling during the preschool years, they reveal themselves as detectives of the written word, having watched parents and teachers make lists, write thank-you notes, or leave written messages. This view of the reader assumes that all children have a drive to make meaning in print and will begin doing it almost on their own if surrounded by a print-rich environment.

Reading Readiness: This is a view which is antithetical to emergent literacy in that it assumes that all children must have mastered a sequence of reading skills <u>before</u> they can begin to read. Once a popular notion regarding early reading, this belief is now considered outmoded.

Language Acquisition: It is continuous and never-ending. From the perspective of this notion, all children come to school with a language base which the school must build on. As a consequence of the connection between oral language and reading, it is important that schools build literacy experiences around the language the child brings to the school.

Prior Knowledge, Schemata, Background, and Comprehension

Schemata are structures which represent generic concepts stored in our memory (Rumelhart, 1980). Young children develop their schemata through experiences. Prior knowledge and the lack of experiences in some cases influence comprehension. The more closely the reader's experiences and schemata approximate those of the writer, the more likely the reader is to comprehend the text. It is obvious that for many children from non-native English language speaking backgrounds and perhaps for those from struggling socioeconomic family structures schemata deficits indicate the need for intense teacher support as these children become emergent and early readers.

Often the teacher will have to model and scaffold for the child the steps to form a schemata from the information provided in a text.

Comprehension

Cooper defines comprehension as: "a strategic process by which readers construct or assign meaning to a text by using the clues in the text and their own prior knowledge." Comprehension is a process where the reader transacts with the text to construct or assign meaning. Reading and writing are both interconnected and mutually supportive. Comprehension is a strategic process in which readers adjust their reading to suit their reading purpose and the type or genre of text they are reading. Narrative and expository texts require different reading approaches because of their different text structures. Strategic readers also call into play their metacognitive capacities as they analyze texts so that they are aware of the skills needed to construct meaning from the text structure.

The Role of Literature in Developing Literacy

The balanced literacy approach advocates the use of "real literature"—recognized works of the best of children's fiction and non-fiction trade books and winners of such awards as the Newbery and Caldecott medals for helping children develop literacy.

Balanced literacy advocates argue that:

- Real literature engages young readers and assures that they will become lifelong readers.

- Real literature also offers readers a language base that can help them expand their expressiveness as readers and as writers.

- Real literature is easier to read and understand than grade-leveled texts.

There are districts in the United States where the phonics-only approach is still heavily embedded. However, the majority of school districts would describe their approach to reading as the balanced literacy approach which includes phonics work as well as the use of real literature texts.

It is important to go online and to visit the key resources of the NCTE, National Council of Teachers of English, and the IRA, International Reading Association, to keep abreast of the latest research in the field.

Skill 3.3 **Demonstrate familiarity with relevant reading research from general education and how it has influenced literacy education.**

See skill 3.1, 3.2 and 3.4

Skill 3.4 **Demonstrate knowledge of trends, controversies, and issues in reading education.**

As in all areas of education, reading instruction has seen its swing of the pendulum. There have been many different suggested approaches to teaching reading over the years.

Phonetic Reading Instruction: From the 1950s into the 1970s, most reading instruction was based on phonics. Students were taught, mostly through workbooks, the sounds the letters and letter combinations made and then applied them to very controlled texts. These _Dick and Jane_ type of readers were found in almost every school and many adults remember learning to read using these types of books.

Reading for Meaning: Then in the 1970s and the 1980s the understanding of children as individuals began to take forefront. In this way, teachers began to focus on providing children with books with more meaning available. Use of phonics slipped into the background as teachers began to look at other methods for determining what struggles children were having in texts. Based on new knowledge about language development, teachers approached reading from a more linguistic stance, using the semantic, syntactic and graphophonemic cueing systems to teach students to read. This developed into making the connection to writing. Teachers began to realize the importance of the reading and writing connection

Whole Language Instruction: The whole language movement reached its height in the 1990s. In this method, reading instruction was taught through trade books and authentic literature. Individual skills were taught as they came up in context. Reading and writing were seen as interrelated and mutually reinforcing. The focus was on reading as a linguistic act.

Each time a new thinking process has erupted; teachers, parents and students have either accepted innovations in reading instruction or clamored for a return to what worked in the past. In recent times, the government has become more and more involved in the instructional process and the term *research based reading instruction* has become a part of the daily vocabulary in schools. There are controversies about the implementation of the most appropriate methods for teaching reading to students and this will continue in the future. However, the key isn't picking one method, but knowing the students and their needs and implementing the best strategies to create what works best for those children in your class.

Skill 3.5   Recognize reading skills and strategies and the role each plays in reading development.

When the National Reading Panel came out with their report identifying major ideas within reading instruction, the field of reading changed. Now teachers have a better understanding of what skills are necessary for the appropriate development of reading in students. The paramount skills of reading are:

- Phonemic Awareness
- Phonics
- Fluency
- Comprehension
- Vocabulary

These skills are the foundational areas in which instruction must be provided to ensure reading development and progress.. Phonemic awareness is the earliest level of skill. It is an understanding of the oral sounds of language and how they work together and later relate to reading. It involves such subskills as rhyme, identification of initial and final sounds, and segmenting words into syllables.

Phonics is the next level of development. Students make the connection between the sounds letters make and how they are written. Sometimes referred to as decoding, this is when students begin to apply their oral skills to the print on the page.

Once students become proficient at developing the ability to decode, they must increase their skills to a fluent level. Fluency is a combination of the pace of reading and the prosody (tone and inflection,) with which passages are read. Research shows that students who are able to read in a fluent manner usually have increased comprehension. Comprehension is the understanding of what has been read, which is the goal of reading. Vocabulary development is pervasive across all areas of reading and begins with a sight word reading vocabulary and progresses throughout the levels into more complex meaning-based understanding of words and their purpose in text.

All of these skills should be the focus of quality reading instruction. In special education, the same reading skills must be in place to ensure success. However, the manner in which they are presented may vary significantly. Additionally, it may be necessary to vary the order, materials or other factors to help students progress.

Skill 3.6   Recognize the scope and sequences for reading instruction at all developmental levels, pre-K through grade 12.

Though within any district there will be a specific reading curriculum required to to ensure all students are making appropriate progress toward achieving state and federal standards, there is a general progression of skills the teacher should keep in mind.

Pre-K- Kindergarten: Teachers help students ages of four through six build phonemic awareness skills. Children master the alphabetic principle, learn a bank of sight words, book handling skills, and build schema of the story structures of narrative. They will also come to love telling and hearing stories both orally and in written form.

First and Second Grade: The shift occurs here from phonemic awareness to phonics. Students associate oral sounds with written letters and through both decoding and encoding, become readers and writers. Sight vocabulary is important at this time as well, as students need to be able to read words quickly and efficiently.

Third, Fourth, and Fifth Grades: Third grade is a transitional year for beginning readers. It is here that the first shift from learning to read to reading to learn occurs. Phonics skills become solidified and a greater emphasis is placed on vocabulary, fluency, and comprehension skills.

Middle School: In middle school, students analyze literature and expand their selections of reading. In literary study, more figurative texts are read, with many fewer literal interpretations possible. During this time content area reading expands and becomes a much greater part of day-to-day instruction than the reading of literature.. Writing across the curriculum is a method teachers use to consolidate students' understanding in many different subjects.

High School: High school reading is centered on learning from reading. It is expanded to all content areas as the central method for delivering information to the students. In English classes, students read and discuss both the classics and modern literature.. Students develop their thinking skills through the process of trying to understand texts presented. The notion of "text" expands to include film and other media. Technological literacy becomes as important as traditional ideas of literacy. Preparing students to be critical thinkers in and out of the school setting is the most important learning that occurs in high school.

COMPETENCY 4.0   UNDERSTAND THE NATURE OF READING AND THE LANGUAGE ARTS.

Skill 4.1   **Recognize reading as the process of constructing meaning through the interaction of the reader's existing knowledge, the information suggested by the written language, and the context of the reading situation, and recognize that reading should be taught as a process.**

Reading is a complex set of skills for students to master. The end result is comprehension. Students can decode the text, read with fluency, have an adequate vocabulary, yet if they are unable to transform all of those skills into something meaningful, they have accomplished nothing.

In order to create meaning, students must interact with the text. They must use the skills of decoding and comprehension to make connections to information they have within their own life experiences and those in the text in order to bring meaning to life. This is an ongoing, recursive process that is its own reward. That is, students who read widely become better readers. Or put another way, students learn how to read by reading.

Skill 4.2   **Demonstrate knowledge of emergent literacy and the experiences that support it.**

See skill 7.3

Skill 4.3   **Demonstrate an understanding of the interrelation between reading and writing and between listening and speaking.**

See skill 2.3

Skill 4.4   **Demonstrate an understanding of the role of metacognition in reading and writing and in listening and speaking.**

The word "metacognition" means thinking about one's own thinking. The prefix "meta" means above. When students think metacognitively, they metaphorically stand above their own reasoning, observing and analyzing it. Teachers invite students to think metacognitively when making a miscue (as in reading "the large gray goose" as "the large gray goods"), asking, "Does that make sense?" The student then applies his/her implicit knowledge of semantics and concludes that another word fits better and self-corrects, changing goods to goose.

When reading a passage written in chronological order, the student uses a metacognitive strategy if after reading points first and second, and then losing track of the third point, the student stops herself to search the text for a marker for the third point and then goes on, confident she is following the author's developing ideas. When writing a simple essay, the student thinks metacognitively when they re-read the body of their paper and ask themselves, "Does the reader need to have a paraphrase of my topic sentence at about this point?" Or when a student writer asks, "Can my reader really SEE what I'm describing in this section?" When a student listens to another's persuasive speech and mentally asks, "How in heavens name did he reach THAT conclusion?" we once again see metacognitive thinking

Skill 4.5   Recognize the importance of promoting the integration of language arts into all content areas.

Whether a student is learning social studies, science, or mathematics, reading and writing in particular are vital to understanding those subject areas. Teachers of biology, for example, will help their students learn if they teach students how to READ biology texts. Coaching and modeling for students how to read figures, graphs, and text structures such as cause-and-effect and hierarchical relationships will assist learners in a biology context. Similarly, a history teacher will assist students' comprehension when he/she teaches text structures such as chronological ordering or cause-and-effect. Also, having students make presentations (using reading, writing, speaking, and listening) in the content areas will further solidify their learning. Simply put, every teacher is a teacher of reading.

COMPETENCY 5.0 UNDERSTAND THE INFLUENCE OF INDIVIDUAL DIFFERENCES AND DIVERSITY ON LANGUAGE DEVELOPMENT AND READING ACQUISITION.

Skill 5.1 Demonstrate an understanding of the impact of physical, perceptual, emotional, social, cultural, environmental, and intellectual factors on learning, language development, and reading acquisition.

There are several educational learning theories that can be applied to classroom practices. One classic learning theory is Piaget's stages of development, which consists of four learning stages: sensorimotor stage (from birth to age 2); pre-operation stages (ages 2 to 7 or early elementary); concrete operational (ages7 to 11 or upper elementary); and formal operational (ages 7-15 or late elementary/high school). Piaget believed children passed through this series of stages to develop from the most basic forms of concrete thinking to sophisticated levels of abstract reasoning.

Some of the most prominent learning theories in education today include brain-based learning and the Theory of Multiple Intelligences. Supported by recent neurological research, brain-based learning suggests that knowledge about the way the brain processes and retains information can enable educators to design effective learning environments. What follows are twelve principles about the brain that may have implications for teaching practices:

- The brain is social
- The brain is a complex adaptive system
- The search for meaning is innate
- We use patterns to learn more effectively
- Emotions are crucial to developing patterns
- Each brain perceives and creates parts and whole simultaneously
- Learning involves focused and peripheral attention
- Learning involves conscious and unconscious processes
- We have at least two ways of organizing memory
- Learning is developmental
- Complex learning is enhanced by challenge (and inhibited by threat)
- Every brain is unique

Educators can use these principles to help design methods and environments in their classrooms to maximize student learning in the area of reading.

Howard Gardner's theory of multiple intelligences, suggests that students learn in (at least) eight different ways. These include visually/spatially, musically, verbally, logically/mathematically, interpersonally, intrapersonally, bodily/kinesthetically. and naturally (i.e., through an understanding of the natural world)..

The theory of constructivism posits that students actively construct knowledge by using mental schema, background knowledge, and experience. Teachers facilitate this process, not by "pouring" knowledge into the waiting vessel of the student, but instead by the student actively shaping and formulating knowledge in a social situation with stimulating materials created or assembled by the teacher. Teachers further scaffold or support student learning within the "zone of proximal development," (Vygotsky) that place where the student can, with assistance, comprehend and master the material. Researchers have shown that the constructivist model is based on four assertions:

1. The learner creates knowledge.
2. The learner constructs and relates new knowledge to existing knowledge.
3. The learner shapes and constructs knowledge in terms of life experiences and social interactions.
4. In constructivist learning communities, the student, teacher and classmates establish knowledge cooperatively on a daily basis.

Kelly (1969) states "human beings construct knowledge systems based on their observations parallels Piaget's theory that individuals construct knowledge systems as they work with others who share a common background of thought and processes." Constructivist learning for students is dynamic and ongoing. For constructivist teachers, the classroom becomes a place where students are encouraged to interact with the instructional process by asking questions and posing new questions to old theories. The use of cooperative learning that encourages students to work in supportive learning environments using their own ideas to stimulate questions and propose outcomes is a major aspect of a constructivist classroom.

Metacognitive learning theory deals with "the study of how to help the learner gain understanding about how knowledge is constructed and about the conscious tools for constructing that knowledge" (Joyce and Weil, 1996). The metacognitive approach to learning involves teaching the student to process his/her own learning and to think about his/her own thinking reflectively. For example, once students solve a math problem, they then reflect on how they analyzed the problem and the steps of their solution. They might also think about alternative ways to reach the same destination. If they discover errors in their own problem solving, student can be taught not only to find the errors in their thinking but also WHY they made such errors. Thus the student becomes an active participant in the learning process and the teacher facilitates a process of higher level thinking.

Social and behavioral theories look at the social interactions of students in the classroom that instruct or impact learning opportunities in the classroom. The psychological approaches behind both theories are subject to individual variables that are learned and applied either proactively or negatively in the classroom. The stimulus of the classroom can promote conducive learning or evoke behavior that is counterproductive for both students and teachers. Students are social beings that normally gravitate to action in the classroom, so teachers must be cognizant in planning classroom environments that are provide both focus and engagement in maximizing learning opportunities.

Designing classrooms that provide optimal academic and behavioral support for a diversity of students in the classroom can be daunting for teachers. The ultimate goal for both students and teachers is creating a safe learning environment where students can construct knowledge in an engaging and positive classroom climate of learning.

No one of these theories will work for every classroom, and a good approach is to incorporate a range of learning styles in a classroom. Still, under the guidance of any theory, good educators will differentiate their instructional practices to meet the needs of their students' abilities and interests in reading using various instructional practices.

Reading and the ELL Learner

Research has shown that there is a positive and strong correlation between a child's literacy in his/her native language and his/her learning of English. The degree of native language proficiency and literacy is a strong predictor of English language development. Children who are literate and engaged readers in their native language can easily transfer their skills to a second language (i.e. English).

What this means is that teacher educators should not approach the needs of ELL learners in reading the same as they do native speakers. Those children whose families are not from a focused oral literacy and reading culture in the native language will need additional oral language rhymes, read-alouds, and singing as supports for reading skills development in both their native and the English language.

Visual and auditory perceptions, in particular, are very important in the reading process. Inaccurate visual perception can lead to misidentification of letters, which in turn will inhibit the application of phonics skills. For instance, a child who looks at a letter o and sees a letter c will have difficulty decoding that word correctly, even if it she knows what sound both letters make. There are some typical developmental visual perceptual difficulties in young children. Up until third grade, some reversals, such as p, b, and d are acceptable and part of the normal developing process.

Auditory perceptual difficulties can be as difficult as visual ones in affecting students' reading development. In this case, it may affect both the development of phonemic awareness and phonics skills. Children with reoccurring ear infections or allergies can develop intermittent hearing loss or a jumbling of sounds. In this way, they do not hear the models well and then when asked to reproduce them are inaccurate.

Skill 5.2 **Demonstrate knowledge of how contextual factors in the school (e.g., grouping procedures, school programs, assessment) can influence student learning and reading.**

See skills 13.1 and 14.3

Skill 5.3 **Recognize how differences among students influence their literacy development, and recognize the need to adjust reading instruction to meet the needs of diverse students (e.g., gifted, English as a New Language, special needs) as well as those who speak nonstandard dialects.**

See skills 13.1 and 14.3

Skill 5.4 **Recognize the need to understand, respect, and value cultural, linguistic, and ethnic diversity.**

As previously discussed, meeting the need of all learners provides a challenge to the reading specialist. Assessment data is the key place to begin to determine what appropriate activities should be implemented to help children to become better readers.

Beyond skills and progress, it is imperative that reading be fun and motivating for the students. It is important to select the children's literature that catches the interest of the students. For students lagging behind, publishers now make numerous series of low reading level yet high interest texts to address these issues.

Boys and girls tend to read different types of books as well. Generally, boys may be drawn to more exciting books, even comic books or newspapers. It may not be the typical reading material that you see in schools, but the skills and activities can easily be taught using alternative materials such as these.

It is also necessary to make sure that teachers address different genres of literature. Exposing children to poetry is just as important as reading fiction and nonfiction selections. Reading plays and songs and other less traditional genres not only provide exposure for the children, but can also help address specific skill deficits.

Multicultural reading can help bridge any gaps that might exist with students for whom English is a second language. This type of literature can help them to make personal connections with the text that are essential for good reading comprehension. Also, multicultural materials enrich other students, offering insights into different cultural practices within society.

Selecting a wide range of literature has the promise of becoming meaningful and personal to a wide range of students. Incorporating various reader response activities will continue to engage students with texts. Having the students excited by what they read is what will produce lifelong readers.

COMPETENCY 6.0   **UNDERSTAND STRATEGIES FOR CREATING A CLASSROOM ENVIRONMENT THAT PROMOTES STUDENTS' INTEREST IN READING.**

Skill 6.1   **Demonstrate an understanding of ways to create a literate environment that fosters interest and growth in all aspects of literacy.**

Strategies for Planning, Organizing, Managing, and Differentiating Reading Instruction to Support the Reading Development of All Students

The physical set up of your classroom is exceedingly important to support the effective development of all children. The homey look of the classroom belies its deliberate design as a space where children can experience, practice, share and learn. Some teachers have done away with the large desk and use smaller tables instead. Sharon Taberski advocates for young children K-3 adjusting the height of the table legs so the children can use the tables as writing spaces and sit on the floor. Taberski gives each of her children a personal 12"x 9"x 2" tray on which they place their home possessions, books, homework, and folders. These materials are kept in a small storage unit near the coat closet during the day.

Children put their completed homework in a wire basket and notes from parents or the office in a second wire basket. Supplies such as pencils, markers, crayons, scissors, and erasers are not brought from home, but rather are available for all in the class from "community" containers at the center of each of the children's tables.

All the children's reading, writing, and individual math folders are stored together in plastic bins in the meeting area. Every child has an individual book bag which is kept in one of two large wicker baskets set in different areas of the room.

This storing of materials away from children decreases their "fiddling with" their belongings during class, makes the room look much neater, and frees the children to focus on their learning experiences, rather than where their belongings are at any given time of day.

As you can see on the accompanying diagram, the 10'x10' meeting area is the center of classroom learning. This is where the whole class is gathered at the beginning of the reading and the writing workshop and for sharing sessions. It is also the demonstration and modeling center for both the teacher and for children.

Generally, the presenter sits on the adult chair (in some balanced literacy classrooms, this is a rocking chair) near the easel with the chart. Generally, this chair and the easel are strategically positioned so that the teacher can see the door and any visitors or urgent messages from the office. Rearranging furniture during the day takes away from instruction time and is disruptive. Have a designated comfortable section of the room that can be a gathering place for a literacy community and then organize the rest of the classroom activities around that center.

Understanding Our Role and Goal

The conference table which is at the back of the room (see diagram) is another key piece of classroom furniture. It is the place where the four or five children and the teacher confer, wait, and do their work. Having children come to a set conference table, rather than the teacher's going to them (although some teachers do advocate going to the children) saves time as far as Taberski is concerned. It serves to keep her and the children on task.

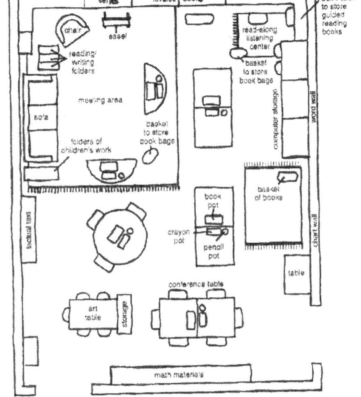

Taberski keeps two separate trays of supplies: a small magnetic board, letters, chalkboard, chalk, sentence strips, index cards, and blank books for her demonstrations during her conferences. She believes that teachers should store materials close to where they are used, so the teacher does not have to take time from the child to get up and get the materials.

The Classroom Library

On the tables, Taberski generally has book crates with books that are not leveled. Children choose from these books during the first independent reading session of her day which is from 8:40-9:00. During the second reading session from 9:30-10:20 the children select books from the leveled reading bins which are stored on the bookcase shelves.

Beyond the leveled books, which have already been discussed, Taberski also maintains a non-leveled, nonfiction library which includes dictionaries, atlases, almanacs, and informational books related to the themes, projects and investigations that the children will undertake throughout the year.

Beyond the leveled books and non-fiction books in the classroom, Taberski and other balanced literacy advocates generally include at least 10-15 big books which they routinely use to engage children with the text.

Since guided reading with groups of 6 children is a major part of the balanced literacy approach, Taberski and other disciplined and dedicated teacher educators "bundle" up six copies of selected books so that they can distribute them to their guided reading groups whenever they choose to do them. Taberski models the concept of a home library collection for the children by keeping books which she particularly likes in a bookcase behind her chair. She sometimes places "her" books on the easel so that they can be shared by the children and returned to her.

Wall Works

Much of creating a family atmosphere lies in the use of the room walls to document the children's learning experiences, skills work, and readings.

Generally at least one wall in a reading classroom is the Chart Wall. Charts with various spelling patterns discussed in class can be posted. If a child later has issues or concerns with that particular pattern, he or she should be directed to look at and to review the chart.

One of the centerpieces of the K-2 classroom is the High Frequency Word Chart. This is a growing list of commonly-used words which the teacher tapes under the appropriate beginning letter according to the children's directions. At the end of each month, the newest high frequency words go into the children's folders and become part of their spelling words. Therefore reading, writing, and spelling are all intricately connected.

Supplies for children K-3 and beyond can include:

A red plastic double pocket reading folder
A blue plastic double pocket reading folder
A four sectioned pressed board spelling/poetry folder
A 4" x 6" assessment notebook for reading
A 4" x 6" assessment notebook for writing
A reading response notebook (loose-leaf- 60 pages)
A handwriting notebook

The Reading Folder contains assessment notebooks, reading response notebooks, a Weekly Reading Log, and strategy sheets the child may be using that particular week.

The Assessment Notebook is a key evaluative tool and a recording document for the conscientious balanced literacy specialist. The teacher uses the notebook to record the child's running record, the retellings of stories shared by the child, and summarizing talks about leveled books read. Within the assessment books, the teacher also has notes about the child's progress, the strategies the child has learned to use well, the books he or she has read, and those strategies the child still needs to practice. These assessment notebooks must be kept accessible so that the teacher can use them to confer with the child, parents, and administrator as needed.

The reading response notebook becomes a compilation of reading strategy sheets and children's writings and art in response to literature.

The Weekly Reading Log allows the child to maintain for himself or herself the titles of books they have read and written a bit about the narrative, style, and genre of that given book.

Book Bags: These are 10" x 12" heavy duty freezer bags which keep 3-10 books a child is "working on" during his/her free time. The teacher generally matches the children to the books and changes these books as needed by the children.

Writing Folders

Children keep several pieces of writing in their folders at a time. Within the writing folder is also a handwriting notebook and a beginning word book as well. The Spelling/Poetry Folder is one which helps children focus on the sequence of letters in words and learn more how words work.

Balanced literacy advocates have a definite schedule for the teaching of reading and writing workshop from which they generally do not deviate. A sample follows.

8:40-9:00- FIRST INDEPENDENT READING/WORD STUDY GROUP

9:00-9:30- MEETING-WHOLE GROUP SESSION in the meeting area
Read Aloud, Shared Reading, or Shared Writing

9:30-10:30- READING WORKSHOP
Reading Conferences or Guided Reading
Second Independent Reading
Reading Share 10:20-10:30

10:30-10:40- Writing Mini Lesson or Writing Share

10:40-11:20- Writing Workshop Writing Conferences, Guided Writing, Modeled Writing, Independent Writing

(11:10-11:20)-Writing Share

Creation of an Environment that Promotes Love of Reading

The aforementioned creation of the meeting area and the reading chair (sometimes a rocking chair) with throw pillows around it promotes a love of reading. Beyond that, some classrooms have adopted an author's hat, decorated with the pictures of famous authors and book characters which children wear when they read from their own works.

Many classrooms also have children's storyboards, artwork, story maps, pop-up books, and "in the style of" writing inspired by specific authors. Some teachers buy calendars for the daily schedule which celebrate children's authors or types of literature. Children are also encouraged to bring in public library books and special books from their home libraries. The teacher can model this habit of sharing beautiful books and inviting stories from his or her home library.

In addition, news stories about children's authors, series books, television versions of books, theatrical film versions of books, stuffed toy book character decorations and other memorabilia related to books can be used to decorate the room.

Various chain book stores including Barnes and Nobles and Borders give out free book marks and promotional display materials related to children's books which can be available in the room for children to use as they read independently or in their guided groups. They might even use these artistic models to inspire their own book themed artifacts.

Skill 6.2 **Identify ways to use texts and trade books to stimulate interest; promote reading growth; foster appreciation for the written word; and increase the motivation of students to read widely and independently for information, pleasure, and personal growth.**

Reading for enjoyment makes it possible to go to places in the world we will never be able to visit, or perhaps when we learn about the enchantments of a particular place, we will set a goal of going there someday. When *Under the Tuscan Sun* by Frances Mayes was published, it became a best seller. It also increased tourism to Italy. Many of the readers of that book visited Italy for the first time in their lives.

In fiction, we can live through experiences that we will never encounter. We delve into feelings that are similar to our own or are so far removed from our own that we are filled with wonder and curiosity. In fact, we read because we're curious—curious to visit, experience, and know new and different things. The reader lives with a crowd of people and a vast landscape. Life is constantly enriched by reading, and the mind is constantly being expanded. To read is to grow. Sometimes the experience of reading a particular book or story is so delicious that we go back and read it again and again, such as the works of Jane Austen. We keep track of what is truly happening in the world when we read current best-sellers because they not only reflect what everyone else is interested in right now, they can influence trends. By reading publications like *Time* and *Newsweek* we can know in-depth what television news cannot cram in.

How do we model this wonderful gift for our students? We can bring those interesting stories into our classrooms and share the excitement we feel when we discover them. We can relate things that make us laugh so students may see the humor and laugh with us. We can vary the established curriculum to include something we are reading that we want to share. The tendency of students nowadays is to receive all of their information from television or the Internet. It's important for the teacher to help students understand that television and the internet are not substitutes for reading. They should be an accessory, an extension, a springboard for reading.

Another thing teachers can do to inspire students to become readers is to assign a book that you have never read before and read along with them, chapter by chapter. Run a contest and the winner gets to pick a book that you and they will read chapter by chapter. If you are excited about it and are experiencing satisfaction from the reading, that excitement will be contagious. Be sure that the discussion sessions allow for students to relate what they are thinking and feeling about what they are reading. Lively discussions and the opportunity to express their own feelings will lead to more spontaneous reading.

You can also hand out a reading list of your favorite books and spend some time telling the students what you liked about each. Make sure the list is diverse. It's good to include nonfiction along with fiction. Don't forget that a good biography or autobiography may encourage students to read beyond thrillers and detective stories.

When the class is discussing the latest movie, whether formally as a part of the curriculum or informally and incidentally, if the movie is based on a book, this is a good opportunity to demonstrate how much more can be derived from the reading than from the watching. Or how the two combined make the experience more satisfying and worthwhile.

Share with your students the excitement you have for reading. Successful writers are usually good readers. The two go hand-in-hand.

In order to discover multiple layers of meaning in a literary work, the first step is a thorough analysis, examining such things as setting, characters and characterization, plot (focusing particularly on conflicts and pattern of action), theme, tone, figures of speech, and symbolism. It's useful in looking for underlying themes to consider the author's biography, particularly with regard to setting and theme, and the date and time of the writing, paying particular attention to literary undercurrents at the time as well as political and social milieu.

Once the analysis is complete and data accumulated on the historical background, determine the overt meaning. What does the story say about the characters and their conflicts, where does the climax occur, and is there a denouement? Once the forthright, overt meaning is determined, then begin to look for undercurrents, subthemes that are related to the author's life and to what is going on in the literary, political, and social background at the time of writing.

In organizing a presentation, it's usually best to begin with an explication of the overt level of meaning and then follow up with the other messages that emerge from the text.

To *interpret* means essentially to read with understanding and appreciation. It is not as daunting as it is made out to be. Simple techniques for interpreting literature are as follows:

- **Context:** This includes the author's feelings, beliefs, past experiences, goals, needs, and physical environment. Incorporate an understanding of how these elements may have affected the writing to enrich an interpretation of it.
- **Symbols:** Also referred to as a sign, a symbol designates something which stands for something else. In most cases, it is standing for something that has a deeper meaning than its literal denotation. Symbols can have personal, cultural, or universal associations. Use an understanding of symbols to unearth a meaning the author might have intended but not expressed, or even something the author never intended at all.
- **Questions:** Asking questions, such as "How would I react in this situation?" may shed further light on how you feel about the work.

Skill 6.3   Identify ways to provide opportunities for students to select from a variety of written materials; to read extended texts; to offer creative and personal responses to literature, including storytelling; and to read for many authentic purposes.

See skill 6.2

Skill 6.4   Recognize the importance of modeling and discussing reading and writing as valuable, lifelong activities.

The goal of reading education is to encourage students to develop dispositions and attitudes toward lifelong learning. Teachers can encourage these in students by demonstration. Teachers who are readers and writers inspire their students as well. Sharing one's excitement about reading a recent bestseller, discussing the pros and cons of a novel brought to life in a film, and mentioning how one uses one's own journal will show students the importance of reading and writing in the teacher's life. Both modeling and oral discussions of how reading and writing help us solve problems and deal with issues are strategies that can be implemented in classrooms.

Another way to encourage lifelong reading is by exposing students to book clubs or or online literature discussion groups. This provides them with a community of readers from whom they can gain valuable insights into what they are reading.

Teaching the students that sometimes everyone has trouble understanding what they have read is a rationale for entering a discussion group to gain clarity. Simply talking to another person about the information can be the key to greater comprehension, whether in college or at the workplace.

Additionally, brain research shows that the most effective method for truly internalizing information is to teach a skill to someone else. In this way, modeling can be used to share information among people. In the work place, this can involve helping a coworker obtain a skill. This constant give and take of information is crucial for the success of a company, and companies will respect and utilize workers willing to help everyone in the company more than self-serving workers. Sharing this information and making these connections for students can better prepare them for the transition from school to work.

Skill 6.5   Identify strategies for using instructional and informational technologies to support reading and writing instruction.

When students are reading and something does not make sense, they should start with using the strategies described in detail in skill 19.1 like context clues, syntax, decoding and semantics. However, there are other times when the reader may need to look outside of the text at additional resources to ensure accurate. Students might begin with the glossary, if included in the same text. However, at other times, students may need to refer to some other mode of finding the meaning or pronunciation of words. Students may use a dictionary to help with these skills.

Dictionary skills are important for students to learn and use regularly. The dictionary can provide the reader with several different meanings for the word. The student can use the different meanings provided along with the contextual information they gained from the text to find the one that is most appropriate. They can also use the pronunciation guide to determine how to say the word, which will help later in reading.

Sometimes it is helpful to use synonyms or antonyms to help clarify meaning. A thesaurus is formatted similarly to a dictionary in design and layout. This can help the student to put the passage in more reader-friendly terms, or terms with which they are very familiar. The use of synonyms and antonyms is an excellent way to build vocabulary.

In today's society all of these tools can be found in various technological forms. There are online dictionaries and thesauruses. Additionally, there are pocket personal electronic dictionaries with built in thesauruses. There is also a reading pen, which you use to help you determine unknown words. The tip of the pen is rubbed lightly across the unknown word. The computer generated voice built into the pen speaks the word orally with the correct pronunciation for the student to hear. Then it provides the definition, synonyms, and antonyms on a digital display. On some models this information can also be repeated orally.

COMPETENCY 7.0 UNDERSTAND STRATEGIES FOR PROMOTING STUDENTS' WORD IDENTIFICATION, SPELLING, AND VOCABULARY SKILLS AND FLUENCY.

Skill 7.1 **Identify strategies for teaching students to monitor their own word identification through the use of syntactic, semantic, and graphophonemic relations.**

When using running records as a form of informal assessment, it is important to be sure and look at the types of errors the child is making. In this way, one can examine the strategies and errors the student makes in order to plan instruction, monitor progress, and assess skill levels. Even if not using a running record, teachers can use even more informal methods of using the errors a student makes to find significant ways to help the student improve in their reading.

Miscue analysis can be multi-faceted and provide both the teacher and reader with a wealth of important information. First, examining the methods a student uses to figure out unknown words helps the teacher to understand which methods require further instruction, fine tuning or have already been mastered. Typically, students use phonics skills (letter-sound correspondences), contextual clues (the other words in the sentence/passage), semantic analysis, or structural analysis techniques to solve problems in reading. It is not through one of these methods that a reader becomes more proficient, but rather through using a combination of all of the approaches.

After collecting the running record, teachers can then go back and look at which of strategies the students are using with success. Tallying is one method to use; in this way, the educator can see not only strategies used but also if one seems to be more dominant than others. This method points out specific strategies which are very weak for the student and would require more instruction. After this analysis, the teacher can develop an instructional plan to address weak areas

Additionally, the teacher can look at the student's ability to monitor their own reading and comprehension. Noting these self-monitoring attempts allows the teacher to see if the student recognizes when he/she made a mistake which does not make sense. This is a very important skill for readers to develop. Once they realize something does not make sense, are they able to go back and apply a correction strategy so as to not hinder comprehension. This becomes more important as the complexity of text increases.

Self-corrections by students begin to show a maturity of reading skills. However, students who make a tremendous number of self-corrections lack fluency in reading and will eventually lose some comprehension. Self-correction is an important step for readers, but during the learning process, we want students to pass through this stage rapidly, leaving in its place fluent, well comprehended reading.

Skill 7.2 **Demonstrate an understanding that spelling is developmental and is based on students' knowledge of the phonological system and of the letter names, students' judgments of phonetic similarities and differences, and students' ability to abstract phonetic information from letter names.**

Spelling itself is a developmental process. Students typically begin making squiggles or random symbols on paper to represent words. From here, they realize that letters are used to represent sounds, so they begin to write random strings of letters to convey meaning. At this point, the connection between letter sounds and the symbols begin to solidify. Students begin to write words as they sound, which is called "invented spelling." While spelling may not be accurate at this stage, children are encoding sounds in a way logical to them. Invented spelling looks somewhat like it sounds. Children first are able to encode beginning sounds (d for dog), ending sounds (bd for bed), and only later, middle sounds (big for big). They go through a period of "letter name" spelling in which letters literally stand for their sounds (tray written as tra; bee written as be; lazy written as laze). This is a very phonetic stage most children progress through on their way to transitional spelling, when children's writing comes closer to standard spelling but with identifiable error patterns. In this period children have assimilated some rules that they often overuse (for example, transitional spellers often may overuse the silent e rule). The last stage is conventional spelling. Children are helped to become conventional spellers by knowing Greek and Latin roots, affixes, word families, "demon words," and the like. The best way to become a good speller, however, is to read and write voraciously.

Skill 7.3   **Identify strategies for using phonics to teach students to use their knowledge of letter–sound correspondence to identify sounds as they construct meaning.**

Phonological Awareness

Phonological awareness means the ability of the reader to recognize the sounds or phonemes of spoken language. This recognition includes how these sounds can be blended together, segmented (divided up), and manipulated (switched around). This awareness eventually leads to phonics, a method for decoding language by unlocking letter-sound or grapheme-phoneme relationships.

Development of phonological skills for most children begins during the pre-K years. Indeed by the age of 5, a child who has been exposed to fingerplays and poetry can recognize a rhyme. Such a child can demonstrate phonological awareness by filling in the missing rhyming word in a familiar rhyme or rhymed picture book. The procedure of filling in a missing word is called the cloze procedure. It can be used in oral or print literacy activities.

One teaches children phonological awareness by directly pointing out the sounds made by letters singly (as in /b/) or in combination (as in /bl/), and to recognize individual sounds in words.

Phonological awareness skills include but are not limited to the following:

I. Rhyming and syllabification
2. Blending sounds into words—such as pic-tur-bo-k
3. Identifying beginning or initial phonemes and ending or final phonemes in short, one-syllable words
4. Breaking words down into sounds- which is also called "segmenting" words
5. Removing initial sounds, and substituting others. An example is /bat/ minus the /b/ with an /m/ substituted becomes /mat/.

The Role of Phonological Awareness in Reading Development

Instructional methods to teach phonological awareness may include any or all of the following:

1. Auditory games during which children recognize and manipulate the sounds of words, separate or segment the sounds of words, take out sounds, blend sounds, add in new sounds, or take apart sounds to recombine them in new formations.
2. Snap game- the teacher says two words. The children snap their fingers if the two words share a sound, which might be at the beginning or end of the word. Children hear initial phonemes most easily, followed by final ones. Medial or middle sounds are most difficult for young children to discriminate. One sees this in their oral responses as well as in their invented spelling. Silence occurs if the words share no sounds. Children love this simple game and it also helps with classroom management.
3. Language games model for children identification of rhyming words. These games help inspire children to create their own rhymes.
4. Read books that rhyme such as *Sheep in a Jeep* by Nancy Shaw or *The Fox on a Box* by Barbara Gregorich.
5. Share books with children that use alliteration (words that begin with the same consonant sound) such as *Avalanche, A to Z.*

Assessment of Phonological Awareness

These skills can be assessed by having the child listen to the teacher say two words. Then ask the child to decide if these two words are the same word repeated twice or two different words. When making this assessment, when using two different words, make certain that they only differ by only one phoneme, such as /d/ and /g/. Children can be assessed on words which are not real words that are familiar to them. Words used can be make-believe words.

The Role of Phonological Processing in the Development of Individual Students

Children who are raised in homes where English is not the first language and or where standard English is not spoken may have difficulty with hearing the difference between similar sounding words like "send" and "sent." Any child who is not in a home, day care, or preschool environment where English phonology operates may have difficulty perceiving and demonstrating the differences between English language phonemes. If children cannot hear the difference between words that "sound the same" like "grow" and "glow," they will be confused when these words appear in a print context. This confusion will of course, impact their comprehension.

Considerations for teaching phonological processing to ELL children include recognition by the teacher that what works for the English language speaking child from an English language speaking family does not necessarily work in other languages.

Research recommends that ELL children learn to read initially in their first language. It is critical that ELL learn to speak English before being taught to read English. Research supports that oral language development lays the foundation for phonological awareness.

All phonological instruction programs must be tailored to the children's learning backgrounds. Rhymes and alliteration introduced to ELL children should be read or shared with them in their first language, if at all possible.

Struggling Readers

"Students who cannot read by age 9 are unlikely to become fluent readers and have a greater tendency to drop out"
Beth Antunez

Among the causes of reading difficulties for some children (and adults) are auditory trauma or ear infections that affect their ability to hear speech. Such children need one-on-one support with articulation and perception of different sounds. When a child says a word such as "parrot" incorrectly, repeat it as a question using the correct pronunciation as a model. If the child "gets" the sound correctly after your question, all is well. Extra support was needed. If the child still has difficulty with pronunciation after repeated instances, then consult with a speech therapist or audiologist. Early identification of medical conditions that affect hearing is crucial to reading development.

Points to Ponder

Phonological awareness is auditory.
It does not involve print.
It begins before children have learned letter-sound relationships.
It is the basis for the successful teaching of phonics and spelling.
It can and must be taught and nurtured.
It precedes and must be in place before the alphabetic principle can be taught.

Phonemic Awareness

"The two best predictors of early reading success are alphabetic recognition and phonemic awareness."
  Marilyn Jager Adams

"In order to benefit from formal reading instruction, children must have a certain level of phonemic awareness. . . phonemic awareness is both a prerequisite for and a consequence of learning to read."
  Hallie Kay Yopp

Phonemic awareness is a specific skill within the broader category of phonological awareness. Probably developing fairly late, it is the knowledge that words are composed of individual phonemes that can be blended.

Theorist Marilyn Jager Adams who researches early reading has outlined five basic types of phonemic awareness tasks.

Task 1- Ability to hear rhymes and alliteration.
For example, the children would listen to a poem, rhyming picture book or song and identify the rhyming words heard which the teacher might then record or list on chart.

Task 2- Ability to do oddity tasks (recognize the member of a set that is different (odd)among the group. For example, the children would look at the pictures of grass, a garden and a rose, answering, Which one starts with a different sound?

Task 3 –The ability to orally blend words and split syllables.
For example, the children say the first sound of a word and then the rest of the word and put it all together as a single word.

Task 4 –The ability to orally segment words.
For example, the ability to count sounds. The child would be asked to count or clap the sounds in "hamburger."

Task 5- The ability to do phonics manipulation tasks.
    For example, replace the "r" sound in rose with a "p" sound.

The Role of Phonemic Awareness in Reading Development

Children who have problems with phonics generally have not acquired or been exposed to phonemic awareness activities at home or in preschool-grade 2. This includes extensive songs, rhymes and read–alouds.

Instructional Methods

Since the ability to distinguish between individual sounds, or phonemes, within words is a prerequisite to association of sounds with letters and manipulating sounds to blend words—a fancy way of saying "reading," the teaching of phonemic awareness is crucial to emergent literacy (early childhood K-2 reading instruction). Children need a strong background in phonemic awareness in order for phonics instruction (sound –spelling relationship-printed materials) to be effective.

Instructional methods that may be effective for teaching phonemic awareness can include:

- Clapping syllables in words

- Distinguishing between a word and a sound

- Using visual cues and movements to help children understand when the speaker goes from one sound to another

- Incorporating oral segmentation activities which focus on easily distinguished syllables rather than sounds

- Singing familiar or "piggyback" songs (e.g. Happy Birthday, Knick Knack Paddy Wack) and replacing key words with those of a different ending

- Dealing children a deck of picture cards and having them sound out the words for the pictures on their cards or calling for a picture by asking for its first and last sound.

Consideration for ELL Students

Given the demographics of our country with its influx of New Americans, the likelihood is that you will be teaching at least some children who are from a non-native English speaking background. Therefore, as a conscientious educator, it is important that you understand the special factors involved in supporting children's second language literacy development.

Not all English phonemes are present in various ELL native languages; for example, the sound of /th/ does not appear in Spanish. Some native language phonemes may and do conflict with English phonemes.

It is recommended that all teachers of reading and particularly those who are working with ELL students use meaningful, student-centered, and culturally customized activities. These activities may include the following: language games, word walls, and poems. Some of these activities might, if possible, be initiated in the child's first language and then reiterated in English.

Assessment of Phonemic Awareness

Teachers can maintain ongoing logs and rubrics for assessment throughout the year of phonemic awareness for individual children. Such assessments would identify particular stated reading behaviors or performance standards, the date of observation of the child's behavior (in this context-phonemic activity or exercise), and comments.

The rubric or legend for assessing these behaviors might include the following descriptors:
- demonstrates or exhibits reading behavior consistently,
- makes progress/strides toward this reading behavior, and
- has not yet demonstrated or exhibited this behavior.

Depending on the particular phonemic task the teacher models, the performance task might include:

- Saying rhyming words in response to an oral prompt
- Segmenting a word spoken by the teacher into its beginning, middle and ending sounds
- Counting correctly the number of syllables in a spoken word

Phonological awareness involves the recognition that spoken words are composed of a set of smaller units such as onsets and rimes, syllables, and sounds.

Phonemic awareness is a specific type of phonological awareness which focuses on the ability to distinguish, manipulate and blend specific sounds or phonemes within an individual word.

Think of phonological awareness as an umbrella and phonemic awareness as a specific spoke under this umbrella.

Phonics deals with printed words and the learning of sound-spelling correlations, while phonemic awareness activities are oral.

In reviewing reading research and theory, new distinctions and definitions appear often. The body of reading knowledge changes over time. The information and definitions in this guide are those accepted in the year of its publication and the time of its authoring and updating. As changes occur in accepted theories, they will be made in the guides and in the certification exams.

"If you believe that you learn to read by reading, you must learn to want to read. Reading to children, therefore models both the "how" and "why" of reading."
Helen Depree and Sandra Iversen-Early Literacy in the Classroom

"The long talk that parents have put off about the ways of the world might need to be an introduction to the facts about the English alphabet."
Terrence Moore-Ashbrook Center Fellow-Principal of Ridgeview Classical Schools in Fort Collins, Colorado

Use of Reading and Writing Strategies for Teaching Letter-sound Correspondence

Provide children with a sample of a single letter book (or create one from environmental sources, newspapers, coupons, circulars, magazines or your own text ideas). Make sure that your already published or created sample includes a printed version of the letter in both upper and lower case forms. Make certain that each page contains a picture of something that starts with that specific letter and also has the word for the picture. The book you select or create should be a predictable one in that when the picture is identified, the word can be read.

Once the children have been provided with your sample and have listened to it being read, challenge them to each make a one letter book. Often it is best to focus on familiar consonants for the single letter book or the first letter of the child's first name. Using the first letter of the child's first name invites the child to develop a book which tells about him or her and the words that he or she finds. This is an excellent way to have the reading and writing workshop enhance the teaching of the alphabetic principle. Encourage children to be active writers and readers by finding words for their book on the classroom word wall, in alphabet books in the special alphabet book bin and in grade and age appropriate pictionaries, (dictionaries for younger children which are filled with pictures).

Of course, the richest resource within the reading and writing workshop classroom for teaching and fostering the alphabetic principle lies in the use of alphabet books as anchor books for inspiring students writing. While young children in grades K-1 will do better with the one letter book authoring activity, children in grades 2 and beyond can truly be inspired and motivated by alphabet books to enhance their own reading, writing and alphabetic skills. Furthermore, use of these books which have and are being produced in a variety of formats to enhance social studies, science and mathematical themes, provide an opportunity for even young children to create a meaningful product that authenticates their content study as it enhances alphabetic skills and, of course, print awareness

An annotated bibliography of selected alphabet books has been provided in the bibliography section of this guide. It was limited by space considerations, but the teacher can with no expense and with much pleasure catch up on the latest titles and identify those most appropriate for the grade taught by visiting a bookstore. Hold the print book in hand and then consider selecting an alphabet book that has a particularly inviting concept, art style, or adaptable format within the children's capacity to use as a model.

For instance, Tina Hoban uses actual color photographs of letters in her *26 Letters and 99 Cents*. Children may want to make clay letters or create letter sculptures that develop their own alphabet book similar to Hoban's. If nutrition is the science topic, children might want to examine Ehlert's very accessible *Eating the Alphabet: Fruits and Vegetables from A to Z*. This, combined with an examination of the fruits and vegetables in a local store (perhaps a pleasant walk from the school and a quick break from the routine) can yield a wonderful alphabet book on fruits and vegetables which can also include those fruits and vegetables eaten in various cultures (i.e. mangos, plantains, pomegranates).

The alphabet book can also offer the class a chance to work collaboratively using a template page created by the teacher. Completion of this collaborative work can be shared with peers in another class and parents and be kept in the classroom library as a model for the following year's class with their recognition and acceptance of the authors!

Assessment Throughout the Year of Graphophonemic Awareness

The teacher will want to maintain individual records of children's reading behaviors demonstrating alphabetic principle/graphophonemic awareness.

The following performance standards should be part of a record template form for each child in grades K-1 and beyond as needed (depending on ELL or special needs):

- Match all consonant and short vowel sounds.
- Read one's own name.
- Read one syllable words and high frequency words.
- Demonstrate ability to read and understand that as letters in words change, so do the sounds.
- Generate the sounds from all letters including consonant blends and long vowel patterns. Blend those different sounds into recognizable words.
- Read common sight words.
- Read common word families.
- Recognize and use knowledge of spelling patterns when reading: run/running, hop/hopping.

Any record kept of an individual child's progress should include each date of observation and some legend or rubric detailing the level of performance, standard acquisition, or mastery.

The following template can be used by teachers to record student progress for each child in grades K-1 and beyond as needed (depending on ELL or special needs):

Reading Progress

Skill Area	Mastered	Making Progress	Not Yet	Comments
Matches all consonant and short vowel sounds				
Reads one's own name				
Reads one syllable words and high frequency words				
Demonstrates ability to read and understand that as letters in words change, so do the sounds				
Generates the sounds from all letters including consonant blends and long vowel patterns. Blend those different sounds into recognizable words				
Reads common sight words				
Reads common word families				
Recognizes and uses knowledge of spelling patterns when reading: run/running, hop/hopping				

Any record kept of an individual child's progress should include each date of observation and some legend or rubric detailing the level of performance, standard acquisition, or mastery.

Development of Alphabetic Knowledge in Individual Students

Researchers Laura M. Justice and Helen K. Ezell (2002) evaluated alphabetic knowledge and print awareness in pre-school children from low income households. In their post-tests, children who had participated in shared reading sessions that emphasized a print focus outperformed their control group peers (other Head Start children) on three measures of print awareness: words in print, print recognition, and alphabetic knowledge.

Other researchers including Chaney (1994) have demonstrated a statistically significant and inverse relationship between household income and children's performance on measures of print awareness and the alphabetic principle. Lonigan (l999) found that substantial group differences existed on a variety of pre literacy tasks administered to 85 preschool children from lower and middle income households. The researchers looked at environmental print, print and book reading conventions, and alphabet knowledge. Results showed that preschool children from middle income households showed significantly higher levels of skill across all print awareness tasks in comparison with preschoolers from low income households.

Obviously this data highlights the importance of extensive alphabetic knowledge activities and print awareness opportunities for some children from low income households in grades K-1 and even beyond if necessary.

Two other studies undertaken by Ezell and Justice (in the year 2000) suggested that structuring adult-child shared book reading interactions to include an explicit print awareness and alphabetic principle focus resulted in a substantial increase in children's verbal interactions with print.

This work highlights the importance of not only classroom and preschool emphasis on print awareness and alphabetic principle routines, but also the need for teachers to reach out to parents and to model for them these shared reading experiences so that family life can parallel the classroom experiences. Many schools currently have parent volunteers and reading buddy programs. Training of these volunteers, particularly in high need, low economic income status communities is certainly warranted.

David J. Chard and Jean Osborn (l999) have reflected on the guidelines necessary for teachers to use in selecting supplemental phonics and word-recognition materials for addressing students with learning disabilities. They note that an important way to help children with reading disabilities figure out the system underlying the printed word is leading them to understand the alphabetic principle. Children with learning disabilities (LD) in particular benefit from organized instruction that centers on letters, sounds, and the relations between sounds and letters. They also benefit from word-recognition pattern instruction that offers practice with word families that share similar letter patterns.

Children who are LD also benefit from opportunities to apply what they are learning to the reading and re-reading of stories and other texts. Such texts contain a high portion of words which reflect the letters, sounds, and spelling patterns the children are learning.

For special needs children, a beginning reading program should include the following elements of alphabetic knowledge instruction:

1. A variety of alphabetic knowledge activities in which the children learn to identify and name both upper and lower case letters.
2. Games, songs, and other activities that help children to learn to name the letters quickly.
3. Writing activities that encourage children to practice the letters which they are writing.
4. A sensible sequence of letter introduction that can be adjusted to the needs of the children.

"Reading is a meaning making, problem solving activity"
Marie Clay

Sequence of Phonics Skills

- Letter Naming
  - Lower Case Letters
  - Upper Case Letters
- Letter Sounds
  - Continuous Sounds
  - Stop Sounds
  - Both Consonant and Vowel Sounds
- Short Vowels in CVC Words
- Short Vowels with Digraphs and –tch Trigraph
- Short Vowels and Consonant Blends
- Long Vowels
- Variant Vowels and Diphthongs
- R- and L- Controlled Vowels
- Multisyllabic Words

Explicit and Implicit Strategies for Teaching Phonics

Uta Frith has identified three phases which describe the progression of children's phonic learning from ages four through eight. These are:

Logographic Phase
Children recognize whole words that have significance for them such as their own names or the names of stores they frequent or products that their parents buy. Examples are McDonald's, SuperValu, and the like. Strategies which nurture development in this phase include explicit labeling of class room objects, components, furniture and materials and showing the children's names in print as often as possible. Toward the end of this phase children start to notice initial letters in words and the sounds that they represent.

Analytic Phase
During this phase the children begin to make associations between the spelling patterns in the words they know and new words-they encounter. Children in this phase of reading development are able to generalize that hat and cat are going to be read in a similar manner because they recognize that the /at/ portions of the words are the same. This is helpful with word families and can be transferred to encoding words through many activities. Some teachers find it helpful to add word families or family houses to their word walls around the room. In this way, students can begin to make these generalizations more rapidly. As the students find more complex words that fall into the family/house, they add them.

Orthographic Phase
In this phase, children recognize words almost automatically. They can rapidly identify an increasing number of words. Students are able to apply many different strategies in a seamless manner to help them decode unknown words. This may include: phonics, structural analysis, syntax, semantics, and contextual clues. Students at this level are fluent readers with good prosody. They are reading to make the shift from learning to read to reading to learn. It is a critical shift for children.

To best support these phases and the development of emergent and early readers, teachers should focus on elements of phonics learning which help children analyze words for their letters, spelling patterns, and structural components. The children need to be involved in activities in which they use what they know about words to learn new ones.

The teacher needs to build on what the children know to introduce new spelling patterns, vowel combinations, and short and long vowel investigations. The teacher must do this and be aware that these will be reintroduced again and again as needed.

Keep in mind that children's learning of phonics and other key components of reading is not linear, but rather falls back to review and then flows forward to build new understandings.

Among suggested activities to support phonics instruction to address the needs of these three phases of phonics learning are:

(These activities have specifically been provided in detail so that the educator can study them and use them in the sample constructed response questions which have been provided at the end of the guide. Since the role of phonics in promoting reading development is so crucial, it is highly likely that a constructed response question on the certification test will focus on the use of such strategies. Therefore it is a good idea for the certification candidate to study them closely. As a bonus, the detail with which these strategies are set forth also makes them readily useful with classes the teacher is currently teaching).

Sorting Words

This activity allows children to focus closely on the specific features of words and to begin to understand the basic elements of letter sound relationships. Start with one syllable (monosyllabic) words. Have the children group them by their length, common letters, sound, and/or spelling pattern.

Prepare for the activity by writing ten to fifteen words on oaktag strips and place them randomly on the sentence strip holder. These words should come from a book previously shared in the classroom or a language experience chart.

Next begin to sort out the words with the children, perhaps by where a particular letter appears in a word. While the children sort the place of a particular letter in a given word, they should also be coached (or facilitated) by the teacher to recognize that sometimes a letter in the middle of the word can still be the last sound that we hear and that some letters at the end of a word are silent (such as "e").

Children should be encouraged to make their own categories for word sorts and to share their own discoveries as they do the word sorts. The children's discoveries should be recorded and posted in the rooms with their names so they have ownership of their phonics learning.

Spelling Pattern Word Wall

One of the understandings emergent readers come to about a word is that if they know how to read, write, and spell one word, they can write, read, and spell many other words as well.

Create in your classroom a spelling pattern word wall. The spelling word wall can be created by stapling a piece of 3" x 5" butcher block paper to the bulletin board. Then attach spelling pattern cards around the border with thumbtacks, so that the cards can be easily removed to use at the meeting area.

Once you decide on a spelling pattern for instruction, remove the corresponding card from the word wall. Then take a 1"x 3" piece of a contrasting color of butcher block paper and tape the card to the top end of a sheet the children will use for their investigation.

After the pattern is identified the children can try to come up with other words that have the same spelling pattern. The teacher can write these on the spelling pattern sheet, using a different color marker to highlight the spelling pattern within the word. The children have to add to the list until the sheet is full, which might take two days or more.

After the sheet is full, the completed spelling pattern is attached to the wall.

Letter Holder Making Words

Use a 2" x 3" piece of foam board to make a letter holder. On the front of the board, attach 16 library pockets –one for each letter from A to P. Use the back of the board to attach another 10 pockets for the rest of the alphabet.

Write the letter name on each pocket and use clear bookbinding tape to secure each row of cards with clear tape. Make twelve cards for each letter. On the front of each 2"x 6" strip, make a capital letter and on its back write that letter in lower case. Write consonants in, say, black marker and vowels in red marker.

Through use of this letter holder, children can experience how letters can be rearranged, added, or removed to make new words. They can use these cards also to focus as needed on letter sequences and to support them in recognizing spelling patterns in words.

The words you choose to use for this activity can be selected from Patricia Cunningham and Dorothy P. Hall's, *Making Words* (l994). Select a word that is called the "secret word." Build up toward the creation of that word through a focus on the smaller words within it. Words should be chosen which reflect the spelling patterns being studied by the class.

You can create letter holders for the children by folding up the bottom third of a used manila file folder and taping the ends to form a shallow pocket. Give them letter cards which are made of 2"x 6" oaktag. So, for example, if the secret word is bicycle, the children would be given the separate letter cards which would make up that word. The children keep the letters on the floor in front of them and only place them in the holder when they are actually making a word.

Making words should begin with making two letter words and then progress as the individual child is ready to make larger words. The teacher provides the instruction of which two letters the child is to use to make a word. After the instruction is given, the children select the correct letters and make the word in their folder. The teacher then writes the word down and the children check their letter holder word against it. The teacher goes around checking through and reviewing the letter holders to see which children are "getting it" and then continues to build up words with more letters if the children are ready.

Word Splits

Splitting compound words. Through working with compound words, children can actually experience bigger words that are often made up of smaller words. By working with five to ten compound words on oaktag cards, children can analyze letter-sound relationships and meaning.

Before children meet in a group, write five to ten words on oaktag cards and arrange them on the sentence strip holder. After the words have been read, cut each of the words into its two smaller words and randomly arrange them on the sentence strip holder. Allow the children to randomly take turns arranging the small words back into the original compound words. Also, encourage them to form new compound words. For example, if one of two original compound words is "rainbow" and the other is "dropping," the children should be able to come with "raindrop." The new words the children come up with should be written on blank oaktag cards with the names of the children who came up with them attached. In this way the children can add to their growing bank of new words and have ownership in the words that they have added.

Role of Phonics in Developing Rapid, Automatic Word Recognition, Decoding, and Reading Comprehension

To decode means to change communication signals into messages. Reading comprehension requires that the reader learn the code within which a message is written and be able to decode it to get the message.

Although effective reading comprehension requires identifying words automatically (Adams, 1990; Perfetti, 1985), children do not have to be able to identify every single word or know the exact meaning of the every word in a text to understand it. Indeed, Nagy (1988) says that children can read a work with a high level of comprehension even if they do not fully know as many as 15 percent of the words within a given text.

Children develop the ability to decode and recognize words automatically. They then can extend their ability to decode to multi-syllabic words.
J. David Cooper (2004) and other advocates of the Balanced Literacy Approach, feel that children become literate, effective communicators and able to comprehend by learning phonics and other aspects of word identification through the use of engaging reading texts. Engaging texts contain highly predictable elements of rhyme, sound patterns, and plot. Researchers, such as Chall (1983) and Flesch (1981), support a phonics-centered foundation before the use of engaging reading texts. This is at the crux of the phonics versus whole language/ balanced literacy/ integrated language arts, teaching of reading controversy.

It is important for the new teacher to be informed about both sides of this controversy, as well as the work of theorists who attempt to reconcile these two perspectives, such as Kenneth Goodman (1994). There are powerful arguments on both sides of this controversy, and each approach works wonderfully with some students and does not succeed with others.
As far as the examinations are concerned, all that is asked of you is the ability to demonstrate that you are familiar with these varied perspectives. If asked on a constructed response question, you need to be able to show that you can talk about teaching some aspect of reading using strategies from one or the other or a combination of both approaches.

This guide is designed to provide you with numerous strategies representing both approaches.

The working teacher can, depending on the perspective of his /her school administration and the needs of the particular children he or she serves, choose from the strategies and approaches which work best for the children concerned.

Blending Letter Sounds

Prompts for Graphophonic Cues

You said (the child's incorrect attempt). Does that match the letters you see?
If it were the word you just said, (the child's incorrect attempt), what would it have to start with?

If it were the word you just said (the child's incorrect attempt), what would it have to end with?

Look at the first letter/s . . . look at the middle letter/s
. . . the last letter. . What could it be?

If you were writing (the child's incorrect attempt) what letter would you write first?
What letters would go in the middle?
What letters would go last?

A good strategy to use in working with individual children is to have them explain how they finally correctly identified a word that was troubling them. If prompted and habituated through one-on-one teacher/tutoring conversations, they can be quite clear about what they did to "get" the word.

If the children are already writing their own stories, the teacher might say to them: "You know when you write your own stories, you would never write any story which did not make sense. You wouldn't and probably this writer didn't either. If you read something that does make sense, but doesn't match the letters, then it's probably not what the author wrote. This is the author's story, not yours right now, so go back to the word and see if you can find out the author's story. Later on, you might write your own story."

Letter Sound Correspondence and Beginning Decoding

Use this procedure for letter-sound investigations that support beginning decoding.

First, focus on a particular letter/s which you want the child to investigate. It is good to choose one from a shared text which the children are familiar with. Make certain that the teachers' directions to the children are clear and either focuses them on looking for a specific letter or listening for sounds.

Next, begin a list of words that meet the task given to the children. Use chart paper to list the words that the children identify. This list can be continued into the next week as long as the children's focus is maintained on the list. This can be easily done by challenging the children with identifying a specific number of letters or sounds and "daring" them as a class team to go beyond those words or sounds.

Third, continue to add to the list. Focus the children at the beginning of the day on the goal of their individually adding to the list. Give them an adhesive note (sticky pad sheet) on which they can individually write down the words they find. Then they can attach their newly found words with their names on them to the chart. This provides the children with a sense of ownership and pride in their letter-sounding abilities. During shared reading, discuss the children's proposed additions and have the group decide if these meet the directed category. If all the children agree that they do meet the category, include the words on the chart.

Fourth, do a word sort from all the words generated and have the children put the words into categories that demonstrate similarities and differences. They can be prompted to see if the letter appeared at the beginning or the end of the word. They might also be prompted to see that one sound could have two different letter representations. The children can then "box" the word differences and similarities by drawing colors established in a chart key.

Finally, before the children go off to read, ask them to look for new words in the texts which they can now recognize because of the letter-sound relationships on their chart. During shared reading, make certain that they have time to share these words they were able to decode because of their explorations.

Strategies for Helping Students Decode Single Syllable Words that Follow Common Patterns and Multi-syllable Words

(This activity is presented in detail so it can actually be implemented with children in an intermediate classroom and also to provide detail for a potential constructed response question on a certification examination.)

The CVC phonics card game developed by Jackie Montierth, a computer teacher in South San Diego for use with 5th and 6th grade students, is a good one to adapt to the needs of any group with appropriate modifications for age, grade level and language needs.

The children use the vehicle of the card game to practice and enhance their use of consonants and vowels. Their fluency in this will increase their ability to decode words. Potential uses beyond whole classroom instruction include use as part of the small group word work component of the reading workshop and as part of cooperative team learning. This particular strategy also is particularly helpful for grade four and beyond English Language learners who are in a regular English Language classroom setting.

The card game works well because the practice of the content is implicit for transfer as the children continue to improve their reading skills. In addition, the card game format allows "instructional punctuation" using a student centered high interest exploration.

Card Design: The teacher can use the computer or use 5"x 8" index cards or actual card deck sized oaktag cards to create a deck. For repeated use and durability, it is recommended that the deck be laminated.

The deck should consist of the following:
44 consonant cards (including the blends)
15 vowel cards (including 3 of each vowel)
5 wild cards (which can be used as any vowel)
6 final e cards

The design of this project can also focus on particular CVC words that are part of a particular book, topic, or genre format. In advance of playing the game, children can also be directed to review the words on the word wall or other words on a word map.

Procedure:

The game is best introduced first as part of a mini lesson with the teacher reading the rules, and a pair of children demonstrating step by step when the game is played before the class for the first time. Have the children divide into pairs or small groups of no more than 4 per group. Each group needs one deck of C-V-C cards.

Have each group choose a dealer. The dealer shuffles the cards and deals 5 cards to each player. The remaining cards are placed face down for drawing during the play. One card is turned over to form the discard pile. Players may not show their cards to the other players. The first player to the left of the dealer looks at his/her cards and if possible, puts down three cards which make a consonant-vowel-consonant word. For more points, four cards forming a consonant-vowel-consonant word can be placed down. The player must then say the word and draw the number of cards he or she laid down. If he or she is unable to form a word, he/she draws either a card from either the draw or discard pile. The player then discards one card. All players must have 5 cards at all times. Play moves to the left.

The game continues until one or more of the following happens:
1. There are no more cards in the draw pile
2. All players run out of cards.
3. All players cannot form a word

The winner is the player who has laid down the most cards during the game.

Players may only lay down words at the beginning of their turn.
Proper names may not be counted as words.

Other ways the game may be played:

The game can be played with teams of individuals in a small group of four or fewer competing against one another (Excellent for special needs or resource room students). It can also be done as a whole class activity where all the students are divided into cooperative teams or small groups who compete against one another. This second approach will work well with a heterogeneous classroom that includes special needs and/or ELL children.

Teachers of ELL learners can do this game in the native language first and then transition it into English, facilitating native language reading skills and second language acquisition. They can develop their own appropriate decks to meet the vocabulary needs of their children and to complement the curricula.

Using Phonics to Decode Words in Connected Text

Identifying New Words

Some strategies to share with children during conferences or as part of shared reading include the following prompts:

- Look at the beginning letter/s... What sound do you hear?

- Stop to think about the text or story. What word with this beginning letter would make sense here?

- Look at the book's illustrations. Do they provide you with help in figuring out the new word?

- Think of what word would make sense, sound right, and match the letters that you see. Start the sentence over, making your mouth ready to say that word.

- Skip the word, read to the end of the sentence, and then come back to the word. How does what you've read help you with the word?

- Listen to whether what you are reading makes sense and matches the letters (asking the child to self-monitor). If it doesn't make sense, see if you can correct it on your own.

- Look for spelling patterns you know from the spelling pattern wall.

- Look for smaller words you might know within the larger word.

- Read on a little, and then return to the part that confused you.

Use of Semantic and Syntactic Cues to Help Decode Words

Semantic Cues

Students will need use their base knowledge of word meanings, semantics, to help them decipher unknown words or text as well as to clarify reading when it does not seem to make sense. Some prompts the teacher can use which will alert the children to semantic cues include:
- Does that sentence make sense?
- Which word in that sentence does not seem to fit?
- Why doesn't it fit?
- What word might make sense in that sentence?

Syntactic Cues

The first strategy good readers use from their own knowledge base to help determine misreading is syntactic cues. Syntactic cues use the order of words and the student's knowledge of the oral English language to help determine if what was read could be accurate. Some prompts the teacher can use to encourage and develop syntactic cues in reading include:

- You read (child's incorrect attempt). Does that sound right?
- You read (child's incorrect attempt). When we talk, do we talk that way?
- How would we say it?
- Recheck that sentence. Does it sound right the way you read it?

Specific Terminology Associated With Phonics

It is important to have a clear understanding of the terms associated with phonics. Here are some definitions, which are helpful in having a clear understanding of phonic development in children.

Phoneme – a phoneme is the smallest unit of sound in the English language. In print phonemes are represented by the letter and a slash. So, /b/ represents the sound the letter b would make.

Morpheme- a morpheme is the smallest unit of grammar in the English language. In other words, it is the smallest unit of meaning, not just sounds.

Consonant Digraph – a consonant digraph are two consonants of the English language who when placed together in a word make a unique sound that neither makes when alone. Examples: ch, th, sh, and wh.

Consonant Blend- a consonant blend is when two consonants are put together, but each retains their individual sound. The two sounds go together in a seamless manner to produce a blended sound. Examples: st, br, cl.

Schwa sound- schwa sound is a vowel sound which is neutral. It typically occurs in the unaccented syllable of a word. An example would be the sound of the a at the end of the word sofa. It is represented in print by an upside down e

Development of Phonics Skills with Individual Students

In *ON SOLID GROUND* (2000), researcher and educator Sharon Taberski said that it is much harder for children from ELL backgrounds and children from homes where other English dialects are spoken to use syntactic cues to attempt to self-correct.

These children, through no fault of their own, do not have sufficient experience hearing Standard English spoken to use this cueing system as they read. The teacher should sensitively guide them through by modeling the use of syntactic and semantic cues.

Highly proficient readers can be paired as buddy tutors for ELL or special needs classroom members or to assist the resource room teacher during their reading time. They can use the CVC Game developed by Jacki Montrieth to support their peers and can even modify the game to meet the needs of classroom peers. Of course, this also offers the highly proficient reader the opportunity to do a service learning project, while still in elementary school. It also introduces the learner to another dimension of reading, the role of the reader as trainer and recruiter of other peers into the circle of readers and writers!.
If the highly proficient readers are so motivated or if their teachers so desire, the peer tutors can also maintain an ongoing reading progress journal for their tutees. This will be a wonderful way to realize the goals of the reading and writing workshop.

There are many different strategies to help children who are struggling with their phonics skill development. A beginning step is to identify the area of difficulty within phonics. A simple assessment to help determine the exact area of difficulty is the CORE Phonics Survey which can be downloaded free. Once the area of deficit has been identified, small group instruction can be developed around these areas to increase specific skills.

When working on specific phonics skills, it is important to utilize decodable texts. There are numerous publishers who have available a variety of different skills and texts for use within the classroom. If students continue to struggle, it may be necessary to utilize a more specific systematic and explicit phonics program. Some examples of these include: Wilson Reading, Early Intervention Reading, and Open Court.

Skill 7.4   Identify methods for teaching students to use context to identify and define unfamiliar words.

Identification of Common Morphemes, Prefixes, and Suffixes

This aspect of vocabulary development is to help children look for structural elements within words which they can use independently to help them determine meaning.

Some teachers choose to directly teach structural analysis. In particular, those who teach by following the phonics-centered approach for reading do this. Other teachers, who follow the balanced literacy approach, introduce the structural components as part of mini lessons that are focused on the students' reading and writing.

Structural analysis of words as defined by J. David Cooper (2004) involves the study of significant word parts. This analysis can help the child with pronunciation and constructing meaning.

The list of terms below is generally recognized as the key structural analysis components.

Root Words

This is a word from which another word is developed. The second word can be said to have its "root" in the first, such as *vis, to see,* in visor or vision. This structural component can be illustrated by a tree with roots to display the meaning for children. Children may also want to literally construct root words using cardboard trees to create word family models.

ELL learners can construct these models for their native language root word families, as well for the English language words they are learning. ELL learners in the 5th and 6th grade may even appreciate analyzing the different root structures for contrasts and similarities between their native language and English.

Learners with special needs can focus in small groups or individually with a paraprofessional on building root word models.

Base Words
These are stand-alone linguistic units which cannot be deconstructed or broken down into smaller words. For example, in the word *re-tell*, the base word is "tell."

Contractions

These are shortened forms of two words in which a letter or letters have been deleted. These deleted letters have been replaced by an apostrophe.

Prefixes

These are beginning units of meaning which can be added (the vocabulary word for this type of structural adding is "affixed") to a base word or root word. They cannot stand alone. They are also sometimes known as "bound morphemes," meaning that they cannot stand alone as a base word. Examples are *re-, un-,* and *mis-*.

Suffixes

These are ending units of meaning which can be "affixed" or added to the ends of root or base words. Suffixes transform the original meanings of base and root words. Like prefixes, they are also known as "bound morphemes," because they cannot stand alone as words. Examples are *-less, -ful,* and *-tion*.

Compound Words

These occur when two or more base words are connected to form a new word. The meaning of the new word is in some way connected with that of the base word. Examples are *firefighter, newspaper,* and *pigtail*.

Inflectional Endings

These are types of suffixes that impart a new meaning to the base or root word. These endings in particular change the gender, number, tense, or form of the base or root words. Just like other suffixes, these are also termed "bound morphemes." Examples are *–s* or *-ed*.

Comments

Definitions are included because the structural analysis components are explicitly taught in schools which advocate the phonics-centered approach and are also incorporated into the word work component of the schools which advocate the balanced literacy approach for instruction.

Definition questions, that is multiple choice questions which have only a single right answer, test whether the teacher candidate has memorized the appropriate terminology. They constitute no less than 15% of the multiple choice question on the test. Therefore by taking the time to memorize these easy definitions, scores are likely to improve.

Some of these activities are presented in detail to help answer the constructed response questions of the test.

Knowledge of Greek and Latin Roots That Form English Words

Knowledge of Greek and Latin roots which comprise English words can measurably enhance children's reading skills and can also enrich their writing.

Word Webs

Sharon Taberski (2000) does not advocate teaching Greek and Latin derivatives in the abstract to young children. However, when she comes across specific Greek and Latin roots while reading to children (as is common and natural), she uses that opportunity to introduce children to these rich resources.

For example, during readings on rodents (a favorite of first and second graders), Taberski draws her class's attention to the fact that beavers gnaw at things with their teeth. She then connects the "dent" root or derivative to other words the children are familiar with or experience. The children then volunteer "*dentist,*" "*dental,*" "*denture.*" Taberski begins to place these in a graphic organizer, or word web.

When she has tapped the extent of the children's prior knowledge of "dent" words, she shares with them the fact that *dens/dentis* is the Latin word for teeth. Then she introduces the word "indent," which she has already previewed with them as part of their conventions of print study. She helps them to see that the "indenting" of the first line of a paragraph can even be related to the "teeth" Latin root in that it looks like a "print" bite was taken out of the paragraph.

Taberski displays the word web in the Word Wall Chart section of her room. The class is encouraged throughout, say, a week's time to look for other words to add to the web. Taberski stresses that for her, as an elementary teacher of reading and writing, the key element of the Greek and Latin word root web activity is the children's coming to understand that if they know what a Greek or Latin word root means, they can use that knowledge to figure out what other words mean.

She feels the key concept is to model and demonstrate for children how fun and fascinating Greek and Latin root study can be.

Greek and Latin Roots Word Webs With an Assist from the World Wide Web

Older children in grades 3-6 can build on this initial print activity by searching online for additional words with a particular Greek or Latin root which has been introduced in class.

They can easily do this in a way that authentically ties in with their own interests and experiences by reading reviews for a book which has been a read-aloud online or by just reading the summaries of the day's news and printing out those words which appear in the stories online that share the root discussed.

The children can be encouraged to circle these instances of their Latin or Greek root and also to document the exact date and URL for the citation. These can be posted as part of their own online web in the word wall section study area. If the school or class has a website or webpage, the children can post this data there as a special Greek and Latin root word page.

Expanding the concept of the Greek and Latin word web from the printed page to the world wide web nicely inculcates the child in the habits of lifelong reading and researching online. This beginning expository research will serve them well in intermediate level content area work and beyond.

Use of Syllabification as a Word Identification Strategy

Strategy: Clap Hands, Count those Syllables as They Come!! (Taberski, 2000)

The objective of this activity is for children to understand that every syllable in a polysyllabic word can be studied for its spelling patterns in the same way that monosyllabic words are studied for their spelling patterns.

The easiest way for the K-3 teacher to introduce this activity to the children is to share a familiar poem from the poetry chart (or to write out a familiar poem on a large experiential chart).

First the teacher reads the poem with the children. As they are reading it aloud, the children clap the beats of the poem and the teacher uses a colored marker to place a tic (/) above each syllable.

Next, the teacher takes letter cards and selects one of the polysyllabic words from the poem which the children have already "clapped" out.

The children use letter cards to spell that word on the sentence strip holder, or it can be placed on a felt board or up against a window on display. Together the children and teacher divide the letters into syllables and place blank letter cards between the syllables. The children identify spelling patterns they know.

Finally and as part of continued small group syllabification study, the children identify other polysyllabic words they clapped out from the poem. They make up the letter combinations of these words. Then they separate them into syllables with blank letter cards between the syllables.

Children who require special support in syllabification can be encouraged to use many letter cards to create a large butcher paper syllabic representation of the poem or at least a few lines of the poem (in letter cards with spaces). They can be told that this is for use as a teaching tool for others. In this way, they authenticate their study of syllabification with a real product that can actually be referenced by peers.

Techniques for Identifying Compound Words

The teaching of compound words should utilize structural analysis techniques. (See above section on structural analysis).
Here are some other strategies for helping students to identify and read compound words.
- Use songs and actions to help children understand the concept that compound words are two smaller words joined together to make one bigger word
- Use games like concentration, memory and go fish for students to practice reading compound words
- Use word sorts to have students distinguish between compound words and nonexamples of compound words

Identification of Homographs

Homographs are words that are spelled the same but have different meanings. A subgroup within this area includes words that are spelled the same, have different meanings, and are pronounced differently. Some examples of homographs include:
- Lie
- Tear
- Bow
- Fair
- Bass

Teaching homographs can be interesting and fun for the students. Incorporate them into passages where the students can use the context clues to decipher the different meanings of the homographs. Games are also a good strategy for using to help students understand multiple meaning words. Jokes and riddles are usually based on homographs, and students love to make collections or books of these.

Semantic Feature Analysis: This technique for enhancing vocabulary skills by using semantic cues is based on the research of Johnson and Pearson (1984) and Anders and Bos (1986). It involves young children in setting up a feature analysis grid of various content words which is an outgrowth of their discussion about these words.

For instance, Cooper (2004) includes a sample of a Semantic Features Analysis Grid for Vegetables. .

Vegetables	Green	Have Peels	Eat Raw	Seeds
Carrots	-	+	+	-
Cabbage	+	-	+	-

Note the use of the + for yes, - for no, and possible use for + and - if a vegetable like squash could be both green and yellow.

Teachers of children in grade one and beyond can design their own semantic analysis grids to meet their students' needs and to align with the topics they are learning. Select a category or class of words (could be planets, winter words, weather words).

Use the left side of the grid to list at least three if not more items that fit this category. The number of actual items listed will depend on the age and grade level of the children with three or four items fine for K-1 and up to 10-15 for grades 5 and 6. Brainstorm with the children or if better suited to the class, the teacher may list on his/her own features that the items have in common. As can be noted from the example excerpted from *Cooper's Literacy -Helping Children Construct Meaning* (2004), these common features such as vegetables' green color, peels, and seeds are usually fairly easy to identify.

Show the children how to insert the notations +, -, and even ? (If they are not certain) on the grid. The teacher might also explore with the children the possibility that an item could get both a + and a -. For example, a vegetable like broccoli might be eaten cooked or raw depending on taste.

Whatever the length of the grid when first presented to the children (perhaps as a semantic cue lesson in and of itself tied in to a text being read in class), make certain that the grid as presented and filled out is not the end of the activity.

Children can use it as a model for developing their own semantic features grids and share them with the whole class. Child-developed grids can become part of a Word Work center in the classroom or even be published in a Word Study Games book by the class as a whole. Such a publication can be shared with parents during open school week and evening visits and with peer classes.

Contextual Redefinition

This strategy encourages children to use the context more effectively by presenting them with sufficient context BEFORE they begin reading. It models for the children the use of contextual clues to make informed guesses about word meanings.

To apply this strategy, the teacher should first select unfamiliar words for teaching. No more than two or three words should be selected for direct teaching. The teacher should then write a sentence in which there are sufficient clues supplied for the child to successfully figure out the meaning. Among the types of context clues the teacher can use are compare/contrast, synonyms, and direct definition.

Then the teacher should present the words only on the experiential chart or as letter cards. Have the children pronounce the words. As they pronounce them, challenge them to define each word. After more than one definition is offered, encourage the children to decide as a whole group what the definition is. Write down their agreed-upon definition with no comment as to its accurate meaning.

Then share with the children the contexts (sentences the teacher wrote with the words and explicit context clues). Ask that the children read the sentences aloud. Then have them come up with a definition for each word. Make certain that as they present their definitions, the teacher does not comment. Ask that they justify their definitions by making specific references to the context clues in the sentences. As the discussion continues, direct the children's attention to their previously agreed-upon definition of the word. Facilitate their discussing the differences between their guesses about the word when they saw only the word itself and their guesses about the word when they read it in context. Finally have the children check their use of context skills to correctly define the word by using a dictionary.

Development of Word Analysis Skills by Individual Students

This type of direct teaching of word definitions is useful when the children have dictionary skills and the teacher is aware of the fact that there are not sufficient clues about the words in the context to help the students define them. In addition, struggling readers and students from ELL backgrounds may benefit tremendously from being walked through this process that highly proficient and successful readers apply automatically

By using this strategy, the teacher can also "kid watch" and note the students' prior knowledge as they guess the word in isolation. The teacher can also actually witness and hear how various students use context skills.

Through their involvement in this strategy, struggling readers gain a feeling of community as they experience the ways in which their struggles and guesses resonate with other peers' responses to the text.

"Knowledge of vocabulary will not guarantee vocabulary success, but lack of vocabulary knowledge can ensure failure."
Andrew Biemiller (2003)

Skill 7.5   Identify methods for teaching students to recognize and use various spelling patterns in the English language as an aid to word identification and meaning.

Development of Word Analysis Skills and Strategies, Including Structural Analysis

Structural analysis is a process of examining the words in the text for meaningful word units (affixes, base words, inflected endings). There are six types of word types which are formed and therefore can be analyzed using structural analysis strategies. They include:

1. Common prefixes or suffixes added to a known word ending with a consonant
2. Adding the suffix –ed to words that end with consonants
3. Compound words
4. Adding endings to words that end with the letter e
5. Adding endings to words that end with the letter y
6. Adding affixes to multisyllabic words

When teaching and using structural analysis procedures in the primary grades, teachers should remember to make sound decisions on which to introduce and teach. Keeping in mind the number of primary words in which each affix appears and how similar they are will help the teacher make the instructional process smoother and more valuable to the students.

Adding affixes to words can be started when students are able to read a list of one-syllable words by sight at a rate of approximately twenty words correct per minute. At the primary level, there is a recommended sequence for introducing affixes. The steps in this process are:

- Start by introducing the affix in the letter-sound correspondence format
- Practice the affix in isolation for a few days
- Provide words for practice which contain the affix (word lists, flash cards, etc.)
- Move from word lists to including passage reading, which include words with the affix (and some from the word lists/flash cards).

1. Word Study Group

This involves the teacher taking time to meet with children from grades 3-6 in a small group of no more than 6 children for a word study session. Taberski (2000) suggests that this meeting take place next to the Word Wall. The children selected for this group are those who need to focus more on the relationship between spelling patterns and consonant sounds.

It is important that this not be a formalized traditional reading group that meets at a set time each week or biweekly. Rather the group should be spontaneously formed by the teacher based on the teacher's quick inventory of the selected children's needs at the start of the week. Taberski has templates in her book of *Guided Reading Planning Sheets.* These sheets are essentially targeted word and other skills sheets with her written dated observations of children who are in need of support to develop a given skill.

The teacher should try to meet with this group for at least two consecutive twenty minute periods daily. Over those two meetings, the teacher can model a Making Words Activity. Once the teacher has modeled making words the first day, the children would then make their own words. On the second day, the children would "sort" their words.

Other topics for a word study group within the framework of the balanced literacy approach that Taberski advocates are: inflectional endings, prefixes and suffixes, and/or common spelling patterns. These are covered later in this chapter.

It should be noted that this activity would be classified by theorists as a structural analysis activity because the structural components (i.e. prefixes, suffixes, and spelling patterns) of the words are being studied.

2. Discussion Circles

Cooper (2004) believes that children should not be "taught" vocabulary and structural analysis skills. Flesch and E.D. Hirsch, who are key theorists of the phonics approach and advocates of Cultural Literacy (a term coined and associated with Hirsch), believe that specific vocabulary words at various grade and age levels need to be mastered and must be explicitly taught in schools. As far as J. David Cooper is concerned, all the necessary and meaningful (for the child and ultimately adult reader) vocabulary can't possibly be taught in schools (no apologies to Hirsch). To Cooper it is far more important that the children be made aware of and interested in learning words by themselves. Cooper feels that through the child's reading and writing, he or she develops a love for and a sense of "ownership" of words. All of Cooper's suggested structural analysis word strategies are therefore designed to foster the child's love of words and a desire to "own" more of them through reading and writing.

Discussion Circles is an activity which fits nicely into the balanced literacy lesson format. After the children conclude a particular text, Cooper suggests that they respond to the book in discussion circles. Among the prompts, the teacher-coach might suggest that the children focus on words of interest they encountered in the text. These can also be words that they heard if the text was read aloud. Children can be asked to share something funny or upsetting or unusual about the words they have read. Through this focus on children's response to words as the center of the discussion circle, peers become more interested in word study.

3. Banking, Booking, and Filing It: Making Words My Own

Children can literally realize the goal of making words their own and exploring word structures through creating concrete objects or displays that demonstrate the words they own. Children can create and maintain their own files of words they have learned or are interested in learning.

The files can be categorized by the children according to their own interests. They should be encouraged to develop files using science, history, physical education, fine arts, dance, and technology content. Newspapers and web resources, which the teacher has approved, are excellent sources for such words. In addition, this provides the teacher with the opportunity to instruct the child in appropriate age and grade-level research skills. Even children in grades 2 and 3 can begin simplified bibliographies and webliographies for their "found" words. Children can learn how to annotate and note the page of a newspaper, book, or URL for a particular word.

They can also copy down the word as it appears in the text (print or electronic). If appropriate, the child can place the particular words found for a given topic or content in an actual bank of the child's own making. The words can be printed on cards. This allows for differentiated word study and appeals to those children who are kinesthetic and spatial learners. Of course, children can also choose to create their own word books which include their specialized vocabulary and descriptions of how they identified or hunted down their words. Richard Scarry, watch out! Scarry books can be anchor books to inspire this structural analysis activity.

ELL learners can share their accounts in their native language first and then with the help of the teacher translate these accounts into English with both the native language and the English language versions of the word exploration posted.

4. Write out your Words, Write with your words

Ownership of words can be demonstrated by having the children use them as part of their writings. The children can author a procedural narrative (a step by step description) of how they went about their word searches to compile the words they found for any of the activities. If the children are in grades K-1, or if the children are struggling readers and writers, their procedural narratives can be dictated. Then they can be posted by the teacher.

ELL students can share their accounts in their native language first and then with the help of the teacher translate these accounts into English with both the native language and the English language versions of the word exploration posted.

Children with special needs may model a word box on a specific holiday theme, genre or science/social studies topic with the teacher. Initially this can be done as a whole class. As the children become more confident, they can work with peers or with a paraprofessional to create their own individual or small team/pair word boxes.

Special needs children can create a storyboard with the support of a paraprofessional, their teacher or a resource specialist. They can also narrate their story of how they all found the words, using a tape recorder.

5.- Word Study Museum Within the Classroom

This strategy has been presented in detail so it can be used by the teachers within their own classrooms. In addition, the way the activity is described and the mention at the end of the description of how the activity can address family literacy, ELL, and special needs children's talents provides an example of other audiences a teacher should consider in curriculum design.

Almost every general education teacher and reading specialist will have to differentiate instruction to address the needs of special education and ELL learners. Family or shared literacy is a major component of all literacy instruction.

Children can create either a single or multiple exhibits, museum style, within their classrooms celebrating their word study. They can build actual representations of the type of study they have done including word trees (made out of cardboard or foam board), elaborate word boxes and games, word history timelines or murals, and word study maps. They can develop online animations, Kids Spiration graphic organizers, quick movies, digital photo essays, and PowerPoint presentations to share the word they have identified. The classroom or the gym or cafeteria can be transformed into a gallery space. Children can author brochure descriptions for their individual, team or class exhibits. Some children can volunteer to be tour guides or docents for the experience. Other children can work to create a banner for the Museum. The children can name the Museum themselves and send out invitations to its opening. Invitations can be sent to parents, community, staff members and peer or younger classes.

Depending on their age and grade level, children can also develop interactive games and quizzes focused on particular exhibits. An artist or a team of class artists can design a poster for the exhibit, while other children choose to build the exhibits. Another small group can work on signage and a catalogue or register of objects within the exhibit. Greeters who will welcome parents and peers to the exhibit can be trained and can develop their own scripts.

If the children are in grades 4-6, they can also develop their own visitor feedback forms and design word-themed souvenirs. The whole museum within the school or classroom can be captured digitally or with a regular camera. The record of this event can be hung near the word walls. Of course, the children can use many of their newly-recognized and owned words to describe the event.

The Word Study Museum activity can be used with either a phonics-based or a balanced literacy approach. It promotes additional writing, researching, discussing, and reading about words.

It is also an excellent family literacy strategy in that families can develop their own Word Exhibits at home. This activity can also support and celebrate learners with disabilities. It can be presented in dual languages by children who are ELL learners and fluent in more than a single language.)

Relationship between Word Analysis Skills and Reading Comprehension

The explicit teaching of word analysis requires that the teacher pre-select words from a given text for vocabulary learning. These words should be chosen based on the storyline and main ideas of the text. The educator may even want to create a story map for a narrative text or develop a graphic organizer for an expository text. Once the story mapping and/or graphic organizing have been done, the educator can compile a list of words which relate to the storyline and/or main ideas.

The number of words that require explicit teaching should only be two or three. If the number is higher than that, the children need guided reading and the text needs to be broken down into smaller sections for teaching. When broken down into smaller sections, each text section should only have two to three words which need explicit teaching.

Some researchers, including Tierney and Cunningham, believe that a few words should be taught as a means of improving comprehension.

It is up to the educator whether the vocabulary selected for teaching needs review before reading, during reading, or after reading.

Introduce vocabulary BEFORE READING if. . .

- Children are having difficulty constructing meaning on their own. Children themselves have previewed the text and indicated words they want to know.

- The teacher has seen that there are words within the text which are definitely keys necessary for reading comprehension

- The text, itself, in the judgment of the teacher, contains difficult concepts for the children to grasp.

Introduce vocabulary DURING READING if . . .

- Children are already doing guided reading.

- The text has words which are crucial to its comprehension and the children will have trouble comprehending it if they are not helped with the text.

Introduce vocabulary AFTER READING if. . .

- The children themselves have shared words which they found difficult or interesting

- The children need to expand their vocabulary

- The text itself is one that is particularly suited for vocabulary building.

Strategies to support word analysis and enhance reading comprehension include:

- Use of a graphic organizer such as a word map
- Semantic mapping
- Semantic feature analysis
- Hierarchical and linear arrays
- Preview in context
- Contextual redefinition
- Vocabulary self-collection

(Note that these terms are in the Glossary.)

Skill 7.6   Demonstrate knowledge of effective techniques and strategies for the ongoing development of independent vocabulary acquisition.

The Relationship Between Oral and Written Vocabulary Development and Reading Comprehension

Biemiller's (2003) research documents that those children entering 4th grade with significant vocabulary deficits demonstrate increasing reading comprehension problems. Evidence shows that these children do not catch up, but rather continue to fall behind.

Strategy One: Word Map Strategy

This strategy is useful for children grades 3-6 and beyond. The target group of children for this strategy includes those who need to improve their independent vocabulary acquisition abilities. The strategy is essentially teacher-directed learning where children are "walked through" the process. They are helped by the teacher to identify the type of information that makes a definition. They are also assisted in using context clues and background understanding to construct meaning.

The word map graphic organizer is the tool teachers use to complete this strategy with children. Word map templates are available online from the Houghton Mifflin web site and from READWRITETHINK, the web site of the NCTE (see webliography section). The word map helps the children to visually represent the elements of a given concept.

The children's literal articulation of the concept can be prompted by three key questions: What is it?; What is it like? What are some examples?

For instance, the word "oatmeal" might yield a word map with "What?", and in a rectangular box a hot cereal you eat in the morning; "What is it like?"; hot, mushy, salty; "What are some examples?", instant oatmeal you make in a minute, apple-flavor oatmeal, Irish Oatmeal.

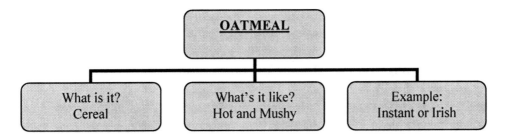

The procedure to be used in sharing this strategy with children is to select three concepts the children are familiar with. Then show them the template of a word map. Tell them that the three questions asked on the map and the boxes to fill in beneath them helps readers and writers to see what they need to know about a word. Next, help the children to complete at least two word maps for two of the three concepts that were pre-selected. Then have the children select a concept of their own to map either independently or in a small group. As the final task for this first part of the strategy, have the children, in teams or individually, write a definition for at least one of the concepts using the key things about it listed on the map. Have the children share these definitions aloud and talk about how they used the word maps to help them with the definitions.

For the next part of this strategy, the teacher should pick up an expository text or a textbook the children are already using to study mathematics, science or social studies. The teacher should either locate a short excerpt where a particular concept is defined or use the content to write model passages of definition on his/her own.

After the passages are selected or authored, the teacher should duplicate them. Then they should be distributed to the children along with blank word map templates. The children should be asked to read each passage and then to complete the word map for the concept in each passage. Finally, have the children share the word maps they have developed for each passage. Give them a chance to explain how they used the word in the passage to help them fill out their word map. End by telling them that the three components of the concept-class, description, example- are just three of the many components for any given concept.

This strategy has assessment potential because the teacher can literally see how the students understand specific concepts by looking at their maps and hearing their explanations. The maps the students develop on their own demonstrate whether they have really understood the concepts in the passages. This strategy serves to ready students for inferring word meanings on their own. By using the word map strategy, children develop concepts of what they need to know to begin to figure out an unknown word on their own. It assists the children in grades 3 and beyond to connect prior knowledge with new knowledge.

This word map strategy can be adapted by the teacher to suit the specific needs and goals of instruction. Illustrations of the concept and the comparisons to other concepts can be included in the word mapping for children grades 5 and beyond. This particular strategy is also one that can be used with a research theme in other content areas.

Strategy Two: Preview in Context

This is a direct teaching strategy which allows the teacher to guide the students as they examine words in context prior to reading a passage. Before beginning the strategy, the teacher selects only two or three key concept words. Then the teacher reads carefully to identify passages within the text that evidence strong context clues for the word.

Then the teacher presents the word and the context to the children. As the teacher reads aloud, the children follow along. Once the teacher has finished the read aloud, the children re-read the material silently. After the silent re-reading, the children will be coached by the teacher to a definition of one of the key words selected for study. This is done through a child-centered discussion. As part of the discussion, the teacher asks questions which get the children to activate their prior knowledge and to use the contextual clues to figure out the correct meaning of the selected key words. Make certain that the definition of the key concept word is finally made by the children.

Next, help the children to begin to expand the word's meaning. Do this by having them consider the following for the given key concept word: synonyms, antonyms, other contexts or other kinds of stories/texts where the word might appear. This is the time to have the children check their responses by having them go to the thesaurus or the dictionary for confirmation. In addition, have the children place the synonyms or antonyms they find in their word boxes or word journals. The recording of their findings will guarantee them ownership of the words and deepen their capacity to use contextual clues.

The main point to remember in using this strategy is that it should only be used when the context is strong. It will not work with struggling readers who have less prior knowledge. Through listening to the children's responses as the teacher helps them to define the word and its potential synonyms and antonyms, the teacher can assess their ability to successfully use context clues. The key to this simple strategy is that it allows the teacher to draw the child out and to grasp through the child's responses the individual child's thinking process. The more talk from the child the better.

The Role of Systematic, Noncontextual Vocabulary Strategies

Strategy One: Hierarchical and Linear Arrays

The very complexity of the vocabulary used in this strategy description, may be unnerving for the teacher. Yet this strategy included in the Cooper (2004) literacy instruction is really very simple once it is outlined directly for children.

By using the term "hierarchical and linear" arrays, Cooper really is talking about how some words are grouped based on associative meanings. The words may have a "hierarchical" relationship to one another. For instance, an undergraduate or a first grader is lower in the school hierarchy than the graduate student and second grader. Within an elementary school, the fifth grader is at the top of the hierarchy and the pre K or kindergartener is at the bottom of the hierarchy. Think of a hierarchical relationship like classification, with classes, subclasses, and small units beneath subclasses. By the way, the term for this strategy obviously need not be explained in this detail to K-3 children, but might be shared with some grade and age appropriate modifications with children in grades 3 and beyond. It will enrich their vocabulary development and ownership of arrays they create.

Words can have a linear relationship to one another in that they run a spectrum from bad to good-for example from K-3 experiences, pleased-happy-overjoyed. Think of these relationships like seriation with words varying along one dimension. These relationships can be displayed in horizontal boxes connected with dashes. Below is another way to display hierarchical relationships.

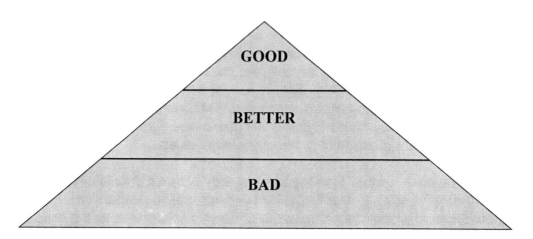

Once you get past the seemingly daunting vocabulary words, the arrays turn out to be another neat, graphic organizer tool which can help children "see" how words relate to one another.

To use this graphic organizer, the teacher should pre-select a group of words from a read aloud or from the children's writing. Show the children how the array will look using arrows for the linear array and just straight lines for the hierarchy. In fact invite some children up to draw the straight hierarchy lines as it is presented, so they have a role in developing even the first hierarchical model. Do one hierarchy array and one linear array with the pre selected word with the children. Talk them through filling out (or helping the teacher to fill out) the array. After the children have had their own successful experience with arrays, they can select the words from their independent texts or familiar, previously-read favorites to study. They will also need to decide which type of array, hierarchical or linear, is appropriate. For 5th and 6th graders, this choice can and should be voiced using the now "owned" vocabulary words "hierarchical array" and "linear array."

This strategy is best used after reading, since it will help the children to expand their word banks.

Contextual Vocabulary Strategies

Vocabulary Self-Collection. This strategy is one in which children, even on the emergent level from grade 2 and up, take responsibility for their learning. It is also by definition a student centered strategy which demonstrates student ownership of their chosen vocabulary.

This strategy is one that can be introduced by the teacher early in the year, perhaps even the first day or week. The format for self-collection can then be started by the children. It may take the form of a journal with photocopied template pages. It can be continued throughout the year.

To start, ask the children to read a required text or story. Invite them to select one word for the class to study from this text or story. The children can work individually, in teams or in small groups. The teacher can also do the self-collecting so that this becomes the joint effort of the class community of literate readers. Tell the children that they should select words which particularly interest them or which are unique in some way.

After the children have had time to make their selections and to reflect on them, make certain that they have time to share them with their peers as a whole class. When each child shares the word which he or she has selected, have them provide a definition for the word. Each word that is given should be listed on a large experiential chart or even in a BIG BOOK format, if that is age and grade appropriate. The teacher should also share the word he or she selected and provide a definition. The teacher's definition and sharing should be somewhere in the middle of the children's recitations.

The dictionary should be used to verify the definitions. When all the definitions have been checked, a final list of child-selected (and single teacher-selected) words should be made.

Once this final list has been compiled, the children can record it in their word journals or they may opt to record only those words they find interesting in their individual journals. It is up to the teacher at the onset of the vocabulary self-collection activity to decide whether the children have to record all the words on the final list or whether they can eliminate some. The decision made at the beginning by the teacher must be adhered to throughout the year.

To further enhance this strategy children, particularly those in grades 3 and beyond, can be encouraged to use their collected words as part of their writings or to record and clip the appearance of these words in newspaper stories or online. This type of additional recording demonstrates that the child has truly incorporated the word into his/her reading and writing. It also habituates children to be lifelong readers, writers, and researchers.

One of the nice things about this simple but versatile strategy is that it works equally well with either expository or narrative texts. It also provides children with an opportunity to use the dictionary.

Assessment is built into the strategy. As the children select the word for the list, they share how they used contextual clues and through the children's response to the definitions offered by their peers, their prior knowledge can be assessed.

What is most useful about this strategy is that it documents that children can learn to read and write by reading and writing. The children take ownership of the words in the self-collection journals and that can also be the beginning of writer observation journals as they include their own writings. They also use the word lists as a start for writers' commonplace books. These books are filled with newspaper, magazine, and functional document clippings using the journal words.

This activity is a good one for demonstrating the balanced literacy belief that vocabulary study works best when the words studied are chosen by the child.

The Relationship between Oral Vocabulary and the Process of Identifying and Understanding Written Words

One way to explore the relationship between oral vocabulary and the comprehension of written words is through the use of Oral Records (which are discussed at length in the appendix).

In *On Solid Ground: Strategies for Teaching Reading K-3*, Sharon Taberski (2000) discusses how oral reading records can be used by the K-3 teacher to assess how well children are using cueing systems. She notes that the running record format can also show visual depictions for the teacher of how the child "thinks" as the child reads. The notation of miscues in particular shows how a child "walks through" the reading process. They indicate if and in what ways the child may require "guided" support in understanding the words he or she reads aloud. Taberski notes that when children read they need to think about several things at once. First, they must consider whether what they are reading makes sense using semantic or meaning cues. Next, they must know whether their reading "sounds right" in terms of Standard English, the use of syntactic and structural cues. Third, they have to weigh whether their oral language actually and accurately matches the letters the words represent (visual or graphophonic cues).

In taking the running record and having the opportunity first-hand to listen to the child talk about the text, the teacher can analyze the relationship between the child's oral language and word comprehension. Information from the running record provides the teacher with a road map for differentiated cueing system instruction.

For example, when a running record is taken, a child often makes a mistake but then self-corrects. The child may select from various cueing systems when he or she self-corrects. These include: "M" for meaning, "S" for syntax, and "V" for visual. The use of a visual cue means that the child is drawing on his or her knowledge of spelling patterns. Of course, Taberski cautions that any relationship between oral language and comprehension that the teacher infers from an examination of the oral-reading records must be drawn using a series of three or more of the child's oral reading records taken over time, not just one.

A teacher can review children's running records over time to note their pattern of miscues and which cues they have the greatest tendency to use in their self-corrections. Whichever cueing system the children use to the greatest extent, it is necessary for the teacher to offer support in also using the other cueing systems to construct correct meaning. Taberski suggests that while assessing running records to determine the relationship between oral language and meaning, the children read from "just right" books.

Strategies for Promoting Oral Language Development and Language Comprehension

Read-Alouds (This is the cornerpiece of the balanced literacy approach for teaching reading. Therefore it is advised that the teacher candidate and new teacher read this material carefully. This may well appear as an essay topic in the Constructed Response section).

Comments:

Within the context of the Balanced Literacy Approach and the Literacy Block, the Read Aloud is part of the Whole Class Activities. The book selected should be one taken from the classroom library which is appropriate for a read aloud. Before reading the book to the class, the teacher needs to be familiar with it. The teacher should also "plan" or at least "know" what nuances of content, style, rhythm, and vocabulary will be emphasized in the reading.

In addition, specifically for the younger grades, the teacher should select a text which also enhances the development of phonemic awareness. This might include a text that can be used to teach rhyming, alliteration, or poetry.

Sometimes, read-aloud texts are selected for their tie-ins with the science, social studies and mathematics curriculum.

Generally teachers aim to teach one strategy during the read-aloud, which the children will practice in small groups or independently. Among these strategies for the first grader could be print strategies and talking about books.

As the teacher reads aloud, the teachers' voice quality should highlight his or her enjoyment of the read-aloud and involvement with the text. Often in a balanced literacy classroom, the teacher reads from a specially decorated Reader's Chair, as do the guest readers. This chair's decorativeness, complete with comfortable throwback pillows or rocking chair style frame, is meant to set an atmosphere that will promote the children's engagement in and love for lifelong reading.

The balanced literacy approach also advocates that teachers select books which children will enjoy reading aloud. Particularly accessible texts for the elementary school classroom read-alouds are collections of poetry.

Teachers must allow time for discussion during and after each Read Aloud period. After the children have made comments, the teacher should also talk about the reading.

Knowledge of Common Sayings, Proverbs and Idioms

Strategy: The Fortune Cookie Strategy (Reissman, 1994). Grades 3 and up

Distribute fortune cookies just before snack to the children. Have them eat the cookies and then draw their attention to the fortunes which are enclosed.

First, the teacher models by reading aloud and sharing his/her own fortune. After reading the fortune aloud, the teacher will explain what the fortune means using its vocabulary as a guide. Finally the teacher can share whether or not the teacher agrees with the statement made in the fortune.

Children can either volunteer to share their fortunes or each can read the fortune aloud, explain the saying and tell whether he or she agrees with the proverb.

Next, children can be asked to interview their parents or community members to collect family proverbs and common sayings.

Once the children return with the sayings and proverbs, they can each share them and explain their meanings. The class as a whole can discuss to what extent these sayings are true for everyone. Proverbs and Sayings can become part of a word wall or be included in a special literacy center. The teacher can create fill in, put together, and writing activities to go with the proverbs. They tie in nicely with cultural study on the grade 3-6 level including Asian, Latin American, and African nations.

What makes proverbs particularly effective for vocabulary development are the limited number of words in their texts and the fact these short texts allow for guided and facilitated reading instruction.

This strategy also highlights in a positive way the uniqueness and commonality of the family proverbs which are contributed by children from ELL backgrounds. If possible their proverbs can also be posted in their native languages as well as in English.

See for further proverbs: **http://www.serve.com/shea/germusa/prov1.htm**

Write like a Babylonian:
http://www.upennmuseum.com/cuneiform.cgi

Write like an Egyptian:
http://www.upennmuseum.com/hieroglyphsreal.cgi

Knowledge of Foreign Words and Abbreviations Commonly Used in English (e.g. RSVP)

Strategy: RSVP your foreign language in English literacy

Of course, the English language is replete with abbreviations that are shortened forms of words from other languages. Not only can this be used for expanding children's vocabulary and writing variety; but also it can help to positively highlight the bilingual and sometimes trilingual abilities of ELL students.

The teacher should develop a word strip mix and match game with commonly found foreign words and abbreviations. These items should, if possible, be cut out of newspapers and flyers to highlight their authenticity as part of everyday life. Among those common words and abbreviations might be: perfume, liqueur (chocolate, of course), latte, cappuccino, brioche, latkes, etc. Food, local coffee houses, and bakeries are excellent sources of these abbreviations. To get sufficient material to cut out to start the game, just get an extra Sunday newspaper or pick up a few circulars from a large supermarket.

Model for the children how to play the game and find out the common words or abbreviations' meaning and foreign derivation using the dictionary.

Next have the children as a whole class or in small groups work to identify the derivations of the foreign words and even map them on a world map.

As part of additional, foreign word center activities, children can opt among a number of choices. These can include maintaining a BIG BOOK OF FOREIGN WORDS or ABBREVIATIONS, to which many contribute, using the weekly food circulars and collecting labels with foreign words which can then be collaged with an accompanying product list, or authoring stories and true accounts featuring as many foreign words as possible.

What is productive about this strategy is that it enhances vocabulary development while it also highlights the extent to which the English language as spoken, used and written in the United States currently is embedded with foreign language words and terms. This of course, makes the native language talents of the ELL child positive and important ones.

Extending a Reader's Understanding of Familiar Words

Dictionary Use:

Dictionaries are useful for spelling, writing, and reading. It is very important to initially expose and habituate students to enjoy using the dictionary.

Cooper (2004) suggests that the following be kept in mind as the teacher of grades K-6 invites children into a lifelong fascination with the dictionary and vocabulary acquisition.

Requesting or suggesting that children look up a word in the dictionary should be the beginning of a wonderful exploration, not a punishment or busy work that has no reference to their current reading assignment.

Model the correct way to use the dictionary for children even as late as third to sixth grade. Some children have never been taught proper dictionary skills. The teacher needs to demonstrate to the children that as an adult reader and writer, he or she routinely and happily uses the dictionary and learns new information that makes him or her better at reading and writing.

Cooper believes in beginning dictionary study as early as kindergarten and this is now very possible because of the proliferation of lush picture dictionaries which can be introduced at that grade level. He also suggests that children not only look at these picture dictionaries, but also begin to make dictionaries of their own at this grade level filled with pictures and beginning words. As children join the circle of lexicographers, they will begin to see themselves as compilers and users of dictionaries. Of course, this will support their ongoing vocabulary development.

In early grade levels, use of the dictionary can nicely complement the children's mastery of the alphabet. They should be given whole class and small group practice in locating words.

As the children progress with their phonetic skills, the dictionary can be used to show them phonetic re-spelling using the pronunciation key.

Older children in grades 3 and beyond need explicit teacher demonstrations and practice in the use of guide words. They also need to begin to learn about the hierarchies of various word meanings. In the upper grades, children should also explore using special content dictionaries and glossaries in the backs of their books.

Strategies for Promoting Comprehension Across the Curriculum by Expanding Knowledge of Content Area Vocabulary

Key Words

Cooper (2004) feels that it is up to the teacher to preview the content area text to identify the main ideas. Then the teacher should compile a list of terms related to the content thrust. These terms and words become part of a key concepts list. Next, the teacher sees which of the key concept words and terms are already defined in the text. These will not require direct teaching. Words for which children have sufficient skills to determine their meaning through base, root, prefixes or suffixes also will not require direct teaching.

Instruction in the remaining key words, which should not be more than two or three in number, can be provided before, during or after reading. If students have previewed the content area and identified those words they need support on, the instruction should be provided before reading. Instruction can also easily be provided as part of guided reading support. After reading support is indicated, the text offers the children an opportunity to enrich their own vocabularies.

Having children work as a whole class or in small groups on a content specific dictionary for a topic regularly covered in their grade level social studies, science, or mathematics curriculum offers an excellent collaborative opportunity for children to design a dictionary/word resource that can celebrate their own vocabulary learning. Such a resource can then be used with the next year's classes as well.

Development of Vocabulary Knowledge and Skills in Individual Students

Hierarchical and linear array vocabulary development strategies lend themselves well to support the struggling learners or second language learners. The use of the arrays allows these learners to use a visual format to "see" and diagram word relationships. Furthermore the diagrams are easy to make, and they can be illustrated. With sufficient support and modeling, many special needs children can do simple linear and hierarchical arrays on their own. The arrays can also be attractively displayed in resource rooms and in regular education classrooms as a demonstration of these individual students' ownership of their words.

English Language Learners should first demonstrate their capacity to fill out hierarchical and linear arrays in their native language and then work with this same format to hone their English Language vocabulary development. Their native language hierarchical relationships and arrays can be displayed in their general education classrooms. Teachers may also want to encourage children grades 3 and beyond to make connections between some of the native words and those derived from them in English. This could be a rich "buddy" (ELL child and native English Language speaker) investigation or it could be one for ELL children alone. At any rate, use of the array with the ELL child's native language makes that child a second language vocabulary owner which immediately includes the child positively in ongoing vocabulary development.

Cooper (2004) suggests that teachers who have children from different language backgrounds use any unscheduled or "extra" time that emerges for read-alouds.

Using the Semantic Feature Analysis Grid

Highly proficient readers can be asked to help same grade peers or better yet younger peers with their word analysis skills by having them work with these struggling readers on filling out teacher developed semantic analysis grids. Some 5th and 6th grade highly proficient readers may also evidence the aptitude and desire to create their own semantic analysis grids for their peer or younger peer tutees. In this way, highly proficient readers can gain insights into the field of teaching reading at an early age and younger struggling readers can be supported by working with a peer or an older student. For both individual students the experience is one that promotes and celebrates word analysis skills and nurtures the concept of a literate and caring community of readers.

ELL students can also add in deliberate items to the categories which reflect their cultures. For instance, Latino children can add in plantains and guava to the fruits their non-Latino peers might list. This provides the ELL learners with an opportunity to enrich the knowledge base of their peers' subject category inventory and puts them in a positive spotlight. The easy notations on the grid make it accessible even for ELL children with limited English language writing and speaking capacities.

Special needs learners can benefit from the grid. It can be developed by teachers, paraprofessionals, and tutors. It can be notated by the children themselves. They can also illustrate it. It can be posted or kept in the word center. The grid provides these learners who are often spatial learners with a concrete demonstration of their word analysis achievement.

Biemiller's research indicates that the listening vocabulary for a 6th grader who tests at the 25 percentile in reading is equivalent to that attained by the 75th percentile 3rd grader. This deficit in vocabulary presents a formidable challenge for the 6th grader to succeed, not only on reading tests, but in various content subjects in elementary school and beyond.

Skill 7.7   Demonstrate knowledge of effective techniques and strategies for the development of fluency.

Use of Oral Reading Fluency in Facilitating Comprehension

At some point it is crucial that just as the nervous, novice bike rider finally relaxes and speeds happily off, so too must the early reader integrate graphophonic cues with semantic and structural ones. Before this is done, the oral quality of early readers has a stilted beat to it, which of course does not promote reading engagement and enjoyment.

The teacher needs to be at his/her most dramatic to model for children the beauties of voice and nuance that are contained in the texts whose print they are tracking so anxiously. Children love nothing more than to mimic their teacher and can do so legitimately and without hesitation if the teacher takes time each day to recite a poem with them. The poem might be posted on chart paper and be up on the wall for a week.

First the teacher can model the fluent and expressive reading of this poem. Then with a pointer, the class can recite it with the teacher. As the week progresses, the class can recite it on their own.

COMPETENCY 8.0 UNDERSTAND STRATEGIES FOR PROMOTING STUDENTS' READING COMPREHENSION SKILLS.

Skill 8.1 **Demonstrate an understanding of ways to provide explicit instruction as well as ways to model when and how to use multiple comprehension strategies.**

Knowledge of Reading as a Process to Construct Meaning

If there were two words synonymous with reading comprehension as far as the balanced literacy approach is concerned, they would be "constructing meaning."

Cooper, Taberski, Strickland, and other key theorists and classroom teachers conceptualize the reader as interacting with the text and bringing his/her prior knowledge and experience to it. Writing is interlaced with reading and is a mutually integrative and supportive parallel process. Hence the division of literacy learning into reading workshop and writing workshop, with the same anchor "readings" or books being used for both.

Consider the sentence, "The test booklet was white with black print, but very scary looking." According to the idea of constructing meaning as the reader reads this sentence, the schemata (generic information stored in the mind) of tests the reader had experienced was activated by the author's notion that tests are scary. Therefore the ultimate meaning that the reader derives from the page is from the reader's own responses and experiences coupled with the ideas the author presents. The reader constructs a meaning that reflects the author's intent and also the reader's response to that intent.

It is also to be remembered that generally readings are fairly lengthy passages, composed of paragraphs which in turn are composed of more than one sentence. With each successive sentence, and every new paragraph, the reader refocuses. The schemata are reconsidered, and new meanings are constructed.

Knowledge of levels of reading comprehension and strategies for promoting comprehension of imaginative literary texts at all levels

Sharon Taberski (2000) recommends that initially strategies for promoting comprehension of imaginative literary texts be done with the whole class.

Here are Taberski's four main strategies for promoting comprehension of imaginative literary texts. She feels that if repeated sufficiently during the K-3 years and even if introduced as late as grade 4, these strategies will even serve the adult lifelong reader in good stead.

Strategy One: "Stopping to Think" –reflecting on the text as a whole.
As part of this strategy, the reader is challenged to come up with the answer to these three questions:

What do I think is going to happen? (Inferential)
Why do I think this is going to happen? (Evaluative and inferential)
How can I prove that I am right by going back to the story? (inferential)

Taberski recommends that teachers introduce these key strategies with books that can be read in one sitting and recommends the use of picture books for these instructive strategies.

Taberski also suggests that books which are read aloud and used for this strategy also contain a strong storyline, some degree of predictability, a text that invites discussion and a narrative with obvious stopping points.

Strategy Two: story mapping, for promoting comprehension of imaginative/literary texts.

For stories to suit this strategy, they should have distinct episodes, few characters and clear-cut problems to solve. In particular, Taberski tries to use a story where a single, central problem or issue is introduced at the beginning of the story and then resolved or at least followed through by the close of the story. To make a story map of a particular story, Taberski divides the class into groups and asks one group of children to illustrate the "Characters" in the book. Another group of children are asked to draw the "Setting," while a third and fourth group of children tackle "Problem " and "Resolution." The story map may also help children hold together their ideas for writing in the writing workshop as they take their reading of an author's story to a new level.

Strategy Three: The Character Mapping strategy also used by Taberski focuses the children as readers on the ways in which the main character's personal traits can determine what will happen in the story. Character mapping works best when the character is a non-stereotypical individual, has been featured perhaps in other books by the same author, has a personality that is somewhat predictable, and is capable of changing behavior as a consequence of what happens. Using writing to share, deepen, and expand understanding of literary texts is a cornerstone of the balanced literacy approach.

Strategy Four: Taberski advocates reading sections of stories aloud and then having the teacher pause to reflect on what's happened in the story and model writing down a response to it. The teacher can use a chart to record his/her response to the events or characters of a particular story being read and the children can contribute their comments as well. Later on, the children can start reflective reader's notebooks or journals recording their reactions to their readings independently.

The best types of texts for this type of response are those that relate to age appropriate issues for young children (i.e. homework, testing, bullies, and friendship), a plot that can be interpreted in different ways, a text that is filled with questions, and a text full of suspense or wonder.

Knowledge of Levels of Reading Comprehension (Literal, Inferential, and Evaluative) and Strategies for Promoting Comprehension of Informational/expository Texts at All Three Levels

There are several key strategies for child reading of informational/expository texts.

1.   Inferencing is a process that involves the reader making a reasonable judgment based on the information given and engages children in literally constructing meaning. In order to develop and enhance this key skill in children, they might have a mini lesson where the teacher demonstrates this by reading an expository book aloud (i.e. one on skyscrapers for young children) and then demonstrates for them the following reading habits: looking for clues, reflecting on what the reader already knows about the topic, and using the clues to figure out what the author means/intends.

2.   Identifying main ideas in an expository text can be improved when the children have an explicit strategy for identifying important information. They can make this strategy part of their everyday reading style, "walking" through the following exercises during guided reading sessions. The child should read the passage so that the topic is readily identifiable to him or her. It will be what most of the information is about.

Next the child should be asked to be on the lookout for a sentence within the expository passage that summarizes the key information in the paragraph. Then the child should read the rest of the passage or excerpt in light of this information and also note which information in the paragraph is less important. The important information the child has identified in the paragraph can be used to formulate the author's main idea. The child reader may even want to use some of the author's own language in stating that idea.

3.   Monitoring means self-clarifying: As one reads, the reader often realizes that what he or she is reading is not making sense. The reader then has to have a plan for making sensible meaning out of the excerpt. Cooper and other balanced literacy advocates have a stop-and-think strategy which they use with children. The child reflects, "Does this make sense to me?" When the child concludes that it does not, the child then either re-reads, reads ahead in the text, looks up unknown words or asks for help from the teacher.

What is important about monitoring is that some readers ask these questions and try these approaches without ever being explicitly taught them in school by a teacher. However, these strategies need to be explicitly modeled and practiced under the guidance of the teacher by most, if not all, child readers.

4.   Summarizing engages the reader in pulling together into a cohesive whole the essential bits of information within a longer passage or excerpt of text. Children can be taught to summarize informational or expository text by following these guidelines. First they should look at the topic sentence of the paragraph or the text and ignore less important ideas. Then they should search for information which has been mentioned more than once and make sure it is included only once in their summary. Find related ideas or items and group them under a unifying heading. Search for and identify a main idea sentence. Finally, put the summary together using all these guidelines.

5.   Generating questions can motivate and enhance children's comprehension of reading in that they are actively involved. The following guidelines will help children generate meaningful questions that will trigger constructive reading of expository texts. First children should preview the text by reading the titles and subheadings. Then they should also look at the illustrations and the pictures. Finally they should read the first paragraph. These first previews should yield an impressive batch of specific questions.

Next, children should get into a Dr. Seuss mode and ask themselves a "THINK" question. Make certain that the children write down the question. Then have them read to find important information to answer their "think" question. Ask that they write down the answer they found and copy the sentence or sentences where they found the answer. Also have them consider whether, in light of their further reading through the text, their original question was a good one or not.

Once the children have answered their original "think" question, have them generate additional ones and then find their answers and judge whether these questions were "good" ones in light of the text.

Strategies for Identifying Point of View, Distinguishing Facts from Opinions and Detecting Faulty Reasoning in Informational/expository Texts

Expository texts are full of information which may or may not be factual and which may reflect the bias of the editor or author. Children need to learn that expository texts are organized around main ideas. Expository content is commonly found in newspapers, magazines, content textbooks, and informational reference books (i.e. atlas, almanac, yearbook of an encyclopedia).

The five types of expository texts (also called "text structures") to which the children should be introduced through modeled reading and a teacher facilitated walk through are:

Description text: This usually gives the characteristics or qualities of a particular topic. It can be depended upon to be factual. Within this type of text, the child reader has to use all of his or her basic reading strategies, because these types of expository texts do not have explicit clue words.

Causation or Cause- Effect text: This text is one where faulty reasoning may come into play and the child reader has to use inferential and self-questioning skills to assess whether the stated cause-effect relationship is a valid one. Clue words to look for are therefore, the reasons for, as a result of, because, in consequence of, and since. The reader must then decide whether the relationship is valid.

Comparison text: This is an expository text which gives contrasts and similarities between two or more objects and ideas. Many social studies, art, and science text books in class and non-fiction books use this format. Key words to look out for are like, unlike, resemble, different, different from, similar to, in contrast with, in comparison to, and in a different vein. It is important that as children examine texts which are talking about illustrated or photographed entities can review the graphic representations for clues to support or contradict the text.

Collection text: This text presents ideas in a group. The writer presents a set of related points or ideas. This text structure is also called a listing or a sequence. The author frequently uses clue words such as first, second, third, finally, and next to alert the reader to the sequence. Based on how well the writer structures the sequence of points or ideas, the reader should be able to make connections. It is important the writer make clear in the expository text how the items are related and why they follow in that given sequence. Simple collection texts that can be literally modeled for young children include recipe making. A class of first graders, beginning readers and writers, were literally spellbound by a teacher's presentation of a widely known copyrighted collection text. The children were thrilled as the author followed the sequences of this collection text, and the children finally took turns stirring it until it was creamy and smooth. The children enjoyed eating their Cream Farina from a commercial cereal box which had cooking directions on it.

The children had constructed meaning from this five minute class demonstration and would now pay close attention to collection texts on other food and product instruction boxes because this text had become an authentic part of their lives.

Response structure expository text: This presents a question or response followed by an answer or a solution. Of course, entire mathematics text books and some science and social studies text books are filled with this type of structure. Again it is important to walk the child reader through the excerpt and to sensitize the child to the clue words which signal this type of structure. These words include, but are not limited to the problem is, the question is, you need to solve for, one probable solution would be, an intervention could be, the concern is, and another way to solve this would be.

Newspapers provide wonderful features which can be used by the teacher as read-alouds to introduce children grades 3-6 to point of view distinctions-- specifically, editorials, editorial cartoons and key sports editorial cartoons. Children can also come to understand the distinction between fact and fiction when they examine a newspaper advertisement or a supermarket circular for a product they commonly use, eat, drink or wear which includes exaggerated claims about what the product can actually do for the individual in question.

Finally the fact versus opinion distinction can be nicely explored if a teacher takes the children online to look at some film star web sites and walks them through some exaggerated claims made about their particular movie star favorites. It is very important at some point, if the children have access to the Internet, that the teacher show them how to examine web sites, look at who developed a particular web site and consider how credible the developers of the site are.

Use of Reading Strategies for Different Texts and Strategies

As children progress to the older grades (3-6), it is important for the teacher to model for them that in research on a social studies or science exploration, it may not be necessary to read every single word of a given expository information text. For instance, if the child is trying to find out about hieroglyphics, he or she might only read through those sections of a book on Egyptian or Sumerian civilization which dealt with picture writing. The teacher, assisted by a child, should model how to go through the table of contents and the index of the book to identify only those pages which deal with picture writing. In addition other children should come to the front of the room or to the center of the area where the reading group is meeting. They should then, with the support of the teacher, skim through the book for illustrations or diagrams of picture writing which is the focus of their need.

Children can practice the skills of skimming texts and scanning for particular topics that connect with their grade Social Studies, Science and Mathematics content area interests.

Use of Comprehension Skills Before, After, and During Reading

Cooper (2004) advocates that the child ask himself or herself what a text is about before he or she reads it and even when reading the text. The child should be continually questioning himself or herself as to whether the text confirmed the child's predictions. Of course after completing the text, the child can then review the predictions and verify whether they were correct.

Using another strategy, the child reader looks over the expository text subheadings, illustrations, captions and indices to get an idea about the book. Then the child, still before reading the text, decides whether he or she can find the answer to his or her question.

Use of Oral Language Activities to Promote Comprehension

Taberski advocates using the "Stopping to Think About" strategy with expository texts as well as fictional ones.

This strategy is centered on the reader's using three "steps" as he or she goes through the expository text. These steps may be expressed as questions.

1. What do I, the reader, think is going to happen?
2. What clues in the text or illustrations or graphics lead me to think that this is going to happen?
3. How can I prove that I am right by going back to the text to demonstrate that this does happen or is suggested by actual clues in the text?

Taberski (2000) deliberately uses expository texts that relate to her grade's Social Studies and Science lessons to model for children how to "stop and think" about the way an expository text is organized. She sometimes deliberately reads a section of a text or a non-fiction book aloud until the end of its chapter, so that the children can consider what they have learned about the topic and how it is organized. Then together as a whole class or as a whole guided reading group, they make predictions about what is coming next.

Development of Reading Comprehension Skills and Strategies of Individual Students

While all child readers can benefit from explicit expository reading strategies, the English Language Learner can truly get a gateway for understanding second language materials by working with a native English language speaking buddy on the question generating strategy. Both the buddy (a peer) and the teacher should alert and walk through with the English Language Learner student how much of a resource illustrations and pictures can be for constructing meaning. If the teacher has time to work individually with the English Language Learner, the day's daily newspaper which is replete with graphics, photos and text is a wonderful tool for honing expository reading skills using these strategies.

The five strategies for enhancing expository reading skills are not beyond use with learners with special needs. However, rather than be offered in an array, these strategies would have to be presented one at a time probably one on one with explicit teacher modeling and then done as shared reading and shared writing with the specific child.

Highly proficient readers might enjoy sharing their skills with other peers and could serve as the newspaper reading buddies for special needs students. They might not only support special needs grade level or younger peers in reading through a designated newspaper section every day, but might also collaborate or oversee their peers or younger peers in designing a word search or crossword puzzle based on that particular section of the newspaper.

Use of editorial sports page cartoons is a good way to introduce special needs learners to opportunities for identifying point of view. They can also create their own takes on the topics of the editorial cartoons using an accessible, non-threatening storyboard format for their commentary.

The Role of Oral Language Fluency in Facilitating the Comprehension of Informational/expository Texts

Children on the middle and secondary levels of education who are studying social studies content have been exposed to what social studies educators call re-enactments. This is a Reader's Theater version of history and cultural study based completely on fact and established historical texts and documents.

Even young children will enjoy and gain tremendous additional expository comprehension facility when they are asked to dramatize a well known historical document or song. They may act out the preamble to the Constitution or read aloud as a chorus the Declaration of Independence or dramatize the Battle Hymn of the Republic. This gives children an opportunity to examine in deep form the vocabulary, syntactic, and semantic clues of these texts. They then have to use their oral instruments (voices) to express appropriate expression for the texts.

If the children are in grades 4 and above, they can also be asked to "explain" in writing how they used the word, syntactic and semantic clues to interpret their oral language recitation. Recitation and writing can be a powerful experience for children grades 4 and up as they build their expository reading and writing skills.

Use of Writing Activities to Promote Comprehension

K-W-L Strategy

This is a graphic organizer strategy which activates children's prior knowledge and also helps them to target their reading of expository texts. This focus is achieved through having the children reflect on three key questions.

Before the child reads the expository passage:
"What do I *Know*?" and
"What do I or we *Want* to find out?"

After the child has read the expository passage:
"What have I or we *Learned* from the passage?"

What is excellent about this strategy, which is broadly used and easily implemented in almost any classroom, is that it is almost totally student- centered and powerfully focuses the child's attention on the actual reading of expository passages. The K-W-L strategy also helps the child prepare for a potential writing task.

When the teacher first introduces the K-W-L strategy, the children should be allowed sufficient time to brainstorm what all of them in the class or small group actually know about the topic. The children should have a three-columned K-W-L worksheet template for their journals and there should be a chart up front to record the responses from class or group discussion. The children can write under each column in their own journal, and should also help the teacher with notations on the chart. This strategy involves the children actually gaining experience in note taking and having a concrete record of new data and information they have gleaned from the passage about the topic.

Depending on the grade level of the participating children, the teacher may also want to channel them into considering categories of information they hope to find out from the expository passage. For instance, they may be reading a book on animals to find out more about the animal's habitats during the winter or about the animal's mating habits.

When children are working on the middle- section (*Want*) strategy sheet, the teacher may give them a chance to share what they would like to learn further about the topic and help them to express it in question format.

K-W-L is useful and can even be introduced as early as grade 2 with extensive teacher support. It not only serves to support the child's comprehension of a particular expository text, but also models for children a format for note taking. Beyond note taking, when the teacher wants to introduce report writing, the K-W-L format provides excellent outlines and question introductions for at least three paragraphs of a report.

Cooper (2004) recommends this strategy for use with thematic units and with reading chapters in required science, social studies, or health text books. In addition to its usefulness with thematic unit study, K-W-L is wonderful for providing the teacher with a concrete format to assess how well children have absorbed pertinent new knowledge within the passage (by looking at the third *Learn* section). Ultimately it is hoped that students will learn to use this strategy, not only under explicit teacher direction with templates of K-W-L sheets, but also on their own by informally writing questions they want to find out about in their journals and then going back to their own questions and answering them after reading.

Use of Text Features (e.g. Index, Glossary) - Graphic Features (e.g. Charts, Maps) and Reference Materials

Traditionally, the aspects of expository text reading comprehension have been taught in a dry format using reference books from the school or public library, particularly, the Atlas, Almanac, and dusty large geography volumes to teach these necessary and meaningful skills.

Although these worthy library and perhaps classroom library books can still be used, it is much easier to take a simple newspaper to introduce and provide children with daily ongoing, authentic experiences in learning these necessary skills as they also keep up with real world events that affect their daily lives.

They can go on a chronological hunt through the daily newspaper and discover the many formats of schedules contained therein. For instance, some newspapers include a calendar of the week with literary, sports, social, movie and other public events. Children can also go on scavenger hunts through various sections of the newspaper and on certain days find full blown timelines detailing famous individual's careers, business histories, and milestones in the political history of a nation or even key movies made by a famous movie director up for an Oscar.

The nature of the newspaper reportage and the public's need to know the why and wherefore behind the story of natural disasters, company takeovers, political downfalls and uprisings leads newspapers to represent events graphically and to use cause /effect diagramming and comparison/contrast wording. If the teacher specifically wants to make certain that the students come away with this material, he or she can pre-clip "teaching" stories from the news for the child and introduce them in a special NEWS center.

After children have been walked through these comparison/contrast news writings and cause/effect diagramming as it has appeared in the newspaper, they can be challenged to find additional examples of these text structures in the news or challenged to reframe or rewrite familiar stories using these text structures. They can even use desktop publishing to re-author the stories using the same text structures.

If a class participates in a local Newspaper in Education program, where the children receive a free newspaper two to three times a week within the classroom, the teacher can teach indexing skills using the index of the newspaper and having children compete or cooperate in small groups to find various features.

Map and chart skills take on much more relevance and excitement when the children work on these skills using sport charts detailing the batting averages and pass completions of their favorite players or perhaps the box scores of their older siblings' football and baseball games. Maps dealing with holiday weather become meaningful to children as they anticipate a holiday vacation.

Ability to Apply Reading Skills for Various Purposes

What is really intriguing about the use of newspapers as a model and an authentic platform for introducing children into recognizing and using expository text structures, features, and references is that the children can demonstrate their mastery of these structures by putting out their own newspapers detailing their school universe using some of these text structures.

They can also create their own timelines for projects or research papers they have done in class using newspaper models.

Application of Comprehension Strategies for Electronic Texts

If the class gets newspapers in the classroom as part of an ongoing Newspapers in Education program, it is natural and easy for the teacher to take the time to show children how the same news is covered online. All of the newspapers have e-news. Children can first do a K-W-L on what they know or think they know about e-news and then actually review their specific daily newspaper's site. With the support of the teacher or an older peer, they can examine the resource and perhaps note the following differences in electronic text:

- Use of moving pictures and video to document events
- Use of sound clips in addition to written text
- Use of music/sound effects not in printed text
- Links to other web resources and to other archived articles

Of course, this can lead to much rich discussion and to further detailed web versus print news resource analysis. For children in grades 5 and 6, this might even include a research investigation of a particular news story or event including broadcast media coverage.

Development of Reading Comprehension Skills and Strategies of Individual Students

Both English Language Learners and struggling readers can benefit from the structure and format of the K-W-L approach. It allows them to share their prior experiences and knowledge of the topics covered in the expository text through natural conversation. It provides them with a natural device for the teacher or tutor to customize and to scaffold instruction to meet their linguistic and experiential backgrounds. Through the discussion and sharing of other children's comments, struggling readers and children from ELL backgrounds have an opportunity to learn how to use questions to "walk through" and take notes on expository writing.

Highly proficient readers can do a comparative expository news event study between print accounts, e-news reportage, and broadcast media coverage. They can prepare charts and their own news mock-up to show the similarities and contrasts between what aspects of the event get covered in what media format. They may also want to write to actual reporters and editors from the different media to share their insights and see if these professionals are willing to respond.

"If we want children to become strategic readers, then we create classrooms that reinforce the strategies we've demonstrated and allow children to practice on books that match their needs."
Sharon Taberski

Skill 8.2 Identify ways to model questioning strategies.

Several well known researchers have described different levels of comprehension from the simplest to the more complex. The most basic level of comprehension is literal. At this point, students are able to answer questions which can be directly found in the text. These questions are simple recall and based directly on the text. In this way, students should be able to find the exact answer to the question in their reading. The do not have to make any generalizations.

The next level of comprehension is inferential questioning. At this level the general idea of the question can be found in the text, but the reader must extrapolate some information. This drawing of conclusions requires more understanding of the underlying concepts the author is trying to convey through the writing. An example of an inferential type of question might include, why did the author write this story?

Finally, the most complex comprehension skill is the critical or evaluative level. Here students are asked to use the information the author provided in the text and make judgments about it. In this level, students may decide if a decision the author had a character make was a good or bad decision. It may be to explain ways in which the author could improve the story. This critical thinking level is the highest level of comprehension.

Students need to have experiences answering all forms of comprehension questions. Teachers need to model how to find the answers or construct an answer in the case of the higher levels. This modeling provides a general framework the students can then use to build their own. Another strategy for teaching comprehension is a think-aloud. In this strategy, the teacher orally describes his entire thinking process about answering the questions. Students see how the teacher does it and can then generalize this to themselves. Highlighting pertinent information can also be helpful when answering comprehension questions.

Once the skills have been taught, it is important for the teacher to assess periodically to ensure the students understand their reading. This can be done informally by simply asking questions during or after reading that fall along the entire continuum. Retells are a quick way to assess whether the student has the basic facts of the story. Literature circles and discussion groups can delve more into the higher levels. Formal assessments will most definitely provide questions from all the levels and usually include some open-ended questioning which requires a written response.

Skill 8.3   Demonstrate knowledge of ways to teach students to connect prior knowledge with new information.

Development of Literary Response Skills

Literary response skills are dependent on prior knowledge, schemata and background. Schemata (the plural of schema) are those structures which represent concepts stored in our memory.

Without schemata and experiences to call upon as they read, children have little ability to comprehend. Of course, the reader's schemata and prior knowledge have more influence on the comprehension of plot or character information that is implied rather than directly stated.

Prior Knowledge

Prior knowledge can be defined as all of an individual's prior experiences, learning, and development which precede his/her entering a specific learning situation or attempting to comprehend a specific text. Sometimes prior knowledge can be erroneous or incomplete. Obviously, if there are misconceptions in a child's prior knowledge, these must be corrected so that the child's overall comprehension skills can continue to progress. Prior knowledge of children includes their accumulated positive and negative experiences both in and out of school.

These might come from wonderful family travels, watching television, visiting museums and libraries, to visiting hospitals, prisons and surviving poverty. Whatever the prior knowledge that the child brings to the school setting, the independent reading and writing the child does in school immeasurably expands his/her prior knowledge and hence broadens his/her reading comprehension capabilities.

The teacher must consider as he/she prepares to begin any imaginative/literary text the following about the students' level of prior knowledge:

1. What prior knowledge needs to be activated for the text, theme or for the writing to be done successfully?
2. How independent are the children in using strategies to activate their prior knowledge?

Holes and Roser (1987) have suggested five techniques for activating prior knowledge before starting an imaginative/literary text:

Free Recall: Tell us what you know about...

Unstructured Discussion: Let's talk about...

Structured Question: Who exactly was Jane Aviles in the life of the hero of the story?

Word Association: When you hear these words--hatch, elephant, who, think--What author do you think of?

Recognition: Mulberry Street...What author comes to mind?

Previewing, predicting, and story mapping are also excellent strategies for activating prior knowledge.

Skill 8.4   **Demonstrate knowledge of ways to teach students strategies for monitoring their own comprehension.**

See skill 7.1

Skill 8.5   **Identify methods for ensuring that students can use various aspects of text (e.g., conventions of written English, text structure and genres, intertextual connections) to gain comprehension.**

Development of Literary Analysis Skills

There are many exciting ways to sensitize and to teach children about the features and formats of different literary genres.

Strategy One: Genre Switch-Reader and Writer Transformation

This strategy should be introduced as a read aloud with young children or with children who are struggling readers. In a similar fashion, it would be introduced as a read-aloud for ELL learners. Older children in grades 3-6 might just be "started off" by a teacher prompt and do the required reading on their own.

To begin, the teacher selects a particular genre book. If it is close to Halloween, a goblin or suspense story will do well. The teacher begins to read the story with the open invitation to the students to determine as the story is being read, what type of story it is and what makes it that type of story.

Older children take notes in their reading journals, while younger children and those more in need of explicit teacher support contribute their ideas and responses as part of the discussion in class. Their responses are recorded on a chart.

As the reading continues, the story type components are listed on the chart (most of the responses are those which have been elicited from the children).

At some point in what is either an oral read aloud, guided reading or independent reading, the teacher directs the children's attention to the components which have emerged on the chart. They then use these components -- character, setting, plot, style, conflict, language – to identify the story genre.

The teacher provides the children with an opportunity to expound at length on why this story is an example of the genre which they have identified.

Once they have done so, the teacher challenges them to consider how this story with its set of given characters, plot, and setting would be changed if the genre were different. The teacher can challenge the class as a whole with the idea of changing the story to a radically different genre—i.e. from suspense to a fairy tale or a comedy or allow the children to come up another genre.

Then depending on the children's developed writing abilities, they might be given time to rewrite the story on their own or re-tell it in class prior to writing and illustrating it.

In the balanced literacy approach, this transformation of the story into another genre is done as part of the Writing Workshop which uses the same reading material as the source for writing. The strategy results in the children having had the experience of an in-depth analysis of a particular genre as well as hands-on writing (or telling, if they can not yet write or can not yet write in English) experience of restyling that basic plot and characters into another genre. This authenticates the children's participation as readers and writers.

Strategy Two: Analyzing Story Elements

Story elements include plot (including conflict and resolution, setting (including time and place), characters (flat and round/static and dynamic), and theme (the main idea of the story). Students can use graphic organizers such as story maps, compare/contrast displays, and sequence boxes to display their understanding of these critical features of narration.

Strategy Three: Analyzing Character Development

Characters in children's literature may be flat or round. A flat character is one-dimensional and is often defined by one characteristic. Rosie in *Rosie's Walk* is an example. A round character seems like someone you know, such as Jesse in *Bridge to Terabithia*. Static characters do not change from the beginning to the end of the story, while dynamic ones do. Characters reveal themselves through their actions, their interactions, and through what they say.

Strategy Four: Interpreting Figurative Language

Similes are direct comparisons between two things using "like" or "as." "Her eyes were like stars" is a simile. Metaphors are indirect comparisons, such as "The earth is a big blue marble." Personification is giving human characteristics to non-animal beings. Frances, Shrek, or the animals in *Mr. Gumpy's Outing* are all examples of personification.

Strategy Five: Identifying Literary Allusions

Children can understand allusions best when they read a lot. A literary allusion when it appears in a story is also called *intertextuality*. That is when a reference, character, or symbol from one story appears or is alluded to in another. Recently, many popular children's books use literary allusions, from the Ahlbergs' *Each Peach Pear Plum* to Jon Scieszka's *The True Story of the Three Little Pigs*. Note that any character or plot element can become an allusion, not just references from fairy tales.

Strategy Six: Analyzing the Author's Point of View

In fiction, point of view is the vantage point from which the narrator tells the story. We determine point of view by asking, where is the narrator standing in relation to the characters. Is the narrator inside or outside of the story? If inside, is the narrator one of the characters? This is *first person point of view*. If outside, can the narrator "see" into anyone else's mind besides his/her own? If the narrator cannot see into the mind and heart of other characters, then the point of view is *third person limited*. Narrators who can see what other characters are thinking and feeling are using *third person omniscient point of view*.

Use of Comprehension Strategies Before, During, and After Reading

Cooper (2004), Taberski (2000), Cox (2005) and other researchers recommend a broad array of comprehension strategies before, during, and after reading.

Cooper (2004) suggests a broad range of classroom posters on the walls plus explicit instruction to give children prompts to monitor their own reading. An example follows: My Strategic Reading Guide

1. Do I infer/predict important information, use what I know, think about what may happen or what I want to learn?
2. Can I identify important information about the story elements?
3. Do I generate questions and search for the answers?
4. Does this make sense to me? Does this help me meet my purpose in reading?
5. If lost, do I remember fix-ups?
    (e.g.,Re-read, read further ahead, look at the illustrations, ask for help, and think about the words, and evaluate what I have read.)
6. Do I remember to think about how the parts of the stories that I was rereading came together?

Storyboard panels, which are used by comic strip artists and by those artists who do advertising campaigns as well as television and film directors, are perfect for engaging children K-6 in a variety of comprehension strategies before, during, and after reading. They can storyboard the beginning of a story, read aloud, and then storyboard its predicted middle or end. Of course, after they experience or read the actual middle or ending of the story, they can compare and contrast what they produced with its actual structure. They can play familiar literature identification games with a buddy or as part of a center by storyboarding one key scene or characters from a book and challenging a partner or peer to identify the book and characters correctly.

Use of Oral Language Activities to Promote Comprehension

Retelling

Retelling needs to be very clearly defined so that the child reader does not think that the teacher wants him or her to spill the WHOLE story back in the retelling. A child should be able to talk comfortably and fluently about the story he or she has just read. He or she should be able to tell the main things that have happened in the story.

When a child retells a story to a teacher, the teacher needs ways to help assess the child's understanding. Ironically, the teacher can use some of the same strategies he or she suggests to the child to assess the child's understanding of a book which is not familiar to the teacher. These strategies include: back cover reading, scanning the table of contents, looking at the pictures, and reading the book jacket.

If the child can explain how the story turned out and provide examples to support these explanations, try not to interrupt him or her with too many questions. Children can use the text of the book to reinforce what they are saying and they can even read from it if they wish. It is also important to note that some children need to re-read the text twice and their re-reading of it is out of enjoyment.

When the teacher plans to use the retelling as a way of assessing the child, then the following ground rules have to be set and made clear to the child. The teacher explains the purpose of the retelling to determine how well the child is reading at the outset of the conference.

The teacher maintains in the child's assessment notebook or in his/her assessment record what the child is saying in phrases, not sentences. Just enough is recorded to indicate whether the child actually understood the story. The teacher also tries to analyze from the retelling why the child cannot comprehend a given text. If the child's accuracy rate with the text is below 95 per cent, then the problem is at the word level, but if the accuracy rate for the text is above 95 per cent, the difficulty lies at the text level.

Development of the Reading Comprehension Skills and Strategies of Individual Students

ELL Learners bring to their classrooms different prior knowledge concerns than do their native English language speaking peers. Some of the ELL students have extensive prior knowledge in their native language and can read well on or above their chronological age level in their native language. Other ELL learners come to the United States from cultures where reading was not emphasized or circumstances did not give families native language literacy opportunities.

Rigg and Allen (1999) offer the following four principles regarding the literacy development and prior knowledge of ELL-second language learners:

1. In learning a language you learn to do the things you want to do with people who are speaking that language.
2. A second language, like the first, does not develop linearly, but rather globally.
3. Language can develop in rich context.
4. Literacy develops parallel to language, so as speaking and listening for the second language develop, so do writing and reading.

As far as retelling, it needs to be noted that English language learners have the problem of not bringing rich oral English vocabulary to the stories they are decoding. Therefore, often they "sound the stories out" well, but cannot explain what they are about, because they do not know what the words mean.

Skill 8.6   Identify methods for ensuring that students gain understanding of the meaning and importance of the conventions of standard written English (e.g., pronunciation, usage) for comprehending text.

Semantic, syntax and general grammar skills necessary for students' accuracy in reading have been discussed previously within this book. However, it is important to understand how these conventions along with pronunciation and word usage can be used to develop a more thorough understanding of the text being read.

Reading comprehension is a complex set of skills which takes place within the mind of the reader. As we have already discussed, prior knowledge impacts the meaning drawn from reading and varies from reader to reader. It is therefore important for students to have some general skills and strategies to help all readers reach the same generalizations with regards to underlying understanding of texts.

The conventions of standard written English when applied to reading can help provide this commonality. When students understand the relationship between words, word meanings, pronunciation, and word usage they can have a firm foundation for comprehending the text. Word usage can be of particular importance considering the number of multiple meanings words have within the English language. Students need to understand how the same word may have more than one meaning, and then they can realize how other tools can be used to derive which meaning is appropriate to the situation.

Pronunciation is another key component to this foundation of skills. While the majority of reading and reading comprehension occurs silently, the students are typically hearing their own voice in their head read the story to them. When they come across a word they are unable to pronounce, it can cause a stumbling block to comprehension. Mispronunciations can also provide difficulty to students. In some cases, a mispronunciation can completely change the meaning of what is being read. To assist in this area, teachers should teach the ability to decipher and interpret the decoding of pronunciation guides in dictionaries.

Overall, students and teachers alike need to understand the value and connection between the reading and writing domains and their importance in the comprehension of texts. Students understand and learn a variety of subskills in English and reading classes; the adequate transference of these skills is crucial to providing the best chance of understanding what is being read.

COMPETENCY 9.0 UNDERSTAND METHODS FOR USING LITERATURE TO PROMOTE STUDENTS' LITERACY SKILLS.

Skill 9.1 Demonstrate familiarity with a wide range of classic and contemporary children's and young adults' fictional and informational literature at appropriate levels of interest and readability.

Major Genres:

Children's literature is a genre of its own and emerged as a distinct and independent form in the second half of the 18th century. *The Visible World in Pictures* by John Amos Comenius, a Czech educator, was one of the first printed works and the first picture book. For the first time, educators acknowledged that children are different from adults in many respects. Modern educators acknowledge that introducing elementary students to a wide range of reading experiences plays an important role in their mental/social/psychological development. Some of the most common forms of literature specifically for children follow:

Traditional Literature: Traditional literature opens up a world where right wins out over wrong, where hard work and perseverance are rewarded, and where helpless victims find vindication—all worthwhile values that children identify with even as early as kindergarten. In traditional literature, children will be introduced to fanciful beings, humans with exaggerated powers, talking animals, and heroes that will inspire them. For younger elementary children, these stories in Big Book format are ideal for providing predictable and repetitive elements that can be grasped by these children.

Folktales/Fairy Tales: Some examples: The Three Bears, Little Red Riding Hood, Snow White, Sleeping Beauty, Puss-in-Boots, Rapunzel, and Rumpelstiltskin. Adventures of animals or humans and the supernatural characterize these stories. The hero is usually on a quest and is aided by other-worldly helpers. More often than not, the story focuses on good and evil and reward and punishment.

Fables: Animals that act like humans are featured in these stories and usually reveal human foibles or sometimes teach a lesson. Example: Aesop's Fables.

Myths: These stories about events from the earliest times, such as the origin of the world, are considered true in their own societies.

Legends: These are similar to myths except that they tend to deal with events that happened more recently. Example: Arthurian legends.

Tall tales: Examples: Paul Bunyan, John Henry, and Pecos Bill. These are purposely exaggerated accounts of individuals with superhuman strength.

Modern Fantasy: Many of the themes found in these stories are similar to those in traditional literature. The stories start out based in reality, which makes it easier for the reader to suspend disbelief and enter worlds of unreality. Little people live in the walls in *The Borrowers* and time travel is possible in *The Trolley to Yesterday*. Including some fantasy tales in the curriculum helps elementary-grade children develop their imaginations. These often appeal to ideals of justice and issues having to do with good and evil; and because children tend to identify with the characters, the message is more likely to be retained.

Science Fiction: Robots, spacecraft, mystery, and civilizations from other ages often appear in these stories. Most presume advances in science on other planets or in a future time. Most children like these stories because of their interest in space and the "what if" aspect of the stories. Examples: *Outer Space and All That Junk* and *A Wrinkle in Time*.

Modern Realistic Fiction: These stories are about real problems that real children face. By finding that their hopes and fears are shared by others, young children can find insight into their own problems. Young readers also tend to experience a broadening of interests as the result of this kind of reading. It's good for them to know that a child can be brave and intelligent and can solve difficult problems.

Historical Fiction: *Rifles for Watie* is an example of this kind of story. Presented in a historically-accurate setting, it's about a young boy (16 years) who serves in the Union army. He experiences great hardship but discovers that his enemy is an admirable human being. It provides a good opportunity to introduce younger children to history in a beneficial way.

Biography: Reading about inventors, explorers, scientists, political and religious leaders, social reformers, artists, sports figures, doctors, teachers, writers, and war heroes helps children to see that one person can make a difference. They also open new vistas for children to think about when they choose an occupation to fantasize about.

Informational Books: These are ways to learn more about something you are interested in or something that you know nothing about. Encyclopedias are good resources, of course, but a book like *Polar Wildlife* by Kamini Khanduri shows pictures and facts that will capture the imaginations of young children.

Skill 9.2 Demonstrate knowledge of ways to locate, evaluate, and use literature for readers of all abilities, ages, and backgrounds.

For Example:

These classic and contemporary works combine the characteristics of multiple theories. Functioning at the concrete operations stage (Piaget), being of the "good person," orientation (Kohlberg), still highly dependent on external rewards (Bandura), and exhibiting all five needs previously discussed from Maslow's hierarchy, these eleven to twelve year olds should appreciate the following titles, grouped by reading level. These titles are also cited for interest at that grade level and do not reflect high-interest titles for older readers who do not read at grade level. Some high interest titles will be cited later.

<u>Reading level 6.0 to 6.9</u>

Barrett, William. *Lilies of the Field*
Cormier, Robert. *Other Bells for Us to Ring*
Dahl, Roald. *Danny, Champion of the World; Charlie and the Chocolate Factory*
Lindgren, Astrid. *Pippi Longstocking*
Lindbergh, Anne. *Three Lives to Live*
Lowry, Lois. *Rabble Starkey*
Naylor, Phyllis. *The Year of the Gopher, Reluctantly Alice*
Peck, Robert Newton. *Arly*
Speare, Elizabeth. *The Witch of Blackbird Pond*
Sleator, William. *The Boy Who Reversed Himself*

For seventh and eighth grades

Most seventh and eight grade students, according to learning theory, are still functioning cognitively, psychologically, and morally as sixth graders. As these are not inflexible standards, there are some twelve and thirteen year olds who are much more mature socially, intellectually, and physically than the younger children who share the same school. They are becoming concerned with establishing individual and peer group identities that presents conflicts with breaking from authority and the rigidity of rules. Some at this age are still tied firmly to the family and its expectations while others identify more with those their own age or older. Enrichment reading for this group must help them cope with life's rapid changes or provide escape and thus must be either realistic or fantastic depending on the child's needs. Adventures and mysteries (the Hardy Boys and Nancy Drew series) are still popular today. These preteens also become more interested in biographies of contemporary figures rather than legendary figures of the past.

Reading level 7.0 to 7.9

Armstrong, William. *Sounder*
Bagnold, Enid. *National Velvet*
Barrie, James. *Peter Pan*
London, Jack. *White Fang, Call of the Wild*
Lowry, Lois. *Taking Care of Terrific*
McCaffrey, Anne. The *Dragonsinger* series
Montgomery, L. M. *Anne of Green Gables* and sequels
Steinbeck, John. *The Pearl*
Tolkien, J. R. R. *The Hobbit*
Zindel, Paul. *The Pigman*

Reading level 8.0 to 8.9

Cormier, Robert. *I Am the Cheese*
McCullers, Carson. *The Member of the Wedding*
North, Sterling. *Rascal*
Twain, Mark. *The Adventures of Tom Sawyer*
Zindel, Paul. *My Darling , My Hamburger*

For ninth grade

Depending upon the school environment, a ninth grader may be top-dog in a junior high school or underdog in a high school. Much of his social development and thus his reading interests become motivated by his peer associations. He is technically an adolescent operating at the early stages of formal operations in cognitive development. His perception of his own identity is becoming well-defined and he is fully aware of the ethics required by society. He is more receptive to the challenges of classic literature but still enjoys popular teen novels.

Reading level 9.0 to 9.9

Brown, Dee. *Bury My Heart at Wounded Knee*
Defoe, Daniel. *Robinson Crusoe*
Dickens, Charles. *David Copperfield*
Greenberg, Joanne. *I Never Promised You a Rose Garden*
Kipling, Rudyard. *Captains Courageous*
Mathabane, Mark. *Kaffir Boy*
Nordhoff, Charles. *Mutiny on the Bounty*
Shelley, Mary. *Frankenstein*
Washington, Booker T. *Up From Slavery*

Skill 9.3   Demonstrate familiarity with various tools and methods used to estimate the readability of texts.

The *Spache* readability formula calculates the U.S. grade level of a text sample based on sentence length and number of unfamiliar words. Unfamiliar words are ones that do not appear on a specially designed list of common words that are familiar to most younger readers (4th grade and below).

Spache is generally used for primary age (Kindergarten to 7th grade) readers to help classify school textbooks and literature, whereas Dale-Chall is better meant for secondary age readers.

Because this formula is based on the usage of familiar words (rather than syllable or letter counts), it is often regarded as a more accurate test for younger readers.
Note that the Spache word list and formula were revised in 1974 and this is the version that Readability Studio uses.

The Spache Formula
GL = (.121 * ASL) + (.082 *UW) + .659
Where:

GL	U.S. grade level
ASL	Average sentence length
UW	Number of unique unfamiliar words

This test requires a 100-word sample; however, note that Readability Studio always analyzes your entire document to guarantee the most accurate results and does not use subsamples for any of its test calculations. If a formula requires a subsample of a specific size, then standardization is used.

The *Dale-Chall* readability formula calculates the U.S. grade level of a text sample based on sentence length and the number of unfamiliar words. Unfamiliar words are ones that do not appear on a specially designed list of common words that are familiar to most 4th-grade students.

The original familiar word list was only 763 words; however, Professors Chall and Dale extended this list to 3,000 for the revised version of this formula in 1995. Note that the revised version of this formula is what Readability Studio uses. Because this formula is based on the usage of familiar words (rather than syllable or letter counts), it is often regarded as a more accurate test for younger readers.

The **Fry Readability Formula** (or **Fry Readability Graph**) was developed by Dr. Edward Fry.

The grade reading level (or reading difficulty level) is calculated by the average number of sentences and syllables per hundred words. These averages are plotted onto a specific graph; the intersection of the average number of sentences and the average number of syllables determines the reading level of the content.

The formula and graph are often used to provide a common standard by which the readability of documents can be measured. It is sometimes used for regulatory purposes, such as in healthcare, to ensure publications have a level of readability that is understandable and accessible by a wider portion of the population.

The **Flesch-Kincaid Reading level** tells how easy something is to read by counting the number of syllables in every word and the number of words in every sentence. Then some math is done. The number which results is a grade-school level. For example, a sentence with a score of 8.0 means that someone in 8th grade could understand. Normal writing is usually between a 7 and an 8.
The formula used to calculate the level is as follows:

0.39 x Average No. of words in sentences + 11.8 x Average No. of syllables per word - 15.59

COMPETENCY 10.0 UNDERSTAND METHODS FOR PROMOTING STUDENTS' STUDY AND RESEARCH SKILLS.

Skill 10.1 Identify methods for developing students' strategies for locating and using a variety of print, nonprint, and electronic sources.

Content area subjects often have texts with a great deal of information. In cases like this, it is necessary for the students to develop specific study skills to help them take in the important information while weeding out the less important.

Highlighting is a difficult strategy for students to master. Even at the college level it seems students have a hard time determining what is important and necessary. Key ideas or vocabulary are a good place to start with highlighting. Teaching students to highlight less information, rather than more, is also important. It is not a good study skill if a student highlights an entire page of information.

Outlining is a skill many teachers use to help students understand important facts. Sometimes the teacher can provide an outline for the students to use as a guide when taking their own notes. In this way, the students know the important parts to key into when reading. Developing outlines can be very difficult for some students, for those students mapping might be a more appropriate study aid.

Mapping involves using graphics, pictures, and words to represent the information in the text. The students can personalize and use colors and pictures which have meaning to them. This provides the natural bridge to prior knowledge and frames the information in a more personal way.

Note-taking skills also are something that require direct instruction. Sometimes, teachers assume students understand how to take notes based on a lecture format, when in fact; the majority of students are trying to write down everything they hear. Teachers can help in this process by taking the time to specifically teach and highlight the key factors.

Test-taking skills are another area that may need to be bolstered. Teaching students to eliminate wrong answers first, and then narrowing down the choices is a start. In open-ended questions, students need to be able to restate the question in their answer and understand they need to answer all parts of the question being asked.

Today there are numerous technological methods which can be utilized to increase the ability of students to study. Leap Frog© has study devices which are preprogrammed with textbooks used across the country. These computerized devices allow students to study for tests in yet a different manner. The use of word processing programs, spreadsheets, and the Internet also provides opportunities for students to use technology as part of the study process. In addition to the study process, technology can also be utilized in the direct delivery of instruction as well.

Combining all of these approaches will allow students the opportunity to read, take in new information, and use that information to respond appropriately.

Skill 10.2   Identify methods for teaching students to vary reading rate according to the reader's purpose(s) and the difficulty of the material.

When reading strategically, students need to keep in mind several factors.

Self-Monitoring- When students self-monitor, they keep track of all the factors involved in the process. In this way, they are able to process the information in the manner that is best for them.

Setting the Purpose for Reading- In strategic reading, the child has a specific reason for reading the text. There is information they wish to gain and that should be clear to the student. If it is unclear, the student will not be successful.

Rereading- Rereading is probably one of the most used methods for taking in overwhelming information. By revisiting the text more than once, the student is able to then take in smaller pieces of information that she missed after the first read.

Adjusting Reading Rates and Strategies-Similar to self-monitoring, student s must be able to understand that sometimes it will be necessary to read slower than at other times. Sometimes they will need to make adjustments to the pace at which they are reading in order to be successful at gaining the information they want to gain.

Text Factors-Understanding the arrangement of nonfiction text with section titles and other unique organizational devices can provide the student with other tools to be successful. Knowing the structure of the text can save valuable time and decrease the rereading necessary.

Skill 10.3 Identify methods for teaching students effective time-management strategies.

Teaching students to better manage their time is a difficult skill for many of them to master. Often students are unable to use the time provided appropriately. Even at young ages it is important to begin to instill in students methods for using time effectively.

Providing students with calendars and agendas for long-term assignments, which they can utilize to plan out a strategy for completing their work, provides a visual method of organization many students find helpful. Additionally, many students benefit from setting short-term goals and reminders. They can use the same calendar/agenda for this purpose as well.

For shorter periods of time, students can use things such as a timer to begin to understand the passage of time. Accomplishing tasks before a previously defined time period allows students to begin to build self-reliance and independence. In this way, they are able to attain short-term goals, and this builds a feeling of success. This feeling of success can be transferred into greater periods of time and larger successes.

Managing time is a skill students need to develop to better prepare themselves to be successful at managing the intake of information throughout their education.

Skill 10.4 Identify methods for teaching students strategies to organize, understand, and remember information from verbal and written sources.

Reading does not end when one leaves the reading classroom; it in fact, is an inherent component of every subject taught in schools today. Content area reading (science, social studies) can sometimes be much more difficult for students. Typically, the information is nonfiction and there is a great deal of knowledge contained in smaller amounts of text. Deciphering content area reading requires a unique set of strategies in order to best acquire the necessary information.

Text Format. Teaching children that nonfiction texts are laid out significantly differently from fictional texts is an important realization. Often times the format of the text helps provide an automatic organizational tool to help chunk information. Key words or section headings can help provide students with catch phrases with which they can remember the information. They can also help students to scan a large amount of information to find smaller pieces required to answer comprehension questions. Indexes and table of content skills can provide additional support with this.

Summarizing. As stated before, content subjects generally attempt to convey a great deal of information in a smaller amount of text. This is where summarizing can be valuable and productive. Teaching the students to take larger amounts of information and break it down into four or five sentences allows them to manage more details. It also helps them to make connections and compartmentalize the information.

Graphic Organizers. There a numerous different formats for graphic organizers. They can be defined as a pictorial method of organizing information to help the student remember it more efficiently. Graphic organizers can be complex or simple, provided to the student or drawn from memory. The key is that the method or organizing tool used will help the students classify the information to be learned into smaller pieces with common characteristics. They also help the students to begin to see relationships between concepts. Graphic organizers work well as study aids to help students acquire more information. Some graphic organizers use pictures or other visual cues to help the students remember the items to be learned.

Semantic Mapping. In this strategy of organizing information the students use a visual representation to show how words or concepts are interrelated. This is a form of graphic organizer. In semantic mapping, the new knowledge is directly linked to the prior information. Sometimes called concept mapping, semantic maps allow the learner to see relationships between words or concepts and tie them to their own background knowledge in a meaningful manner.

Graphic Aids - It is important to teach students how to interpret graphic aids which may be included in content area texts. This may involve teaching some other subject area skills (e.g. reading a graph or chart), but it is necessary for students to understand these additions to the text. Graphic aids often help to clarify the text and provide another format to help with accurate interpretation.

Skill 10.5   Identify methods for teaching students test-taking strategies.

With the advent of the Internet the art of research and study skills in texts is becoming lost. It is, however, a skill that needs to be emphasized and explained to students. Understanding reference materials will provide the students with the necessary foundational skills to better prepare them for future learning.

Students need to be able to locate information that they need for projects or to further their learning. In order to be able to find the information they need, students will need knowledge of using indexes, table of contents, and other time saving helpers.

Furthermore, students need to be taught how to read and interpret graphs, charts and maps that will be found within reference materials and content-specific materials. Being able to correctly interpret these types of information will better allow the student to draw appropriate conclusions. These aids will enhance the knowledge the student gains from reading and provide further clarification.

Once the children understand how to access and interpret the information contained in content-specific materials or reference materials they can then begin to analyze it to clarify their thinking and make connections to their own life or to other texts. Sometimes, the students will find conflicting pieces of information that they will be able to then look at in more depth.

Processing information in this way takes the level of reading to an even higher more involved level. It also requires students to find their own method for integrating it into their personal schema for later recall.

Teaching students specific study skills like note taking, summarizing, using graphic organizers, semantic mapping, and time management will allow for effective use of the reference materials available to them.

COMPETENCY 11.0 UNDERSTAND METHODS FOR PROMOTING STUDENTS' WRITING SKILLS.

Skill 11.1 Demonstrate familiarity with methods for teaching students planning strategies most appropriate for particular kinds of writing.

See skill 6.1

Skill 11.2 Demonstrate familiarity with methods for teaching students to draft, revise, edit, and publish their writing.

The writing process is one which is important for students to learn. Writing is not a skill many can achieve perfectly on a first round with no need for improvement. Most authors need to make changes to their writing as it develops, and it's important for students to see the value and necessity of this procedure.
The first step in the process involves a planning stage. This may be through the use of graphic organizers, outlines or other organizational tools. Students need to find a way to brainstorm ideas, organize thoughts, and bring together the jumble of ideas about the topic in their minds.

After the initial planning is completed, the students can begin to write their first draft. During this stage, the student is writing for the flow of the words and ideas. They are not as concerned with grammar, punctuation, and the other rules of language. The purpose is to write the stories and ideas down in a format to share with others. Many teachers call this part of the process the sloppy copy. Using this terminology helps students to better understand that it is okay for this work in progress to have mistakes within it.

Once the draft is complete, it is time for the editing process, which leads to revisions. It is here that mistakes are detected and worked through. Many times it is helpful to proceed through more than one editing process. The student should take the time to self-edit before passing their work tp others to read. In this way, the majority of the mistakes can be found by the author and corrected through revisions. After the student has found most of the errors him or herself, it can be helpful to have a peer editing session. In this way, the student can gain valuable insight from peers as to how a reader will respond to their writing . Suggestions can be made and the writing can be further clarified. Finally, many times it is important for the student to seek out an adult to complete one final round of editing.

When the editing process is completed, a final good copy of the story is typed and then can be published. Students greatly enjoy making their own books or other published written products. Having a finished project of a published quality provides a feeling of satisfaction for students. However, it is important that not all works of writing be taken to this level and stage. All writing is not intended for publication, and it is vital students understand this fact as well.

Skill 11.3 **Demonstrate familiarity with methods for teaching students the conventions of standard written English needed to edit their writing.**

See skill 6.1

COMPETENCY 12.0   UNDERSTAND PURPOSES OF ASSESSMENT AND APPROPRIATE USES OF ASSESSMENT RESULTS.

Skill 12.1   Demonstrate familiarity with a model of reading diagnosis that includes student proficiency with print conventions, word recognition and analysis, vocabulary, fluency, comprehension, self-monitoring, and motivation.

In a typical school setting there is a model in place for the diagnosis of reading proficiency which accounts for all areas of reading development. First, a screening process is completed to obtain a general picture of the student's competency overall. For students who demonstrate proficiency, there is little more individual follow-up. Screening typically measures some the big ideas in reading (phonemic awareness, phonics, vocabulary, fluency, comprehension) at various levels depending on the age of the student.

When students are unsuccessful at demonstrating the necessary benchmarks or other data indicates the need for more specific diagnosis, additional assessment may occur. In these cases, students may be assessed on specific measures of self-correction rates, motivation, behavioral impact on reading, word recognition, and/or print conventions.

The model of assessment, diagnosis, intervention and reassessment is a continuous process throughout the school year.

Skill 12.2   Demonstrate knowledge of the uses and limitations of informal and formal assessments for screening, diagnosis, and progress monitoring.

See Skill 13.2.

Skill 12.3   Demonstrate an understanding that goals, instruction, and assessment should be aligned.

It is imperative for reading instruction to be aligned with the goals of both the district and state. This alignment assures that necessary content is being covered, taught and shared with all of the students. As this alignment occurs, it should be further expanded to include assessment. These three components are the essential process for insuring students are not only receiving the appropriate information, but that the teachers are making the necessary adjustments to that information to insure the success of all parties involved.

Skill 12.4   Demonstrate knowledge of the procedures for screening classes to identify students in need of more thorough reading diagnoses.

There are universal screening tools available from several sources for use school-wide or for entire classes. Two such assessments are: The Dynamic Indicators of Basic Early Literacy Skills (DIBELS) and AIMS. Both of these assessments are timed, quick assessments of reading skills. They are intended to be given to entire schools to provide an overview of the students' skills across various reading subareas. These assessments do not diagnose specific deficits, but instead help determine which students may require additional intervention to successfully complete the curriculum.

**COMPETENCY 13.0   UNDERSTAND THE CHARACTERISTICS AND
CONSTRUCTION OF FORMAL AND INFORMAL
ASSESSMENTS OF STUDENTS' READING.**

**Skill 13.1   Demonstrate an understanding of methods for assessing
strengths and needs of individual students in the areas of
reading, writing, and spelling and determining students'
reading levels (e.g., independent, instructional, frustration).**

**Characteristics and Uses of Criterion-referenced and Norm-referenced
Tests to Assess Reading Development and Identify Reading Difficulties**

Criterion-referenced – tests where the children are measured against criteria or
guidelines which are uniform for all the test takers. Therefore by definition, no
special questions, formats or considerations are made for the test taker who is
either from a different linguistic/cultural background or is already identified as a
struggling reader/writer. On a criterion-referenced test, it is possible that a child
test taker can score 100% because the child may have actually been exposed to
all of the concepts taught and mastered them. A child's score on such a test
would indicate which of the concepts have already been taught and what he or
she needs additional review or support to master.

Two criterion-referenced tests that are commonly used to assess children's
reading achievement are the Diagnostic Indicators of Basic Early Literacy Skills
(DIBELS) and the Stanford Achievement Test. DIBELS measures progress in
literacy from kindergarten to grade three. It can be downloaded from the Internet
free at dibels.uoregon.edu. The Stanford measures individual children's
achievement in key school subjects. Subtests covering various reading skills are
part of this test. Both DIBELS and the Stanford Achievement Test are group-
administered.

DEGREES OF READING POWER (DRP) –This test is targeted to assess how
well children understand the meaning of written text in real life situations.
This test is supposed to measure the process of children's reading, not the
products of reading such as identifying the main idea and author's purpose.

CTPIII- This is a criterion-referenced test which measures verbal and quantitative
ability in grades 3-12. It is targeted to help differentiate among the most capable
students, i.e., those who rank above the 80th percentile on other standardized
tests. This is a test that emphasizes higher order thinking skills and process-
related reading comprehension questions.

Norm-referenced –test in which the children are measured against one another. Scores on this test are reported in percentiles. Each percentile indicates the percent of the testing population whose scores were lower than or the same as a particular child's score. Percentile is defined as a score on a scale of 100 showing the percentage of a distribution that is equal to it or below it. This type of state standardized norm-referenced test is being used in most districts today in response to the No Child Left Behind Act. While this type of test does not help track the individual reader's progress in his/her ongoing reading development, it does permit comparisons across groups.

There are many more standardized norm-referenced tests to assess children's reading than there are criterion-referenced. In these tests, scores are based on how well a child does compared to others, usually on the local, state and national level. IF the norming groups on the tests are reflective of the children being tested (e.g. same spread of minority, low income, gifted students), the results are more trustworthy.

One of the best known norm-referenced tests is the Iowa Test of Basic Skills. It assesses student achievement in various school subjects and has several subtests in reading. Other examples of norm-referenced tests used around the country are the Metropolitan Achievement Tests, the Terra Nova-2, and the Stanford Diagnostic Reading Test-4. These are all group tests. An individual test that reading specialists use with students is the Woodcock Reading Mastery Test.

Techniques for Determining Students' Independent, Instructional and Frustration Reading Levels

Instructional reading is generally judged to be at the 95 percent accuracy level, although, Taberski places it at between 92 and 97 percent. Taberski tries to enhance the independent reading levels by making sure that readers on the instructional reading levels read a variety of genres and have a range of available and interesting books within a particular genre to read.

Taberski's availability for reading conferences helps her to both assess first hand her children's frustration levels and to model ongoing teacher/reader book conversations by scheduling child-initiated reading conferences when she personally replenishes their book bags.

In order to allay children's frustration levels in their reading and to foster their independent reading, it is important to some children that the teacher personally take time out to hear them read aloud and to check for fluency and expression. Children's frustration level can be immeasurably lessened if they are explicitly told by the teacher after they have read aloud that they need to read without pointing and that they should try chunking words into phrases which mimic their natural speech.

Assessment of the Reading Development of Individual Students

For young readers who are from ELL backgrounds, even if they have been born in the United States, the use of pictures validates their story authoring and story telling skills and provides them with access and equity to the literary discussion and book talk of their native English speaking peers. These children can also demonstrate their storytelling abilities by drawing sequels or prequels to the story detailed in the illustrations alone. They might even be given the opportunity to share the story aloud in their native language or to comment on the illustrations in their native language.

Since many stories today are recorded in two or even three languages at once, discussing story events or analyzing pictures in a different native language is a beneficial practice which can be accomplished in the 21st century marketplace.

Use of pictures and illustrations can also help the K-3 educator assess the capabilities of children who are struggling readers if the children's learning strength is spatial. Through targeted questions about how the pictures would change if different plot twists occurred or how the child might transform the story through changing the illustrations, the teacher can begin to assess struggling reader's deficits and strengths.

Children from ELL backgrounds can benefit from listening to a recorded version of a particular story which they can read along with the tape. This gives them another opportunity to "hear" the story correctly pronounced and presented and to begin to internalize its language structures. In the absence of taped versions of some key stories or texts, the teacher may want to make sound recordings her or himself.

Highly proficient readers can also be involved in creating these literature recordings for use with ELL peers or younger peers. This of course develops oral language proficiency and also introduces these skilled readers into the intricacies of supporting ELL reading instruction. When they actually see their tapes being used by children, they will be tremendously gratified.

Skill 13.2   Demonstrate an understanding of methods for developing and conducting assessments that involve multiple indicators of learner progress.

The Use of Data and Ongoing Reading Assessment to Adjust Instruction to Meet Students' Reading Needs

Assessment is the practice of collecting information about children's progress, and evaluation is the process of judging the children's responses to determine how well they are achieving particular goals or demonstrating reading skills.

Assessment and evaluation are intricately connected in the literacy classroom. Assessment is necessary because teachers need ways to determine what students are learning and how they are progressing. In addition, assessment can be a tool which can also help students take ownership of their own learning and become partners in their ongoing development as readers and writers. In this day of public accountability, clear, definite and reliable assessment creates confidence in public education.

There are two broad categories of assessment

Informal assessment utilizes observations and other non-standardized procedures to compile anecdotal and observation data/evidence of children's progress. It includes but is not limited to checklists, observations, and performance tasks.   Formal assessment is composed of standardized tests and procedures carried out under circumscribed conditions. Formal assessments include: state tests, standardized achievement tests, NAEP tests, and the like.

To be effective, assessment should have the following characteristics:

I. It should be an ongoing process with the teacher making informal or formal assessments on an ongoing basis. The assessment should be a natural part of the instruction and not intrusive.

2. The most effective assessment is integrated into ongoing instruction. Throughout the teaching and learning day, the child's written, spoken and reading contributions to the class or lack thereof, need to and can be continually noted.

3. Assessment should reflect the child's actual reading and writing experiences. The child should be able to show that he or she can read and explain or react to a similar literary or expository work.

4. Assessment needs to be a collaborative and reflective process. Teachers can learn from what the children reveal about their own individual assessments. Children, even as early as grade two, should be supported by their teacher to continually and routinely ask themselves questions assessing their reading. They might ask: "Am I understanding what the author wanted to say?" " What can I do to improve my reading?" and "How can I use what I have read to learn more about this topic?"

Teachers need to be informed by their own professional observation AND by children's comments as they assess and customize instruction for children.

5. Quality assessment is multidimensional and may include but not be limited to samples of writings, student retellings, running records, anecdotal teacher observations, self-evaluations, and records of independent reading. From this multidimensional data, the teacher can derive a consistent level of performance and design additional instruction that will enhance the child's reading performance.

6. Assessment must take into account children's age and ethnic/cultural patterns of learning.

7. Assess to teach children from their strengths, not their weaknesses. Find out what reading behaviors children demonstrate well and then design instruction to support those behaviors.

8. Assessment should be part of children's learning process and not done TO them, but rather done WITH them.

Concepts of Validity, Reliability, and Bias in Testing

Validity is how well a test measures what it is supposed to measure. Teacher made tests are therefore not generally extremely valid, although they may be an appropriate measure for the validity of the concept the teacher wants to assess for his/her own children's achievement.

Reliability is the consistency of the test. This is measured by whether the test will indicate the same score for the child who takes it more than once.

Bias in testing occurs when the information within the test or the information required to respond to a multiple choice question or constructed response (essay question on the test) is information that is not available to some test takers who come from a different cultural, ethnic, linguistic or socio-economic background than do the majority of the test takers. Since they have not had the same prior linguistic, social or cultural experiences that the majority of test takers have had, these test takers are at a disadvantage in taking the test and no matter what their actual mastery of the material taught by the teacher, they cannot address the "biased" questions. Generally other "non-biased" questions are given to them and eventually the biased questions are removed from the examination.

For example, on a recent reading test in one school system, the grade four reading comprehension multiple choice section had some questions about the well known fairy tale of the gingerbread boy. These questions were simple and accessible for most of the children in the class. But two children who were recent new arrivals from the Dominican Republic had learned English there. They were reading on grade four level, but in their Dominican grade school, the story of the Gingerbread Boy was not a major one. Therefore a question about this story on the standardized reading test did demonstrate examiner bias and was not fair to these test takers.

Skill 13.3 **Demonstrate an understanding of methods for administering and using information from interest inventories, norm-referenced tests, formal and informal inventories, constructed response measures, portfolio-based assessments, student self-evaluations, work/performance samples, observations, anecdotal records, journals, and other indicators of student progress to inform instruction.**

The Characteristics and Uses of Formal and Informal Assessments

Informal Assessments

A running record of children's oral reading progress in the early grades K-3 is a pivotal informal assessment. It supports the teacher in deciding whether a book a child is reading is matched to his/her stage of reading development. In addition this assessment allows the teacher to analyze a child's miscues to see which cueing systems and strategies the child uses and to determine which other systems the child might use more effectively. Finally the running record offers a graphic account of a child's oral reading.

Generally, a teacher should maintain an annotated class notebook with pages set aside for all the children or individual notebooks for each child. One of the benefits of using running records as an informal assessment is that they can be used with any text and can serve as a tool for teaching, rather than an instrument to report on children's status in class.

Another strength of running records is that they can be taken repeatedly and frequently by the teacher, so that the educator can truly observe a pattern of errors. This in turn provides the educator with sufficient information to analyze the child's reading over time. As any mathematician or scientist knows, the more samples of a process you gather over time, the more likely the teacher is to get an accurate picture of the child's reading needs.

Using the notations which Marie Clay developed and shared in her *An Observation Study of Early Literacy Achievement*, Sharon Taberski offers in her book, *On Solid Ground*, a lengthy walk through keeping a running record of children's reading. She writes in the child's miscue on the top line of her running record above the text word. Indeed she records all of the child's miscue attempts on the line above the text word. Sharon advises the teacher to make all the miscue notations as the child reads, since this allows the teacher to get additional information about how and why the child makes miscue choices. Additionally, the teacher should note, self corrections (coded SC) when the child is monitoring his/her own reading, crosschecks information, and uses additional information.

As part of the informal assessment of primary grade reading, it is important to record the child's word insertions, omissions, requests for help, and attempts to get the word. In informal assessment the rate of accuracy can be estimated by dividing the child's errors by the total words read.

Results of a running record assessment can be used to select the best setting for the child's reading. If a child reads from 95%-100% correctly, the child is ready for independent reading. If the child reads from 92% to 97% right, the child is ready for guided reading. Below 92% the child needs a read-aloud or shared reading activity. Note that these percentages are slightly different from those one would use to match books to readers.

One of the increasingly popular and meaningful forms of informal assessment is the compilation of the literacy portfolio. What is particularly compelling about this type of informal portfolio is that artists, television directors, authors, architects and photographers use portfolios in their careers and jobs. This is a most authentic format for documenting children's literacy growth over time. The portfolio is not only a significant professional informal assessment tool for the teacher, but a vehicle and format for the child reader to take ownership of his or her progress over time. It models a way of compiling one's reading and writing products as a lifelong learner, which is the ultimate goal of reading instruction.

Portfolios can include the following six categories of materials:

Work samples: These can include children's story maps, webs, K-W-L charts, pictures, illustrations, storyboards, and writings about the stories which they have read.

Records of independent Reading and Writing: These can include the children's journals, notebooks or logs of books read with the names of the authors, titles of the books, date completed, and pieces related to books completed or in progress.

Checklists and Surveys: These include checklists designed by the teacher for reading development, writing development, ownership checklists, and general interest surveys.

Self Evaluation Forms: These are the children's own evaluations of their reading and writing process framed in their own words. They can be simple templates with starting sentences such as: "I am really proud of the way I ...

I feel one of my strengths as a reader is _____

To improve the way I read aloud I need to _____

To improve my reading I should _____

Generally at the beginning of a child's portfolio in grade 3 or above there is a letter to the reader explaining the work that will be found in the portfolio and from fourth grade level up, children write a brief reflection detailing their feelings and judgments about their growth as readers and writers.

When teachers are maintaining the portfolios for mandated school administrative review, district review, or even for their own research, they often prepare portfolio summary sheets. These provide identifying data on the children and then a timeline of their review of the portfolio contents plus professional comments on the extent to which the portfolio documents satisfactory and ongoing growth in reading.

Portfolios can be used beneficially for child-teacher and of course, parent/teacher conversations to review the child's progress, discuss areas of strength, set future goals, make plans for future learning activities and evaluate what should remain in the portfolio and what needs to be cleared out for new materials.

Rubrics

Holistic scoring involves assessing a child's ability to construct meaning through writing. It uses a scale called a RUBRIC which can range from 0 to 4.

O- This indicates the piece cannot be scored. It does not respond to the topic or is illegible.

1- The writing does respond to the topic, but does not cover it accurately.

2- This piece of writing does respond to the topic but lacks sufficient details or elaboration.

3- This piece fulfills the purpose of the writing assignment and has sufficient development (which refers to details, examples, and elaboration of ideas).

4- This response has the most details, best organization, and presents a well expressed reaction to the original writer's piece.

MISCUE ANALYSIS

This is a procedure that allows the teacher a look at the reading process. By definition, the miscue is an oral response different from the text being read. Sometimes miscues are also called unexpected responses or errors. By studying a student's miscues from an oral reading sample, the teacher can determine which cues and strategies the student is correctly using or not using in constructing meaning. Of course, the teacher can customize instruction to meet the needs of this particular student.

INFORMAL READING INVENTORIES (IRI)

These are a series of samples of texts prearranged in stages of increasing difficulty. Listening to children read through these inventories, the teacher can pinpoint their skill level and the additional concepts they need to work on.

Characteristics and uses of Group versus Individual Reading Assessments

In assessment, tests are used for different purposes. They have different dimensions or characteristics whether they are given individually or in a group and whether they are standardized or teacher-made. The chart below shows the relationships of these elements.

	Standardized	Teacher-made
Individual	*Characteristics* • is uniformly administered *Uses* • is best for younger children • helps with placement for special services	*Characteristics* • has more flexibility *Uses* • assists teaching decisions • used for diagnostic purposes
Group	*Characteristics* • is uniformly administered • is time efficient *Uses* • permits comparisons across groups • used for policy decisions by administrators	*Characteristics* • has high face validity • is time efficient *Uses* • informs teach-reteach & enrichment decisions • documents students' learning

Techniques for Assessing Particular Reading Skills

Sharon Taberski recommends that the teacher build in one-on-one time for supporting individual children as needed in considering what makes sense, sounds right and matches the letters.

She has noted that emergent and early readers tend to focus on meaning without adequate attention to graphophonic cues. She suggests using the following prompts for children who are having problems with graphophonic cues:

Does what you said match the letters?

If the word were what you said ___, what would it have to start with?
Look carefully at the first letters... then look at the middle letters. . then look at the last letters. What could it be?

If it were ____, what would it end with?
Oral retellings can be used to test children's comprehension.

Children who are retelling a story to be tested for comprehension should be told that that is the purpose when they sit down with the teacher.

It is a good idea to let the child start the retelling on his or her own, because then the teacher can see whether he or she needs prompts to retell the story. Many times more experienced readers summarize what they have read. This summary usually flows out along with the characters, the problem of the story and other details.

Other signs that children understand what they are reading when they give an oral retelling include their use of illustrations to support the retelling, references to the exact text in the retelling, emotional reaction to the text, making connections between the text and other stories or experiences they the readers have had, and giving information about the text without the teacher's asking for it.

Awareness of Text Leveling

The classroom library in the context of the balanced literacy approach to reading instruction is focused on leveled books. These are books which have been leveled with the support of Fountas and Pinnell's Guided Reading: *Good First Teaching for All Children* and *Matching Books to Readers: Using Leveled Reading in Guided Reading, K-3.*

The books which are leveled according to the designations in these reference books need to be stored in bins or crates with front covers facing out. This makes them much easier for the children to identify. In that way the children can go through the appropriate levels and find those books that they are particularly interested in which are also at the right level for them to read. These are those books which the children can read with the right degree of reading accuracy. When young children can see the cover of a book, they are more likely to flip through the book until they can independently identify an appealing book. Then they will read a little bit of the book to see if it's "just right."

"Just right" leveled books that children can read on their own need to be available for them to read during independent reading. The goal is for the more fluent readers to select books on their own. Ultimately the use of leveled books helps the children, in addition to the teacher, decide which books are "good" or "just right" for them.

Levels are indicated by means of blue, yellow, red, and green dot stickers at their right upper corners which parallel emergent, early, transitional, and fluent reading stages. They are then kept in containers with other "blue," "yellow," "red," and "green" books.

Other lists and resources other than Fountas and Pinnell which can be used to match children with "just right" books include the Reading Recovery level list. Ultimately, the teacher has to individualize whatever leveling is used in the library to address the individual child learners' needs.

Awareness of the Challenges and Supports in a Text

Illustrations can be key supports for emergent and early readers. Teachers should not only use wordless stories (books which tell their narratives through pictures alone), but can also make targeted use of Big Books for read-alouds, so that young children become habituated to the use of illustrations as an important component for constructing meaning. The teacher should model for the child how to reference an illustration for help in identifying a word in the text the child does not recognize. Of course, children can also go on a picture walk with the teacher as part of a mini-lesson or guided reading and anticipate the story (narrative) using the pictures alone to construct meaning.

Decodability: Use literature which contains examples of letter sound correspondences you wish to teach. First, read the literature with the children or read it aloud to them. Then take a specific example from the text and have the children reread it as the teacher points out the letter-sound correspondence to the children. Then ask the children to go through the now familiar literature to find other letter-sound correspondences. Once the children have correctly made the letter-sound correspondences, have them share similar correspondences they find in other works of literature.

Cooper (2004) suggests that children can become word detectives so that they can independently and fluently decode on their own. The child should learn the following word detective routines so that he or she can function as an independent fluent reader who can decode words on his/her own. First the child should read to the end of a sentence. Then the child should search for word parts which he or she knows. The child should also try to decode the word from the letter sounds. As a last resort, the child should ask someone for help or look up the word in the dictionary.

Skill 13.4 Demonstrate an understanding of the construction and interpretation of classroom reading tests, including the state assessment.

Often times in the classroom, teachers will need to develop their own curriculum - based assessments to measure student progress. When developing these kinds of assessments, it is important to make sure the skills taught align with and match the questions on the assessment.

In analyzing the results of teacher-constructed tests, it can be beneficial to list all of the student results on one sheet. In this manner, an item analysis can be preformed. For example, if all students missed the same question, it can tell a teacher which items need to be re-taught or that perhaps that question was an invalid one and should be eliminated. Also, this chart can be used to form instructional groups based on skills. All of the students who missed a certain question can be grouped together for a brief period of time for some re-teaching.

Many district core curriculum materials may provide their own assessment materials to be used in the classroom. The above-mentioned procedure can be used to help with the interpretation of this data as well. This can help to determine which aspects of the district curriculum these core programs have addressed well and which will need to be addressed through another format. It is important to keep in mind that no one commercially available program will meet all of the needs of the district level curriculum or all of the students in your classroom.

State assessment data is crucial to review and gain knowledge from as well. However, generally state assessment data is available at a point in time when it is difficult to make general adaptation, which will be effective with a particular group of students. Generally, students may have moved on to another grade level or be ready to move on by the time the results are available. Sometimes this can be frustrating to the teachers involved. However, state assessment data can provide valuable information which should not be ignored.

State assessments can help grade levels better see how their teaching and curriculum are working. It can help to provide areas of strength and weakness within the curriculum as related to achieving state standards. It can also be used to help teachers who have the students in the future by identifying areas of strength and weakness within the students themselves.

All assessment data is important to review and consider in the planning of instruction. It is part of the ongoing cycle of planning, instructing and assessing that occurs in all classrooms to ensure appropriate instruction is provided to students.

COMPETENCY 14.0 UNDERSTAND INSTRUCTIONAL METHODS FOR ADDRESSING STUDENTS' READING DIFFICULTIES.

Skill 14.1 Demonstrate knowledge of the nature and multiple causes of reading and writing difficulties.

No one knows exactly what causes learning disabilities. There is a wide range of possibilities that make it almost impossible to pin point the exact cause. Listed below are some factors that can attribute to the development of a disability.

Problems in Fetal Brain Development - During pregnancy things can go wrong in the development of the brain, which alters how the neurons form or interconnect. Throughout pregnancy, brain development is vulnerable to disruptions. If the disruption occurs early, the fetus may die, or the infant may be born with widespread disabilities and possibly mental retardation. If the disruption occurs later, when the cells are becoming specialized and moving into place, it may leave errors in the cell makeup, location, or connections. Some scientists believe that these errors may later show up as learning disorders.

Genetic Factors - Learning disabilities can run in families, which show that there may be a genetic link. For example, children who do not have certain reading skills, such as hearing the separate sounds of words, are likely to have a parent with a similar problem. A parent's learning disability can take a slightly different form in the child. Due to this, it is unlikely that specific learning disorders are directly inherited.

Environment - Additional reasons for why learning disabilities appear to run in families stem from the family environment. Parents with expressive language disorders may talk less to their children or their language may be muffled. In this case the lack of a proper role model for acquiring good language skills causes the disability.

Tobacco, Alcohol, and Other Drug Use -- Many drugs taken by the mother pass directly to the fetus during pregnancy. Research shows that a mother's usage of cigarettes, alcohol, or other drugs during pregnancy may have damaging effects on the unborn child. Mothers who smoke during pregnancy are more likely to have smaller birth weight babies. Newborns who weigh less than 5 pounds are more at risk for learning disorders..

Heavy alcohol use during pregnancy has been linked to fetal alcohol syndrome, a condition resulting in low birth weigh, intellectual impairment, hyperactivity, and certain physical defects.

Sight Vocabulary- Beginning readers may enjoy outdoing Dolch (1936), who compiled the best known sight vocabulary word list. They can create their own class version of this list with illustrations and even some comments about why they have nominated certain words for the list.

Uses of Large Group, Small Group, and Individualized Reading Instruction

The framework for organizing the balanced literacy classroom is referred to as the one book-whole class mode. What this means is that everyone in the class has experiences with the same book. Everyone in the class discusses the literature. The teacher starts by activating prior knowledge and developing the context or background for the piece of literature. Some of the children within the class may have less prior knowledge or context with which to frame the book. The teacher will need to provide a preview of the book or develop key concepts to provide a stronger base for what the class will read together.

Some children will have to work with a paraprofessional or with a reading tutor before the class studies the book. Different modes of reading are accommodated within the class, by the books being read as a read-aloud, as part of shared reading or as guided reading. Student reader choices can also include: cooperative reading, reading with a partner, or independent reading.

Following the reading, the children respond to it which can be done through a literature circle and/or the whole class or in writing.

Strategies for Selecting and Using Meaningful Reading Materials at Appropriate Levels of Difficulty

Matching young children with "just right" books fosters their reading independently, no matter how young they are. The teacher needs to have an extensive classroom library of books. Books that emergent readers and early readers can be matched with should have fairly large print, appropriate spacing, so that the reader can easily see where each word begins and ends, and few words on each page so that the young reader can focus on all important concerns of top-to bottom, left-to-right, directionality, and the one-to-one match of word to print.

Illustrations for young children should support the meaning of the text, and language patterns and predictable text structures should make these texts appealing to young readers. Most important of all, the content of the story should relate to the children's interests and experiences as the teacher knows them.

Only after all these considerations have been addressed can the teacher select "just right" books from an already leveled bin or list. In a similar fashion, when the teacher is selecting books for transitional and fluent readers, the following ideas need to be taken into account:

The book should take at least two sittings to read, so children can get used to reading longer books. The fluent and transitional reader needs to deal with more complex characters and more intricate plotting. Look for books that set the stage for plot development with a compelling beginning. Age appropriateness of the concepts, plot and themes is important so that the child will sustain interest in the book. Look for book features such as a list of chapters to help children navigate through the book.

Series books are wonderful to introduce at this point in the children's development.

Skill 14.4 Demonstrate knowledge of models and procedures for providing reading diagnosis and educational services to students with reading difficulties.

Awareness of Strategies and resources for supporting individual students (e.g. English language learners, struggling readers through highly proficient readers)

"If you teach reading with phonics, you will have no cases of non-readers."
Rudolf Flesch

Highly proficient readers can sometimes support early readers through a partner relationship. Some children, particularly the emergent and beginning early readers, benefit from reading books with partners. The partners sit side by side and each one takes turns reading the entire text

Use of talking book and author web resources provides special needs learners with visual or auditory disabilities immediate contact with authors, and direct sharing in the joy of their oral language story telling. In addition to the accessibility of the keyboard, their responses to literature can be shared with a broad network of other readers, including close and distanced peers. Technology literally enfranchises special needs learners into the circle of connected readers and writers.

In the classroom, there are numerous ways to determine which students are in need of additional assistance. The most effective methods are to examine the classroom performance assessment data available and to work individually with the student.

Regular classroom teachers often have numerous concerns about the students they are working with in the classroom. They will seek out help from the reading specialist for additional strategies and support to help increase students' reading skills. It is important that the specialist be able to determine what difficulties require additional assistance and in which specific areas of reading to provide that assistance.

As previously discussed, running records are of tremendous value in helping in this area. It is a fast and efficient way to examine the numbers of errors the students are making .. Also, the levels at which the students are able to read can be a warning flag. If a student is struggling with material several grade levels below their current grade it is important to determine the cause.

Once a general warning flag appears, it may be necessary for the specialist to look in depth and administer additional skill specific assessments or examine the data present in more depth. In general, it's good to keep in mind the five larger areas of reading as a method of narrowing down the problem. These include: phonemic awareness, phonics, fluency, comprehension, and vocabulary.

Identifying which of these areas is causing the problems helps the teacher and specialist to determine an appropriate plan of action to address skill deficits. Many children will demonstrate deficits in more than one area, so it is critical to follow the appropriate skill sequence to move the students forward in the most efficient manner possible.

Even knowing the broad area of difficulty may not be enough in itself. Sometimes very skill specific assessment or identification will need to occur before instruction can begin. Other times, a more global approach would be prudent. An example of a time that a global approach would be more beneficial might include a student who has all of the phonics skills in isolation but has difficulty applying them in text. In this case, spending more time teaching the phonics skills will not benefit the child, but rather spending the time helping the child to use other cueing systems beyond phonics in a broader sense through many passages and texts would be a more suitable use of time.

One of the first things that a teacher learns is how to obtain resources and help for his/her students. All schools have guidelines for receiving this assistance especially since the implementation of the Americans with Disabilities Act. The first step in securing help is for the teacher to approach the school's administration or exceptional education department for direction in attaining special services or resources for qualifying students. Many schools have a committee designated for addressing these needs such as a Child Study Team or Core Team. These teams are made up of both regular and exceptional education teachers, school psychologists, guidance counselors, and administrators. The particular student's classroom teacher usually has to complete some initial paper work and will need to do some behavioral observations.

The teacher will take this information to the appropriate committee for discussion and consideration. The committee will recommend the next step to be taken. Often subsequent steps include a complete psychological evaluation along with certain physical examinations such as vision and hearing screening and a complete medical examination by a doctor.

The referral of students for this process is usually relatively simple for the classroom teacher and requires little more than some initial paper work and discussion. The services and resources the student receives as a result of the process typically prove to be invaluable to the student with behavioral disorders.

Collaborative teams play a crucial role in meeting the needs of all students, and they are an important step to identifying students with special needs. Under the Individuals with Disabilities Act (IDEA), which federally mandates special education services in every state, it is the responsibility of public schools to ensure consultative, evaluative and if necessary, prescriptive services to children with special needs. In most school districts, a collaborative group handles this responsibility called the Child Study Team (CST). If a teacher or parent suspects a child to have academic, social or emotional problems, he is she is referred to the CST where educational professionals (including teachers, specialists, the school psychologist, guidance, and other support staff) review the student's case and situation through meetings with the teacher and/or parents/guardians. The CST will determine what evaluations or tests are necessary, if any, and will also assess the results. Based on these results, the CST will suggest a plan of action if one is felt necessary.

One plan of action is an Academic Intervention Plan (AIP). An AIP consists of additional instructional services that are provided to the student in order to help him or her better achieve academically if the student has met certain criteria (such as scoring below the state reference point on standardized tests or performing more than two levels below grade-level).

Another plan of action is a 504 plan. A 504 plan is a legal document based on the provisions of the Rehabilitation Act of 1973 (which preceded IDEA). A 504 plan is a plan for instructional services to assist students with special needs in a regular education classroom setting.

When a student' with physical, emotional, or other impairments (such as Attention Deficit Disorder) impact his or her ability to learn in a regular education classroom setting, that student can be referred for a 504 meeting. Typically, the CST and perhaps even the student's physician or therapist will participate in the 504 meeting and review to determine if a 504 plan will be written.

Finally, a child referred to CST may qualify for an Individualized Education Plan (IEP). An IEP is a legal document, which delineates the specific, adapted services a student with disabilities will receive. An IEP differs from a 504 plan in that the child must be identified for special education services to qualify for an IEP, and ALL students who receive special education services must have an IEP. Each IEP must contain statements pertaining to the student's present performance level, annual goals, related services and supplementary aids, testing modifications, a projected date of services, and assessment methods for monitoring progress. Each year, the CST and guardians must meet to review and update a student's IEP.

At times, the teacher must go beyond the school system to meet the needs of some students. An awareness of special services and resources and how to obtain them is essential to all teachers and their students. When the school system is unable to address the needs of a student, the teacher often must take the initiative and contact agencies within the community. Frequently there is no special policy for finding resources.

It is simply up to the individual teacher to be creative and resourceful and to find whatever helps the student needs. Meeting the needs of all students is certainly a team effort that is most often spearheaded by the classroom teacher

Skill 14.5 **Demonstrate familiarity with methods for developing a variety of reports on and profiles of students with reading difficulties.**

As a reading specialist, it is crucial to develop a method to share information with other staff members, administers, parents, and even the students themselves related to skill weaknesses, strengths, and areas to be developed. As instruction occurs, it is also necessary to provide some form of progress updates as well. The varied nature of the recipients of the information requires that multiple reporting procedures be developed. Obviously, the information shared with parents and students will vary significantly from information colleagues and administrators may require both in details and specificity.

It is also important to consider the method of reporting. It is recommended to consider oral reporting, especially in the case of parents and students. However, it is necessary for the oral report to also have some form of written product. This allows the parents, in particular, to refer to the information later to better support their children. When communicating with parents use simple nontechnical language which can be understood by all parties. Providing examples of the difficulties being experienced as well as ideas for developing these skills are good things to include in the reports.

When talking with students it is important to talk about strengths and provide them with immediate strategies they can implement to improve their skills. Students who are struggling with reading can be very sensitive and frustrated by their own progress. It is necessary to provide remediation, instruction, and suggestions keeping these things in mind.

Administrators generally will want information related to student progress or overall program statistics. In this way, they can use the information to report to school board members or other interested parties to show the value of the reading interventions being delivered in buildings of the district. It is important to keep accurate statistics related to the number of students serviced, the amount of time each student is seen, and the progress made by these students. Keeping this data over years provides a longitudinal look at a program, helping make informed decisions and changes.

Other teachers working with the students need very specific and detailed information in relation to progress of the students in their classrooms. The reading specialist and regular classroom teacher will work hand in hand to ensure the literacy success of the students. Keeping an open line of communication is crucial. Sharing regular struggles and successes also is important. Regular progress monitoring of skills and information provides both parties with enough information to help the students.

COMPETENCY 15.0   UNDERSTAND METHODS FOR WORKING WITH STUDENTS WITH SPECIAL NEEDS WHO HAVE READING DIFFICULTIES.

Skill 15.1   Demonstrate familiarity with the instructional implications of research in reading, special education, psychology, and other fields that deal with the treatment of students with reading and learning difficulties.

In the age of accountability and research-based interventions, reading specialists need to keep abreast of current happenings within their field. One such way is to regularly read the publications of the professional organization in the field, the International Reading Organization, or IRA. While keep abreast can be done in numerous ways, it is important to insure that students are receiving the most appropriate and available instructional strategies.   It also allows the specialist to continue to expand their knowledge base and skill levels.

However, it is necessary to keep in mind other bodies of research may be available which directly impact the teaching of reading. There are other disciplines whose focus may involve the development of literacy skills as well, or on a broader nature the way the brain processes language and language-based tasks. This information can be incorporated into the instruction of literacy skills to students.

The field of special education is one such area. Many students with learning differences struggle with the task of reading in particular. Ongoing research continues in this area and can provide additional information or strategies which may benefit students who are not disabled. By reviewing and keeping up-to-date with what works with the students who are struggling the most, reading specialists can begin to apply this new learning and hopefully prevent some students for struggling.

Psychology researchers study the brain and the way it processes information. School psychology also includes: assessments, interventions, and the response students have to interventions. All of these areas can provide the reading specialist with additional information about appropriate strategies and instructional techniques.

Sometimes the information gleaned from other disciplines, even math, can be applied to the teaching of literacy. General sociological studies also provide information of value. There are other sources of information available as well.

This is why it is important to talk with other specialists within your building and district. No one person can keep up with all of the new information and learning available in all disciplines; however, together a district filled with specialists can share the information learned in their respective areas. This open sharing of information and tasks helps to reach all of the students in the school instead of just a few. A team approach to the meeting of student needs is crucial.

Skill 15.2   Demonstrate knowledge of methods for interpreting diagnostic information to plan instructional programs and explaining diagnostic information to classroom teachers, parents/guardians, and other specialists.

Teachers need to take the information from assessments and understand how to transfer that into instructional objectives and teachable points. This can be a confusing process. As the reading specialist, it is important you be able to work with teachers, other specialists and parents through this process. Taking the time to explain the process and how you arrived at specified instructional objectives will help more than the student.

Looking at the assessment information provided, the reading specialist needs to be able to determine which area of reading is impacted and what skills in that area need to be taught. Keeping in mind the five areas of reading. comprehension, phonemic awareness, phonics, vocabulary, and fluency, the specialist can begin to categorize the information and better plan appropriate instruction.

Skill 15.3   Demonstrate familiarity with the process of developing individual educational plans for students with severe learning problems related to literacy.

Having the knowledge of interpreting and applying formal and informal assessment data is very important to the development of IEPs. An individualized educational instructional program is designed around the child's strengths and weaknesses. An educator must have knowledge of interpreting formal and informal assessment data to assist him in determining some of those strengths and weaknesses.

Formal Assessments:

Results of formal assessments are given in derived scores, which compare the student's raw score to the performance of a specified group of subjects. Criteria for the selection of the group may be based on characteristics such as age, sex, or geographic area. The test results of formal assessments must always be interpreted in light of what type of tasks the individual was required to perform. The most commonly used derived scores follow.

A. Age and Grade Equivalents. These scores are considered developmental scores because they attempt to convert the student's raw score into an average performance of a particular age or grade group.

Age equivalents are expressed in years and months, i.e. 7-3. In the standardization procedure, a mean is calculated for all individuals of the particular age who took the test. If the mean or median number of correct responses for children 7 years and 3 months was 80, then an individual whose raw score was 80 would be assigned an age-equivalent of 7 years and 3 months.

Grade Equivalents are written as years and tenths of years, e.g., 6.2 would read sixth grade, second month. Grade equivalents are calculated on the average performance of the group, and have been criticized for their use to measure gains in academic achievement and to identify exceptional students.

Quartiles, Deciles, and Percentiles indicate the percentage of scores that fall below the individual's raw score. Quartiles divide the score into four equal parts; the first quartile is the point at which 25% of the scores fall below the full score. Deciles divide the distribution into ten equal parts; the seventh decile would mark the point below which 70% of the scores fall. Percentiles are the most frequently used measure, however. A percentile rank of 45 would indicate that the person's raw score was at the point below which 45% of the other scores fell.

B. Standard Scores are raw scores with the same mean (average) and standard deviation (variability of asset of scores). In the standardization of a test, about 68% of the scores will fall above or below 1 standard deviation of the mean of 100. About 96% of the scores will fall within the range of 2 standard deviations above or below the mean. A standard deviation of 20, for example, will mean that 68% of the scores will fall between 80 and 120, with 100 as the mean. The most common are T scores, z scores, stanines, and scaled scores. Standard scores are useful because they allow for direct comparison of raw scores from different individuals. In interpreting scores, it is important to note what type of standard score is being used.

C. Criterion Referenced Tests and Curriculum-based Assessments are interpreted on the basis of the individual's performance on the objectives being measured. Such assessments may be commercially prepared or teacher-made, and can be designed for a particular curriculum or scope and sequence. These assessments are made by selecting objectives, task analyzing those objectives, and selecting measures to test the skills necessary to meet those tasks. Results are calculated for each objective, such as Cindy was able to divide 2-digit numbers by 1-digit numbers 85% of the time and was able to divide 2-digit numbers by 2-digit numbers 45% of the time. These tests are useful for gaining insight into the types of error patterns the student makes. Because the student's performance is not compared to others in a group, results are useful for writing IEPs as well as deciding what to teach.

Informal Assessments:

Some of the most common informal assessments include checklists, observations, and performance assessments/tasks. There are a variety of checklists available. Some, like the Conners Checklist, have standardized procedures for scoring and provide specific details as to the adequate interpretation of the information gained. Other less specific checklists can be interpreted in a broader manner to provide general guidance in writing goals and objectives for the IEP. For example, if on checklists completed by several parties who have regular interaction with the student, the student is rated as having poor organization skills, when writing the IEP a goal might be developed to increase organization.

Observational data and performance assessments can be used in a similar manner as checklists. It is important to keep in mind that one should complete more than one before listing the area in the IEP as either a strength or need. Generally accepted practice looks to at least three measures before considering an area to have validity and reliability.

Sometimes it is necessary to develop assessment strategies specific to the student to build in accommodations for any issues which may be related to the disability. It is important to be very specific when detailing this information to the parents or in reports/IEPs. The reasons behind the need for these individualized strategies, the nature of them, and their scope should all be clearly explained.

As instruction occurs, it is important for the special educator to have a means to evaluate the appropriateness of said instruction. Regular progress monitoring with assessment measures specifically designed for progress monitoring is the most appropriate way to evaluate the success of instruction. Along with the tool, it is important to set realistic goals based on normative data for the rates of growth in specific skills. An example of this can be found in improving reading fluency. If the goal is to improve reading fluency, it is helpful to understand that on average children make about one word more correct per minute each week of instruction. With this information available, one can set an appropriate academic objective within the IEP. Then, progress monitoring using reading fluency measures can occur weekly to ensure the student is making expected growth. If the child is not, then further examination of the reasons need to occur.

SUBAREA IV. PROFESSIONAL ROLES AND RESPONSIBILITIES

COMPETENCY 16.0 UNDERSTAND STRATEGIES FOR IMPLEMENTING AND ENHANCING READING PROGRAMS FOR ALL STUDENTS.

Skill 16.1 Demonstrate an understanding of ways to communicate with students about their strengths, areas for improvement, and ways to achieve improvement.

In education, it is important to not only communicate with other teachers, administrators, parents and other stake holders the strengths and weaknesses of the students, but we must also communicate that information with the students themselves.

If students are not informed, they will have no knowledge or standards by which to judge themselves and to strive for improvement. Communicating with students their individual strengths can help provide them with ways in which they can learn additional information which may be difficult for them at later times. Teaching them to use their strengths and emphasizing them are excellent strategies to build self-esteem as well.

Additionally, students will usually have some basic understanding of areas which are difficult for them. These areas for improvement may be the source of frustration for the student and can be the underlying cause of behavioral issues occurring within the classroom.

Being frank and honest with the students while developing a plan together to address these areas can help the students to feel more in control of situations they may otherwise feel out frustration about. It is often helpful to provide the student with a visual representation of their progress, so they can see small improvements right away. In this way, the student can begin to feel successful about a skill which may have previously been a source of significant frustration previously.

Skill 16.2   Identify ways to differentiate instruction to meet the needs of different students.

Awareness of Strategies and Resources for Supporting Individual Students

Children who come from family backgrounds where English is not spoken lack a solid understanding of its syntactic structure. Therefore as they are being assessed using the oral running record, they may need additional support from their teacher in examining the structure and meaning of English. A child from a non-native English Language speaking background may often pronounce words that make no sense to him or her and just go on reading. They have to learn to stop to construct meaning. This child may have to be prompted to self-correct.

Children from non-native English Language speaking backgrounds can benefit from independent reading opportunities to listen to a familiar story on tape and read along. This also gives them practice in listening to standard English oral reading. Often these children can begin to internalize language structures by listening to a book on tape several times.

Highly proficient readers can sometimes support early readers through a partner relationship. Some children, particularly the emergent and beginning early readers, benefit from reading books with partners. The partners sit side by side and each one takes turns reading the entire text.

Use of talking book and author web resources provides special needs learners with visual or auditory handicapping conditions immediate contact with authors. This can lead to direct sharing in the joy of oral language story telling. In addition to the accessibility of the keyboard, children's responses to literature can be shared with a broad network of other readers, including close and distance peers. Technology literally invites special needs learners into the circle of connected readers and writers.

Skill 16.3   Demonstrate familiarity with methods for implementing programs designed to help students improve their reading and writing, including those supported by federal, state, and local funding.

Funding for materials comes directly through federal and state grants. Sometimes these have specific requirements which must be followed in order for that funding to continue. *Reading First Grants* are an example of this type of situation from federal funding. It is important to understand where the funding is from in order to be sure you are meeting all of the necessary obligations.

COMPETENCY 17.0 UNDERSTAND STRATEGIES FOR PARTICIPATING IN CURRICULUM DEVELOPMENT AND IMPLEMENTATION.

Skill 17.1   Demonstrate knowledge of state and national educational standards relevant to reading education and exemplary programs and practices.

Illinois has its own *Illinois Learning Standards for English Language Arts* which are based on accepted national standards. These standards cover the areas of reading, writing, listening, speaking, and the study of literature. The specific standards can be reviewed at: http://www.isbe.net/ils/ela/standards.htm. These standards provide the direction curriculua in these areas should take for all children in the state. National standards are available from the National Council of Teachers of English and the International Reading Association. They provide the general outline of skills students need in order to be successful readers, writers, listeners and speakers. Following these standards along with keeping abreast with current exemplary programs and practices used in Illinois and across the country will provide the students with the most appropriate educational experience possible.

Skill 17.2   Demonstrate familiarity with curriculum material and instructional technology evaluation guidelines and with methods for selecting and evaluating instructional materials for literacy, including those that are technology based.

Technology is a part of our everyday life, and it is the same for the students we are teaching. It is important to include technology based materials and instructional tools in the reading program. Finding these materials is relatively easy with the use of an Internet search tool. However, evaluating the materials often takes more time and energy. There are programs such as Accelerated Reader which have much documentation and are used as an incentive tool to improve reading. It is important for the teacher to have a specific list of questions against which to compare the various available programs fairly. It is also important to have a specific purpose for the materials. In this way, one can see which materials meet which students' needs in order to use the available resources in the best way possible.

Skill 17.3   Demonstrate an understanding of the importance of participating in the development and implementation of school improvement plans.

As a specialist of any kind within a school building, it is imperative that collaboration among all staff be of top priority. It is not enough to simply service the students who are assigned through whatever means the district or building uses. Current educational trends recognize collaboration as the utmost priority.

In some cases reading specialists are becoming literacy coaches and then are responsible for working closely with regular educators to increase the reading skills of students across the building. This collaborative model has the reading specialist working in the classroom beside the teacher in a team teaching model. At times, lessons may be modeled to demonstrate new or innovative ideas or different ways to structure lessons. Still other times, the two professionals would work together to provide instruction to groups of students.
This coaching model also provides out of classroom time where professional development activities may occur. These may take the form of study groups, individual discussion sessions, or workshop offerings for different strategies. For this to be a successful implementation, it is important for all parties to realize this is a learning session for everyone and one party is not evaluating another.

Another less formal collaboration model simply involves regular meetings where children and their needs are discussed. These meetings may be formal or informal. Usually they revolve around the assessment data gathered on the students. As the data and needs of the students are reviewed, the teachers present will discuss items indicating various needs. This allows for the most appropriate professional development to occur.

As this conversation is directly related to an immediate need for the teacher with his current students, the skills learned are more likely to be implemented. In an informal setting, anyone with knowledge can share his or her ideas, suggestions, strategies or skills.   It is in this format that all parties feel less threatened and comfortable sharing.

As the reading specialist, it is vital to collaborate with other reading specialists as much as possible. Today's use of technology and the availability of email can make this a much less cumbersome task. Collaboration is a vital part of growth for all teachers and should not be seen as a negative. It should instead be viewed as a positive skill that culminates in a team of professionals working together to ensure that all students receive the most appropriate educational experience possible.

Skill 17.4   Demonstrate an understanding of strategies for participating in and facilitating reading curriculum design, revision, and implementation.

As a reading specialist, one duty you will be asked to participate in may be updating the district reading curriculum. Curriculum writing is a skill unto itself and requires an understanding of developmentally appropriate practices, state standards, and materials and resources available.

It is important to understand that curriculum is not the same thing as a program. Many districts have what are called Core Curriculum programs. These commercially developed products are meant to reach the majority of students and provide them with the necessary skills to be successful readers. Companies work hard to look at the state standards and have their products meet these standards. The problem occurs usually due to this all encompassing nature of these materials. The products have so many pieces and parts that certain specific areas may not be taught to the level some students need.

Each district across the country has iits own reading curriculum. While they are aligned with the state standards, they are not exactly the same. Generally, the state provides its guidelines, in the form of standards, for the basic skills needed for students to be productive members of society. Therefore, state standards do not necessarily cover all aspects of reading that a district may feel are important to be taught. In this way. curriculua can be more involved and cover more details than the state requires. However, they should at a minimum address all of the identified state standards at a particular grade level.

Periodically, state departments of education will update and change the standards. This would be a time to revise the district curriculum and incorporate the changes. Additionally, new information may arise through research or through an analysis of testing scores which would further indicate a revision might be necessary. Curriculums should be continuous works in progress. Keeping them current and filled with relevant information is important for the teachers to continue to provide adequate education.

As curriculum changes are made, it's important to update and provide inservice to all teachers. After all, the teachers are the direct personnel responsible for implementing the curriculum on a day-to-day basis. Sometimes, it may be necessary to model or provide professional development activities to the teachers to enable them to properly implement the new curricular changes.

Skill 17.5 **Demonstrate an understanding of strategies for participating in the evaluation and selection of instructional materials, including textbooks, trade books, materials for students with special needs, and technology.**

Uses of Instructional Technology to Promote Reading Development

One of the most interesting ways in which the web complements the Reading and Writing Workshop involves the proliferation of author specific websites. If used judiciously, these web resources allow authors to come into the classroom and allow children to write, question, discuss and share their literacy experiences with the authors themselves. Children can also readily become part of a distanced community of peers who are also reading works by a given author.

For instance, children who have been introduced to the work of Faith Ringgold, the author of *Tar Beach*, can easily visit her online site, www.faithringgold.com. Here they will not only find extensive biographic data on Ringgold, but they will also be able to learn a song inspired by her main character Cassie. They will be able to help illustrate a new story Ringgold has put up on the website, and also see if any of the questions they may have generated in their shared or independent reading of her books have already been answered in the "frequently asked questions" section of her web resource. A few of the author websites respond online to individual children's questions.

There are even some reader response web resources such as the spaghetti review web site where young readers can post their response to different books they are reading. **http://www.book-club-review.com/view.php?cid=1**

COMPETENCY 18.0   UNDERSTAND STRATEGIES FOR COMMUNICATING AND WORKING WITH FAMILIES, THE PUBLIC, AND OTHER PROFESSIONALS.

Skill 18.1   Demonstrate an understanding of the value of community support for school reading programs.

See skill 18.2

Skill 18.2   Identify strategies for communicating effectively about reading to the general public.

Often times in schools, parents, grandparents and other people involved in children's lives want to take a more active role in the educational process. They may also have an opinion on the appropriate method for teaching students how to read. Sometimes this can lead to controversy and misunderstandings.

It is important to provide opportunities for the public to come into the school and participate in activities to encourage reading. During these incentive and fun programs, it is just as important to share tidbits of information about the methodologies and strategies of reading being implemented.

In this way, the public can begin to understand the differences in reading instruction today than perhaps occurred when they attended school, which is often the biggest statement made by adults concerning current educational trends.

Taking the time to educate parents and other family members can not only help provide a better understanding and open communication, but it can also result in more support for students than the school alone would ever be able to provide.

Some strategies for educating parents and family members include:

- Bingo games where the correct answer on the bingo board is a fact about reading instruction
- Small parent workshops offered on various topics
- Newsletter pieces or paragraphs
- Individual parent meetings
- Inviting parents in to observe lessons
- Small pieces of information shared during other social times where parents are invited into the school

Skill 18.3   Demonstrate knowledge of methods for involving parents/guardians in cooperative efforts to support students' reading and writing development and for implementing effective strategies to include parents/guardians as partners in the literacy development of their children.

Strategies for Promoting Independent Reading in the Classroom and at Home

Pre-select books for the children that are just right for them. Provide the children with a quiet, relaxing space within the classroom where they can go to read these books. Don't get upset if they seem to take a break or wander around the room after fifteen minutes. Adults take breaks as well. Regularly providing DEAR (drop everything and read) time for silent reading in the classroom is a way to help students enjoy the process of reading. This will carry over to independent reading at home.

Make certain that the children who are reading independently fill in their weekly logs. Beyond telling what books they were reading and how many pages they have read, have the children respond to the following prompts:

This week I was successful at ...

Next week I plan to...

A response can also be an illustration or a sentence or two about the book.

Deliberately assign a child or a pair of children to read big books. These are a guaranteed success for the children because they have already been shared in class. Some children enjoy reading these independently using big rulers to point at words. This provides them with a sense of mastery over the words and ownership of their independent reading.

Some children enjoy working on their own strategy sheet such as a story map, character map, or storyboard panel, to demonstrate how they can apply a strategy to their own independent learning.

Skill 18.4   Identify strategies for communicating with allied professionals and paraprofessionals in assessing student achievement and planning instruction.

See skill 17.3

Skill 18.5 **Identify ways to communicate information and data about literacy to school personnel, parents/guardians, and the community.**

As previously discussed, communicating general information about reading and appropriate reading instruction is important. It is just as important to share more specific information about students with parents, other school personnel, and the community.

Developing a variety of reporting procedures was previously discussed in skill 14.5. However, once you have the reports and have gathered the information, the next step involves finding appropriate methods to share this information with the people that need the data. Again, depending on the audience the amount and type of information may change.

Some ways to share information with parents/guardians include:

- Individual parent meetings
- Small group meetings
- Regular parent updates through phone calls
- Charts and graphs of progress sent home
- Notes home
-

<u>Some ways to share information with school personnel include:</u>

- Faculty meetings
- Power point or other presentations
- Email
- Conferences
- School board presentation
- Graphs and charts

COMPETENCY 19.0 UNDERSTAND THE VALUE OF AND METHODS FOR PURSUING PROFESSIONAL DEVELOPMENT.

Skill 19.1 Demonstrate an understanding of the value of participating in professional development programs.

It is imperative one keeps up on the current research validated methods for working in the field of reading. This can be best done through membership to professional organizations such as International Reading Association (IRA) or the National Reading Conference (NRC). Joining these or other similar organizations will help the professional stay current with methodologies and provide appropriate literature and other publications for review.

Technology and the availability of the Internet also provide staff with materials and strategies to help keep abreast of the issues and current literature in the field of reading. Online journals, search engines, study groups and chat groups can be integral to ongoing professional development. Coursework at the graduate level will also help educators continue to build their understandings, as does mentoring and collaborative teaching. In fact, finding an experienced mentor in the same field can provide more information as to roles, issues and current topics in the field of reading than a variety of other sources.

Other specific skills in reading, such as Reading Recovery©, require additional training specifically in their program. These types of programs usually have a rigorous ongoing professional development plan that require numerous hours over years.

It is important to seek out conferences and workshops specifically designed for reading specialists because though districts typically provide inservice to the majority of their populations, i.e., regular education teachers, they often overlook the lower incidence employees. Sometimes the standard professional development of the district will not pertain to supporting a specialist's area of expertise. Other times, reading specialists may be asked to provide inservice to groups of teachers.

Having a professional development plan can be an integral component of staying current. In this plan, the reading teacher looks ahead down the road at what skills she would like to attain and then develops a plan over the years to help achieve these goals. Looking into the future as an educator and having a set plan for what goals and objectives the teacher hopes to achieve herself helps tremendously in implementing current research.

As with any educational profession thinking of yourself as an appropriate role model for your students is paramount. Appropriate ethics and demonstration regularly of those ethics is a key component to professionalism.

Skill 19.2   Recognize the importance of using multiple indicators to judge professional growth.

As a teacher you will experience many forms of evaluations. Through student teaching to formal evaluations completed by supervisors, ongoing critical examination of your performance will be a part of the regular process. One area that is often under -utilized but perhaps more valuable than outside evaluations is the self-assessment.

Examining with a critical eye one's own performance is the highest level of reflection. There are several forms that self-assessments can undertake. One format is to videotape yourself completing a lesson with the students. Then replay the tape for yourself at a later time. Before watching the tape, you should have specific questions or areas in mind. Simply watching the tape itself is much less valuable than when you watch it with a purpose. The questions might include things like: Did I keep the students engaged throughout the lesson? Was I clear in explaining the content I wanted them to understand? What could I do to improve the understanding of this concept for the students?

Another method of self-assessment might include providing your students with surveys to complete. When compiling the data from the questions, you will have a better understanding of how you are perceived by your students and what skills you can work on to improve weak areas. Carefully written questions focused on the items you are interested in learning about is necessary.

Sometimes a self-assessment could be as simple as keeping a reflection journal. With this strategy, the teacher simply keeps a regular notebook and after each day or week or even lesson takes a few minutes to write down her thoughts and feelings. Writing down what went well, what did not go well, what could have been done differently, or what was a surprise can provide valuable insight into teaching style and improvement. The drawback to this strategy is finding the time to use this method. Self reflection has been found to provide the most immediate and effective changes to instructional practice. If used authentically and kept confidential, it can be one of the best tools for improvement available to an educator.

Regular use of self-evaluation tools allows the teacher to understand what goals and objectives to include in the personal improvement plan. Remembering to review the state standards and using them as a guide for the self-evaluation will provide further guidance and a place to start for the development of such plans.

Skill 19.3 Demonstrate familiarity with resources for gaining information related to certification and recertification.

One of the most important things a teacher needs to know is how to keep their certification up to date. The rules and procedures for this can change over time and staying current is crucial so as to not lose your certification. On the web, information about Illinois certification can be found at http://www.isbe.net/certification/.

As of 2007, new teachers earn an initial certificate after meeting all of the requirements of certification. They are required to move from this initial certificate to a standard. To make this move new teachers must:

- Complete four valid years of teaching
- Complete one of the following professional development options
    o Advanced degree
    o Approved Induction and mentoring program
    o Obtain National Board Certification
    o Complete at least 12 graduate level credits
    o Complete 12 hours of education related approved professional development
    o Subsequent Illinois certification
    o Becoming highly qualified as described in NCLB in another area
    o Taking an exam

Once these criteria are met, there are other paperwork procedures a new teacher must follow in order to complete the transfer. The paperwork can be obtained from the above referenced website.

Once you have a standard or master level certificate there are additional required professional development activities required every five years for standard and every ten years for master level. They are:

- Advanced degree
- Obtain National Board Certification
- 8 semester hours of graduate credits
- Subsequent Illinois certification
- Becoming highly qualified as described in NCLB in another area
- 4 semester hours of approved graduate work in self assessment or NBPTS certification
- Continuing professional development units or Continuing education units

COMPETENCY 20.0   UNDERSTAND METHODS FOR WORKING WITH PARAPROFESSIONALS.

Skill 20.1   Demonstrate familiarity with methods for planning lessons that involve the participation of paraprofessionals.

Sometimes it is necessary and helpful to include paraprofessionals in the instruction of students. This provides the students with the opportunity to work with more than one adult to improve their reading skills and continues to allow the teacher to direct the instruction.

It is necessary for the teacher to plan all lessons or activities for the paraprofessional to implement. As the paraprofessional is not a trained educator, the teacher is responsible for making sure the necessary curriculum objectives are included and that the activities are well-planned. As the teacher, all responsibility for progression and skill growth is placed in your hands. The paraprofessional is responsible for implementing your plans and objectives.

Therefore, it is imperative that the teacher provide clear plans and activities and at the beginning takes the time necessary to train and ensure a complete understanding of what is to be completed. A little time of clear explanations at the beginning can prevent misunderstandings at a later time.

The paraprofessional should understand clearly how and what the teacher wants implemented. In this way, it is important that the teacher writes lesson plans which can be easily interpreted with no misunderstandings. Clear language should be used and all necessary materials provided. Highlighting is a good strategy for indicating which parts of the lesson the paraprofessional is responsible for within one set of lesson plans.

Communication is probably the most important factor when working with a paraprofessional. Open dialogue can prevent miscommunications and provide valuable input and ideas as to how the students are progressing. Gathering data by another person working with a child can help to reaffirm ideas or thoughts as well as provide the next steps in the instructional process. Teaching the paraprofessional how to keep notes and documentation on students can help record progress.

Skill 20.2 Demonstrate knowledge of strategies for observing paraprofessionals and providing feedback on their performance.

As discussed it is important to work closely with any paraprofessionals involved in providing instruction or support to students. Occasionally, it is important to touch base with the paraprofessional to ensure the lesson plans are being implemented as described.

This can be a sensitive area for both the teacher and paraprofessional. It is important to provide feedback without being punitive or seeming judgmental. With proper training and the open communication previously discussed, a great working relationship with give and take can be achieved. When providing feedback it can help to follow the following suggestions:

- Observe informally first – this can be achieved by working in the same room as when the instruction is being delivered and seems less threatening than a formal observation
- Provide the feedback in the form of additional instruction in the manner in which lessons should be delivered. In this way, there is no blame; it simply becomes a new lesson, not something someone did wrong
- Provide praise frequently
- Use open communication to ask the paraprofessional for his or her suggestions as well, indicating their opinions are valuable to you
- Provide professional training for paraprofessionals
- Schedule a regular meeting to discuss the students being worked with Listen carefully and make time for any questions the paraprofessional may have even if it interrupts your schedule
- Encourage leadership and decision making by the paraprofessional as his or her skills increase.

Skill 20.3 Demonstrate familiarity with methods for guiding and training tutors and volunteers.

Schools, particularly at the elementary level, have a wealth of adults who want to be an active part of the child's education. Parent volunteers and other adults want to come into the schools and are often times willing to help with a broad range of activities the teacher needs completed. These may include copying, giving individual assessments, reading with children, tutoring, gathering and making materials, and many others.

Putting these adults to use in the classroom can be a tremendous benefit, particularly in the area of reading. However, it is important to guide and train both tutors and volunteers. Taking a few minutes at the onset can save time and effort later. This can be done on an individual basis or school wide tutoring training sessions can be offered.

It can be a time saving device to train all adults interested in providing tutoring services at one time. They can work in small groups to develop their skills, and as a specialist, your time is only taken once for the training. It is important to provide the materials for the tutors to maximize their time with the students. This involves organization and a lot of forethought before the actual tutoring begins. There are various resources available to obtain the materials for tutoring, but it is a time-consuming process the first year of set up.

Finding a communication method between the tutors and yourself is also important. One strategy that works well and is rather inexpensive involves a bagged book system. In this strategy, the book and activities to complete with the student are kept in a Ziploc type storage bag with the child and tutor's name on it. Inside the bag, a communication notebook with some general questions can be left. The tutor writes the answers to the guided questions about the activity completed with the student. In this way, the teacher can review the answers as they are changing materials in the bag for the next tutoring session.

Overall, it is important to take the time and effort to be organized for volunteers and tutors before inviting them in to the classroom to maximize their presence in the classroom.

COMPETENCY 21.0 UNDERSTAND PROFESSIONAL CONDUCT FOR THE READING TEACHER.

Skill 21.1 Identify the benefits of participating in professional organizations related to reading education.

See Skill 19.1

Skill 21.2 Demonstrate knowledge of the importance of staying current with developments in reading education and children's and young adults' literature by reading professional journals and publications.

See skill 21.1

Skill 21.3 Demonstrate knowledge of the importance of conducting self-evaluation and reflecting on one's own teaching practices to improve instruction and other services to students.

All teachers should engage in self-reflection no matter how many years of experience they have or what subject areas they teach. Research is continually changing the materials used in the classroom and adherence to state standards is vital to ensure that students learn what they are supposed to in the classroom. Teachers who engage in self-reflection are better able to discover where the instruction was successful and where there was a breakdown in communication with the students. This enables the teacher to determine the areas where students need extra teaching, extra practice or interventions to help them succeed. They can also make changes to the way they teach in the classroom to meet the needs of all learners. What works for one group of students will not work for all groups. Teachers of the same subject may have to use different instructional techniques with different classes studying the same topic. Ways that teachers can engage in this reflection process include:

1 Using a journal to record the events of each day
2 Writing a reflection on each lesson to record what worked and what needs to be changed
3 Reflecting on how various instructional techniques worked with different students

Within the busy day of school life, teachers often do not have the time for this reflection. However, it does not take a long period of time and setting aside even 15 minutes before they start planning lessons for the next day can be really worthwhile. Once the practice is established it will become routine.
Educational journals are full of literacy research. These are often available at the school if the district has a subscription. As the reading specialist you should have a subscription to these, which include:

1   The Reading Teacher
2   Educational Leadership
3   Adolescent Learning
4   Reading Research Quarterly

In addition, experts are writing about the findings of research into literacy and there are many published books on the subject. Consider the writings of:

1   Marie Clay
2   Donald Graves
3   Regie Routman
4   Susan Taberski
5   Lucy Culkins

When administrators provide time for teachers to get together to plan instructional activities geared towards reading, a spirit of collaboration will exist in the school. One way to accomplish this is to provide the teachers with time to visit other schools and observe what is happening in another classroom in the district. Teachers within the same division (e.g., primary, Elementary,) or teachers of one grade in the school can get together on a regular basis to discuss how they are teaching various concepts and to discuss how to best help students that are struggling with reading. The Reading Specialist should be part of this team as well as the teacher giving support to the struggling readers. It may mean after school time or shut down days for the school. Administrators can also schedule the timetable in such a way that these teachers have time off during the school day for this purpose.

Reading specialists, administrators and teachers are always on the lookout for professional development opportunities that will help them in teaching reading. Many school districts offer professional development in many areas and provide an outline of this to the schools at the beginning of the year. However, this often involves travel and for schools that manage their own budgets, this is something that has to be looked at carefully.

With the many demands placed on teachers, it is often not feasible to hold PD sessions after school hours on a regular basis. Teachers do not mind if this is scheduled into the timetable at the beginning of the year and the sessions are only for short periods of time. Using the PD time allowable by the school district to shut down schools for a half or full day is one way of bringing appropriate professional development to the staff. Schools within close proximity to one another can work together to share the cost of bringing in guest speakers and experts in the field of reading.

Another method that has seen success is to add 15 minutes to the school day from Monday to Thursday and give teachers Friday afternoons for professional development. When this becomes a district wide policy, teachers know exactly what is expected of them on Friday. Some of these sessions can be school PD where the teachers get time to plan together, discussing how best to teach the children and how to make sure they are teaching state-mandated outcomes. Some of these Fridays can be a chance for teachers to get together with those from other schools. For example, there could be a PD for Grade 1 teachers, those in middle literacy, high school English teachers, and so on. When small groups are formed in this way, you have professional learning communities within the school district.

Professional development opportunities for teacher performance improvement or enhancement in instructional practices are essential for creating comprehensive learning communities. In order to promote the vision, mission and action plans of school communities, teachers must be given the toolkits to maximize instructional performances. The development of student-centered learning communities that foster the academic capacities and learning styles of all students should be the fundamental goal of professional development for teachers.

The level of professional development may include traditional district workshops that enhance instructional expectations for teachers or the more complicated multiple day workshops given by national and state educational organizations to enhance the federal accountability of skill and professional development for teachers. Most workshops on the national and state level provide clock hours that can be used to renew certifications for teachers every five years. Typically, 150 clock hours is the standard certification number needed to provide a five year certification renewal, so teachers must attend and complete paperwork for a diversity of workshops that range from 1-50 clock hours according to the timeframe of the workshops.

Some states require districts and schools to provide in-service professional development opportunities for teachers during the school year dealing with district objectives/expectations and relevant workshops or classes that can enhance teaching practices for teachers. Clock hours are provided with each class or workshop and the type of professional development being offered to teachers determines clock hours. Each year, schools are required to report the number of workshops, along with the participants attending the workshops, to the Superintendent's office for filing. Teachers collecting clock hour forms are required to file the forms to maintain certification eligibility and job eligibility. The research by the National Association of Secondary Principals,' "Breaking Ranks II: Strategies for Leading High School Reform" created the following list of educational practices needed for expanding the professional development opportunities for teachers:

1 Interdisciplinary instruction between subject areas
2 Identification of individual learning styles to maximize student academic performance
3 Looking at multiple methods of classroom management strategies
4 Providing teachers with national, federal, state and district curriculum expectations and performance outcomes
5 Identifying the school communities' action plan of student learning objectives and teacher instructional practices
6 Helping teachers understand how to use data to impact student learning goals and objectives
7 Teaching teachers on how to disaggregate student data in improving instruction and curriculum implementation for student academic equity and access
8 Develop leadership opportunities for teachers to become school and district trainers to promote effective learning communities for student achievement and success

In promoting professional development opportunities for teachers that enhance student achievement, the bottom line is that teachers must be given the time to complete workshops at no or minimal costs. School and district budgets must include financial resources to support and encourage teachers to engage in mandatory and optional professional development opportunities that create a "win-win" learning experience for students.

See also Skill 19.2.

Skill 21.4   Demonstrate knowledge of the importance of being aware of, adhering to, and modeling ethical standards of professional conduct in reading education.

One of the most important professional practices a teacher must maintain is student confidentiality. This extends far beyond paper records, and goes into the realm of oral discussions. Teachers are expected not to mention the names of students and often the specifics of their character in conversations with those who are not directly involved with them, inside and outside of school.

In the school environment, teacher record keeping comes in three main formats with specific confidentiality rules. All of the records stated below should be kept in a locked place within the classroom or an office within the school:

1) *Teacher's personal notes on a student.*
When a teacher takes notes on a student's actions including behaviors and/or grade performance that are not intended to be placed in a school recorded format, such as a report card, the teacher may keep this information private and confidential to his/her own files. Teachers may elect to share this information or not.

2) *Teacher daily recorded grades and attendance of the student.*
Teacher's grade books and attendance records are to be open to the parent/guardian of that child who wishes to check on their child. Only that child's information may be shared, not that of others.

3) *Teacher recorded/notation on records that appear in the student cumulative file.*
There are specific rules regarding the sharing of the Cumulative Records of students.

      a)   Cumulative files will follow a student that transfers within the school district, from school to school.

      b)   All information placed in a cumulative file may be examined by a parent at any time it is requested. If a parent shows up to review their child's cumulative file, the file should be shown as it is in its current state. (This includes IEPs.)

      c)   When information from a cumulative file is requested by another person/entity outside of the parent/guardian, the information may not be released without the express written consent of the parent/guardian. The parental consent must specify which records may be shared with the other party of interest.

      d)   A school which a student may intend to enroll in may receive the student's educational record without parental consent. However, the school sending that information must make a reasonable attempt to notify the parent/guardian of the request. (FERPA)

Today's world is quickly becoming a digital environment. Teachers now communicate often with Email and are keeping records in digital formats, often within a district mandated program. Teachers should keep in mind that Emails and other electronic formats can be forwarded and are as "indelible" as permanent ink and should maintain a professional decorum just as when they are writing their own records that will be seen outside of their personal notations.

The educator is expected to demonstrate ethical practice in all areas of his teaching responsibilities.

With regard to interaction with students, teaching and discipline practices should reflect practices that are respectful of the student as a person. Researched-based methods should be employed that will provide measurable outcomes. The ethics of education goes beyond methods or materials. With students of a variety of age and/or ability levels and often limited funding, appropriate materials can become difficult to obtain. If possible, students should be included in the head count for ordering general education materials. When alternative materials are needed, it is important to secure those through other funding sources (Title I) in the school. Teaching materials that are copyrighted may not be photocopied unless they are specifically intended for such use as printed on the book. The same is true for musical materials that have a copyright. If materials are intended for reproduction it will be stated.

Information technology brings a world of information to the educator and student's classroom. Careful consideration should be given, however, to the validity of the information before it is incorporated into practice or curricular material. Reputable sources for education practices will have connections to recognized organizations for educators.

Likewise, students should be guided in the finding and use of valid sites for research and learning. It is important to teach the philosophy that not everything on the Internet is reliable or true.

GLOSSARY

These definitions are critical for success on all multiple choice questions on the examinations. Proper use of these terms, is crucial for success in tackling a constructed response involving balanced literacy.

ABILITY GROUPING- grouping of children with similar needs for instructional purposes. Ability groups do not remain constant throughout the year, but change as the children's needs within them change.

ALLITERATION- occurs when words begin with the same consonant sound, as in *Peter Piper picked a pair of pickled peppers.*

ALPHABETIC PRINCIPLE- the idea that written spellings represent spoken words.

ANCHOR BOOK- a balanced literacy term for a book that is purposely read repeatedly and used as part of both the reading and writing workshop.

It is a good idea to use certain books that become the children's familiar and cherished favorites for both reading and then to inspire children's writing.

ASSONANCE- Occurs when words begin with the same vowel sound.

AUTHENTIC ASSESSMENT- assessment activities which reflect the actual workplace, family community and school curriculum.

BALANCED LITERACY LESSON FORMAT- The Balanced Literacy Approach has its own specific format for the delivery of the literacy lesson, whether it is a reading or writing workshop lesson. The format begins with a 10-15 minute mini-lesson which the teacher delivers to the whole class. This mini-lesson is then followed by a thirty-minute small group (when the children break into small groups to work) lesson. It concludes with a 10-minute share during which the whole class reconvenes to share what they have done in the small groups.

One can refer to this format as the whole-small-whole group approach.

BENCHMARKS- school state, or nationally mandated statements of the expectations for student learning and achievement in various content areas.

BICS-BASIC INTERPERSONAL COMMUNICATION SKILLS (ELL term-Bilingual Education)- learning second language skills and becoming proficient in a second language through face to face interaction-translation through speaking, listening, and viewing.

BLENDING- the process of hearing separate phonemes and being able to merge them together to read the word.

BOOK FEATURES- children need to be familiar with the following book features: front and back cover, title and half- title page, dedication page, table of contents, prologue and epilogue, and foreword and after notes. For factual books, children need to be familiar with: labels, captions, glossary, index, headings and subheadings of chapters, charts and diagrams, and sidebars.

CHECKLIST- an assessment form which lists targeted learning and social behaviors as indicators of achievement, knowledge or skill. They can be professionally- or teacher-prepared.

CINQUAIN- a five line poem that can be read and then used as a model for writing. Generally line 1 of this format is a single word, line 2 has 2 words, which describe the title of line 1, line 3 is comprised of 3 words which are movement words, line 4 has 4 words which express feeling and line 5 has a single word which is a synonym for line 1's single word.

COMPREHENSION- this occurs when the reader correctly interprets the print on the page and constructs meaning from it. Comprehension depends on activating prior knowledge, cultural and social background of the reader, and the reader's ability to use comprehension monitoring strategies.

CONCEPTS ABOUT PRINT- include: how to handle a books, how to look at print, directionality, sequencing, locating skills, punctuation, and concepts of letters and words.

CONSONANT DIAGRAPHS- two consecutive consonants that represent one new speech sound. In the word "digraph" the *ph* which sounds like /f/ is a digraph.

CONTEXTS- sentences deliberately prepared by the teacher which include sufficient contextual clues for the children to decipher meaning.

CONTEXTUAL REDEFINITION- using context to determine word meaning.

COOPERATIVE READING- Children read with a partner or buddy. It can be silent or oral reading.

CRISSCROSSERS- an ELL term for second language learners who have a positive attitude toward both first language and second language learning. These second language learners, children from ELL backgrounds, are comfortable navigating back and forth between the two languages as they learn.

CUES- as they self monitor their reading comprehensions, readers have to integrate various sources of information or cues to help them construct meaning from text and graphic illustrations.

DECODING-"sounding out" a printed sequence of letters based on knowledge of letter sound correspondences.

DIPHTHONGS- two vowels in one syllable where the two sounds are heard. For instance in the word *house* both the "o" and the "u" are heard.

DIRECTIONALITY-children use their fingers to indicate left to right direction and return sweep to the next line.

DIFFERENTIATED INSTRUCTION- The need for the teacher, based on observation of individual student's work, progress, test results, fluency, and other reading/literacy behaviors, to provide modified instruction and alternative strategies or activities. These activities are specifically developed by the teacher to address the individual student's different needs.

EARLY READERS- recognize most high frequency words and many simple words. They use pictures to confirm meaning. Using meaning, syntax, and phonics, they can figure out most simple words. They use spelling patterns to figure out new words. They are gaining control of reading strategies. They use their own experiences and background knowledge to predict meanings. They occasionally use story language in their writing. This stage follows emergent reading.

EMERGENT READERS- the stage of reading in which the reader understands that print contains a consistent message. The reader can recognize some high frequency words, names, and simple words in context. Pictures can be used to predict meaning. The emergent reader begins to attend to left to right directionality and features of print and may identify some initial sounds and ending sounds in words.

ENCODE- to change a message into symbols. For example, readers encode oral language into writing.

ENGLISH as a SECOND LANGUAGE- a way of teaching English to speakers of other languages using English as the language of instruction.

EXPOSITORY TEXT-. is non-fiction that provides information and facts. This text type is what newspapers, science, mathematics and history texts use. Currently there is much focus, even in elementary schools, on teaching children how to comprehend and author expository texts. They must produce brochures, guides, recipes, and procedural accounts on most elementary grade levels. The teaching of reading of expository texts requires working with a particular vocabulary and concept structure that is very different from that of the narrative text. Therefore time must be taken to teach the reading of expository texts and contrast it with the reading of narrative texts.

FIRST LANGUAGE- an ELL term for the language any child acquires in the first few years of life. It is through this acquired language that the child acquires phonological and phonemic awareness.

FLUENT READERS- identify most words automatically. They can read chapter books with good comprehension. They consistently monitor, cross-check, and self-correct reading. They can offer their own interpretations of text based on personal experiences and prior reading experiences. Fluent readers are capable of reading a variety of genres independently. Furthermore, they can respond to texts or stories by sharing pertinent examples from their lives. They can also readily make connections to other books which they have read. Finally, they are capable of beginning to create spoken and written writings which are in the style of a particular author.

FORMAL ASSESSMENT- a test or an observation of a performance task which is done under controlled and regulated conditions.

FUNCTIONAL READING- the reading of instructions, recipes, coupons, classified ads, notices, signs, and other documents which we have to read and correctly interpret in school and in society.

GRADE EQUIVALENT/GRADE SCORE- a score transformed from a raw score on a standardized test into the equivalent score earned by an average student in the norming group.

GRAPHIC ORGANIZERS- graphic organizers express relationships among various ideas in visual form including: sequence, timelines, character traits, fact and opinion, main idea and details, differences and likenesses. Graphic organizers are particularly helpful for visual learners.

GUIDED READING- one of the key modes of instruction in the balanced literacy theory approach. During guided reading, the teacher "guides" the child through silent reading of a text by giving them prompts, target questions, and even helping the child start an answer to a specific prompt or question. At the end of each guided reading section or excerpt of the text, the child stops to talk with the teacher about the text. By definition, guided reading is an interactive discussion between the child and the teacher. This mode of reading instruction is generally used when children need extra support in constructing meaning because the text is complex or because their current independent reading capacities are still limited.

.

HIGH FREQUENCY- frequently used words. These words appear many more times than do other words in ordinary reading material. Examples of such words include: *as, in, of,* and *the*. These words are also sometimes called service words. These words are also part of sight vocabulary words. A classic best-known high frequency word list was generated by Dolch (l936).

INDEPENDENT READING- a set period of time within the daily literacy block when children read books with 95%-100% accuracy on their own. This reading of books by themselves which they can understand without teacher support promotes lifelong literacy and love of learning, which enhances reading mileage, builds fluency, and helps children orchestrate integrated cue strategies.

INFORMAL ASSESSMENT- observations of children made under informal conditions; these can include kid watching, checklists, and individual child/teacher conversations.

INFORMAL READING INVENTORY (IRI) - a series of reading excerpts that can be used to determine a child's reading strengths and needs in comprehension and decoding. Many published reading series have an IRI to go with their series.

JUSTIFIED PRINT- the positioning of print on the page so that each line ends either a sentence or a phrase.

KID WATCHING- term used within the balanced literacy approach for the teacher's deliberate, detailed, and recorded observations of individual student and class literacy behaviors., often done during small group work. The teacher then reconfigures lessons on experiences to meet the students' individual and group needs.

KINESTHETIC- learning is tactile; as contrasted with an activity where the learner sits still or attempts to sit still in one place. Cutting and moving syllable or word strips or using sandpaper letters are kinesthetic activities.

LANGUAGE EXPERIENCE- Children giving dictation to the teacher who writes their words on a chart or their drawings. This shows children that words can be written down.

LEARNING LOGS- daily records of what students have learned.

LISTENING POST- sets of headphones attached to a single tape player. Children can go to centers where they listen to audiotapes of books while reading the print book. These posts are in many libraries as well.

LITERATURE CIRCLES- a group discussion involving four to six children who have read the same work of literature (narrative or expository text). They talk about key parts of the work, relate it to their own experience, listen to the responses of others, and discuss how parts of the text relate to the whole.

MANIPULATION- moving around or switching sounds within a word or words within a phrase or sentence.

MEANING VOCABULARY- words whose meanings children understand and can use.

MISCUE- an oral reading error made by a child which differs from the actual printed text.
MISCUE ANALYSIS- the teacher keeps a detailed recording of the errors or inaccurate attempts of a child reader during a reading assessment. These are recorded within a running record. This helps the teacher see whether the cues-syntactic, semantic, or graphophonemic-the child is using are accurate.

MONITORING READING- various strategies that children use to monitor their readings. A sample are maintaining fluency by bringing prior knowledge to the story to make predictions, using these predictions to do further checking, searching, and self-correcting as the story progresses, and using problem-solving word study skills to make links from known words to unknown words.

MORPHEMES- the smallest units of meaning in words. There are two types of morphemes; free morphemes, which can stand alone such as *love,* and bound morphemes, which must be attached to another morpheme to carry meaning such as *ed* in *loved*.

NARRATIVE TEXT- one of the two basic text structures. The narrative text tells or communicates a story. Narrative texts are novels, short stories and plays. Some poems are narratives as well. The narrative text needs to be taught differently than the expository text because of its structure.

ONE TO ONE MATCHING- matching one spoken word with one written word.

ONSET-RIME BLENDING –ONSET-Everything before the vowel and RIME (the vowel and everything after it). For example, the word "sleep" can be broken into /sl/ and /eep/. Word families are build using rimes. The /eep/ word family would include *jeep, keep* and *weep*.

ORTHOGRAPHY- a method of representing spoken language through letters and diacritics.

PERCENTILE- if a child scores at the 56th percentile for his/grade level, his/her score is equal to or above that of 56 percent of the children taking that standardized test and below that of 46 percent of the children on whose scores the test was normed.

PERFORMANCE ASSESSMENT- having children do a task that demonstrates their knowledge, skills and competency. Having children author their own alphabet book on a particular topic would be a performance assessment for knowledge of the alphabet.

PHONEME- The speech sound units that make a difference in meaning. The word "rope" has three phonemes /r/, /o/, and /p/. Change one phoneme, say /r/ to /n/, and you have a different word *nope.*

PHONEMIC AWARENESS- the understanding that words are composed of sounds. Phonemic awareness is a specific type of phonological awareness dealing only with phonemes in a spoken word.

PHONICS- the study of relationships between phonemes (speech sounds) and graphemes (letters) that represent the phonemes. It is also decoding or the sounding out of unknown words. that are written.

PHONOLOGICAL AWARENESS- the ability to recognize the sounds of spoken language and how they can be blended together, segmented, and switched/manipulated to form new combinations and words.

PHONOLOGICAL CUES- readers use their knowledge of letter/sound and sound/letter relationships to predict and confirm reading.

PHONOLOGY- the study of speech structure in language that includes both the patterns of basic speech units (phonemes) and the tacit rules of pronunciation.

PORTFOLIOS- collections of a child's work over time. They include a cover letter, reflections from the child and teacher, and other supportive documents including standards, performance task examples, prompts and sometimes peer comments.

PRIMARY LANGUAGE- (ELL term)- the language an individual is the most fluent in and at ease with. This is usually, but not always the individual's first language.

PROMPTS- when the teacher intervenes in the child's independent reading to help the child pronounce or comprehend a specific word or prompt. On a reading record, the teacher notes the prompt. When the teacher wants to match a child with a particular book or determine the child's stage of reading/level, the teacher does not use prompts.

QUESTION GENERATING STRATEGY FOR AN EXPOSITORY TEXT- first the child previews the text by reading titles, subheads, looking at pictures or illustrations, and reading the first paragraph. Next the child asks a "think" question which he or she records. Then the child reads to find information that might answer the "think" question. The child may write down the information found or think about another question that is answered by what the child is reading. The child continues to read using this strategy.

READING FOR INFORMATION- Reading with the purpose of extracting facts and expert opinion from the text. Children should be introduced to the following information reading resources: web resources that are age and grade appropriate for children, the concept of the table of contents, chapter headings, glossaries, pictures, maps, charts, diagrams and text structures in an information text. They should be taught to use notes, graphs, organizers, and mind maps to share information extracted from a text.

RECODE- To change information from one code into another, as recoding writing into oral speech.

RECOGNITION VOCABULARY- the group of words which children are able to correctly pronounce, read orally and understand on sight.

RECORD OF READING BEHAVIOR – (running record) an objective observation during which the teacher records, using a standard set of symbols, everything the child reader says as the child reads a book selected by the teacher.
REFLECTION- to analyze, discuss, and react to one's learning on any grade or age level.

RETELLING- retelling can be written or oral. Children are expected and encouraged to tell as much of a story as they can remember. Re-telling is far more extensive than just summarizing. Children should include the beginning, middle and end plot lines and should be able to tell about the book's characters.

RUBRIC- a set of guidelines or acceptable responses for the completion of any task. Usually a rubric ranges from 0 to 4 with 4 being the most detailed response and 0 indicating a response to the task which lacked detail or was in other ways insufficient.

SCAFFOLDING- refers to the teacher support necessary for the child to accomplish a task or to achieve a goal which the child could not accomplish on his/her own. Vygotsky termed this window of opportunity the "zone of proximal development." Ultimately as the child becomes more proficient or capable, the scaffold is withdrawn. The goal of scaffolding is to help the child to perform the reading task independently and internalize the behavior. During SHARED READING, the task is scaffolded by the teacher's reading to the children aloud. As the teacher reads, the teacher scaffolds the initial decoding and helps with the meaning making/construction.

SEARCHING- children pause to search in the picture, print, or their memory for known information. This can happen as the child tackles an unknown word or after an error.

SECOND LANGUAGE-(ELL term)-A language acquired or learned simultaneously with or after a child's acquisition of a first language.

SEGMENTING- the process of hearing a spoken word and identifying its separate phonemes or syllables.

SELF-CORRECTION- children begin to correct some of their own reading errors. Generally this behavior is accompanied by the re-reading of the previous phrase or sentence.

SEMANTIC CUES- children use their prior knowledge, sense of the story, and pictures to support their predicting and confirming the meaning of the text.

SEMANTIC WEB- a visual graphic organizer that the teacher can use to introduce a reading on a specific topic. It visually represents many other words associated with a target word. The web can help activate the children's prior knowledge and extend or clarify it. It can also serve to check new learning after guided or independent reading.

SPATIAL LEARNING- Using images, color, or layout to help readers whose learning style is spatial.

STANDARD SCORE- how far a child's grade on a standardized test is from the average score (mean) on the test in terms of the standard deviation. If a child scores 70 on a standardized test and the standard deviation is 5 and the average (mean) score is 65, the child is one standard deviation above the average.

STANDARDIZED TEST- a test given under specified conditions allowing comparisons to be made. A set of norms or average scores on this test will be used for comparisons.

STOP AND THINK STRATEGY- a balanced literacy strategy for constructing meaning. As the text is being read, the child asks himself or herself, does this make sense to me? If it does not make sense to me, I should then try to re-read it or read ahead. I can also look up words that I don't know or ask for help. Generally the teacher models this strategy with the whole class as a mini lesson and then it is posted prominently in the classroom for continued reference by the children.

STRATEGIC READERS- as defined by researchers Marie Clay and Sharon Taberski, strategic readers are self improving and do the following as they read:

(A lengthy glossary explanation of this term has been provided because it can appear in a variety of multiple choice questions on the examination as well as part of a constructed response question).

- Monitor their reading to see if it makes sense semantically, syntactically, and visually.
- Look for and use semantic, syntactic, and visual clues.
- Uncover and identify new things about the text.
  Cross check and use one cueing system against another.
- Self-correct their reading when what they first read does not match the semantic, syntactic and visual clues
- Solve for and identify new words using multiple cueing systems

Beyond these behaviors, a strategic or self-improving reader uses many strategies to construct meaning. When their reading experience is going well-they know the words and understand the text or story-they are working continuously (even if they are not conscious of it) at maintaining meaning. If and when the strategic or self-improving reader runs into an unfamiliar word, then the reader has many strategies to identify that word. Becoming a successful strategic reader is a goal that can and should be shared with children as early as the middle of the first grade, although the term "self-improving reader" might be used at that point.

TEXT FEATURES- children need to be alerted to the following text features which may initially appear strange to them. The features of text include: a period which marks the end of a "telling sentence;" a question mark that is at the end of a sentence that asks a question, an exclamation mark used to express surprise or excitement at the end of a sentence, capital letters which begin a sentence and the names of persons, places, and things; bold italicized or underlined text to highlight key ideas; quotation marks which show dialogue, a hyphen used to break a long word up into its syllables, a dash used to show a break in an idea, or to indicate a parenthetical element or an omission; an ellipse, which shows an omission or break in the text; and a paragraph in nonfiction which shows a new point being made.

TRANSITIONAL READERS- recognize an increasing number of "hard" words that are content related. They can provide summaries of the stories that they read. They are more at ease with handling longer, more complex, connected text with short chapters. Transitional readers can read independent level texts with correct phrasing, expression, and fluency. When they encounter unfamiliar words, they have a variety of strategies to figure out the unfamiliar words. Their reading demonstrates that they are able to integrate meaning, syntax and phonics in a consistent manner so that they can understand the texts they are reading.

VENN DIAGRAM- a diagram consisting of two or three intersecting circles to visually represent similarities and differences for texts, characters and topics. No author study is complete without VENN DIAGRAMS comparing different author's works. This is the most commonly used graphic organizer in elementary schools today. It can be used effectively as part of an answer to a constructed response question.

VISUAL CUES- readers use their knowledge of graphemes to predict and confirm text. The graphemes may be words, syllables or letters.

WORD ANALYSIS- the analysis of words employing letters, phonic structures, contextual clues, or dictionary skills.

WORD IDENTIFICATION- how the reader determines the pronunciation, and the meaning of an unknown word.

WORD RECOGNITION- The process of determining the pronunciation and some degree of the meaning of an unknown word.

WORD WORK- the term that the balanced literacy approach uses for the study of vocabulary.

"An impressive and growing body of authoritative opinion and research evidence suggests that reading failure is preventable for all but a very small percentage of children."
John Jay Pikulski

Directory of Theorists and Researchers

Introduction:
Many questions on the teacher certification examinations can only be correctly answered if you know the theorist or the research that is referenced. The teaching of reading owes much to the work, principles and guidelines of teacher educators and university field researchers who have changed the style, methods and practice of teaching reading. While those listed in this directory are by no means all the major researchers (page constraints would make a complete listing impossible), the individuals listed below are those whose contributions are frequently referenced on the certification tests and whose work is evident in today's elementary classroom teaching and learning of reading.

PHONICS CENTERED APPROACH

In 1955 Rudolph Flesch gained national prominence when he published *Why Johnny Can't Read*. This book went on to become a best seller and has now become a classic which is readable and speaks to current concerns. Flesch became the spokesperson for a war that periodically resurfaces in the reading world.

Flesch, Chall (1967) Stahl (1992), Adams (1990), and Johnson and Bauman (1984) believe that a phonics-based approach is crucial for reading success. Flesch and others feel that the balanced literacy advocates are seriously undermining the crucial role that phonics plays in the children's development as successful decoding readers. However, it must be noted that while balanced literacy does emphasize the use of literature based reading programs, it in no way dismisses phonics from its reading program; indeed phonics is included in the crucial "word work" component of the reading and writing workshop.

The phonics advocates point to the fact that most research shows that early and systematic instruction in phonics skills results in superior reading achievement in elementary school and beyond.

Adams (1990) detailed what type of phonics instruction is needed.

To learn to read skillfully, children need practice in seeing and understanding decodable words in real reading situations and with connected text.... phonics instruction {needs to be} part of a reading program that provides ample practice in reading and writing. Encouraging children with connected text can also show them the importance of what they are learning and make the lessons in phonics relevant and sensible. Phonics centered advocates believe that children should begin to learn letter associations in kindergarten with most useful phonics skills being taught by first grade. These basic skills should then be reviewed in second grade and beyond.

Consonant sounds should be taught first, since they are more reliable in their letter-sound associations.

Short vowel sounds appear more frequently in beginning reading materials, so they should be introduced before long vowels. Phonics advocates believe that most beginning readers need to be taught letter sound associations explicitly. Phonics advocates also believe that beginning readers need to read stories that have words to which phonics skills apply. This allows them to practice their phonics skills as they write and spell words. They should also play lots of letter-sound association games.

Phonics advocates claim that when phonics is abandoned reading scores drop and balanced literacy advocates counter with the fact that they have never advocated abandoning the teaching of phonics.

As Jeanne Chall, a professor at Harvard's Graduate School of Education notes: "a beginning reading program that does not give children knowledge and skill in recognizing and decoding words will have poor results."

Theorists and Researchers:

Adams, Marilyn Jager
Noted for her research on early reading, Adams lists five basic types of phonemic awareness tasks which should be covered by the end of first grade. These include: ability to hear rhymes and alliterations, ability to do oddity tasks, ability to orally blend words, ability to orally segment words, ability to do phonemic manipulation tasks.

Clay, Marie M. Marie
A New Zealand born researcher, in the field of special needs emergent literacy and in the development of assessment tools for these children. Her research in this field is felt throughout the Reading Recovery movement and involves the use of her, *Reading Recovery: A Guidebook for Teachers in Training,* in the majority of graduate emergent literacy courses and in many classrooms in the US including those that do not have a Reading Recovery teacher.

Her doctoral thesis focused on what was to become her life's work, emergent reading behavior. At the crux of her research for the dissertation, Clay reviewed and detailed the progress week by week of one hundred children during their first year of school (1966). An important outcome of the dissertation was her development of reliable observation tools for the assessment and analysis of changes over time in children's literacy learning. These assessments are the crux of *An Observation Survey of Early Literacy Achievement* (1993) which is an essential work for the primary school educator. The assessments have been validated and reconstructed for learners from the Spanish, Maori and French languages. A special appendix in this guide includes the *Record of Reading Behavior* tool she created with Kenneth Goodman.

Reading Recovery is a key Clay contribution to the field of foundations of reading teaching. The movement, which is discussed in detail in this section, was born out of the concerns of classroom educators who were upset that even with excellent programs and expert teaching, they were not able to positively influence the literacy progress of some of their young children. Clay posed the question of investigating what would happen if the design and delivery of traditional reading education were changed for these struggling young learners.

The whole thrust of the Reading Recovery movement has been to improve the early identification and instructional delivery for these struggling young readers. Her goal was to develop a system which would bring those children scoring the lowest in assessment measures to the level of the average readers within their classes.

With the support of Barbara Watson and others, the program was developed in three years. The first field tests of the program took place in the late 1970's in Auckland schools. To date, circa 2005, the program is operating in most English speaking countries and has been reconstructed for use in Spanish and French.

Janet S. Gaffey and Billie Askew have said of Marie Clay (1991) that her contribution "has been to change what is possible for individual learners when teaching permits different routes to be taken for desired outcomes."

Reading Recovery has been identified by the International Reading Association as a program that not only teaches children how to read, but also reduces the number of children who are labeled as "learning disabled." It further lowers the number of children who are placed in remedial reading programs and classes.

Clay Reading Recovery lessons are designed to promote accelerated learning so that children can catch up to their peers and continue to learn independently.

The hallmark of the Reading Recovery program is that the Reading Recovery teacher works with one student at a time over a 12 to 20 week period. Each daily 30 minute lesson is tailored to address the needs of the individual student. Therefore Reading Recovery teachers generally teach no more than four or five students per day in individual lessons.

The Clay Observation of Early Childhood Achievement (l993) is used to assess children's strengths and weaknesses. Reading Recovery teachers devote the first ten minutes of their sessions with individual children to assessment as the children engage in reading and writing. A running record of the child's progress is taken every day and is used to plan future lessons.

The lessons themselves include the use of familiar stories. Children engage in assembling and in sequencing cut up stories. They work with letters or write a story. Teaching style involves the teacher demonstrating strategies and the child then developing effective strategies to continue reading independently. Key components of each lesson include: phonemic awareness, phonics, spelling, and comprehension study. Much time is devoted to problem solving so that the children's decoding is purposeful. Children are given time to practice and demonstrate fluency skills.

Ultimately what sets Reading Recovery aside is the fact that it is one-to-one tutoring. This is also what makes it effective for children, and of course, what raises issues about it are costs for the school systems which may want to adopt it. Obviously the districts and education systems have to decide whether they want to pay the costs of this and other individualized tutoring systems now in the primary school years or pay later as these children become adults whose literacy skills are not sufficient for proactive citizenship.

Fountas, Irene C and Gay Su Pinnell
These two researchers have developed a leveling system for reading texts, which arranges them by level of difficulty. Beyond a specific analysis of set titles, the theorists have explained in several published works how to use their leveling system to meet and assess the progress of various readers. They also provide detailed explanations and support for reading teachers of young children K-3 in using reading records and benchmark texts.

They are the key articulators of the balanced literacy model that includes reading and writing workshop. Among their other contributions to the field are: guidelines for creating sets of leveled books, assessment rubrics, strategies for fostering "word solver" skills in child readers, and methods for teaching phonics and spelling in the literacy classroom.

Routman, Regie

Routman's contributions to Reading Foundations are the result of over three decades of experience as an elementary school teacher, a reading specialist, a learning disabilities tutor, a Reading Recovery teacher, a language arts and mentor teacher and a staff developer. Due to these various experiences, her insights into reading resonate with a broad spectrum of school community members.

Routman's works are conversational, teacher to teacher sharings of her daily experiences in classrooms. In her published books on the teaching of reading (i.e. *Reading Essentials*-Heinemann, 2002), Regie shows teachers how to teach consistent with the findings in reading research, yet also with highly practical "scripted lessons" and teaching tips which make the classroom come alive. She advocates literature based teaching and meaning centered approaches for learning.

In addition, she is a strong advocate of using poetry from grades one and beyond as an integral thread for a reading program. She is the author of *Kids' Poems: Teaching Children to Love Writing Poetry* (Scholastic, 2000) which includes separate volumes of poetry for grades K-4.

Routman believes in teaching reading to meet specific children's needs regardless of the particular reading program in place. She is a strong advocate for the use of small guided reading groups and reading for understanding. Phonics and other word analysis strategies are part of her reading framework, but not at its core. Her focus for the reading classroom is on the development and the use of the classroom library as the center for an independent reading program, shared reading and reading aloud.

Routman has designed informal reading evaluations on books/texts her students are reading (her published works are known for their appendices replete with templates for evaluations, projects, reports, book lists, suggested texts by topics etc.). Her classroom model includes matching children with specific library books as well as linking assessment with instruction. Finally she is a researcher who sees reading as intimately linked to writing.

Routman is also involved with the politics of literacy. This vision of literacy involves the image of the teacher, as an informed professional, who regularly reads the latest professional books, collaborates with colleagues in school and beyond, and deals with the most recent research developments. Interestingly, Routman is one researcher who also feels that an informed professional can and should know when to question research. Other aspects of the politics of literacy as Routman conceptualizes them are: communicating effectively with parents and dealing with testing and standards mandates.

Two of her published works, *Conversations: Strategies for Teaching, Learning, and Evaluating* (Heinemann, 2000) and *Invitations: Changing as Teachers and Learners k-12* (Heinemann, 1991 and 1994) are essential for the elementary reading teacher's bookshelf and can take the teacher through several years of work.

Taberski, Sharon

Taberski is an experienced elementary teacher educator who is also a member of the Primary Literacy Standards Committee run by the National Center on Education and the Economy and the University of Pittsburgh. Her works in the field are served up as wonderfully accessible and necessary advice from "the veteran teacher across the hall" who loves her students and is delighted to help a new colleague.

Unlike many theorists in the field of reading, Taberski's work is not focused around a prescribed set of skills, but rather around a series of interconnected interactions with the learner.

Among these interactions which are detailed and clearly communicated in her book *On Solid Ground* (2000-Heinemann) are:

- Assessment- Procedures for assessing children's reading, and to inform teaching, scheduling and managing reading conferences, taking oral reading records, and using retellings as discussion tools.
- Demonstration- Taberski developed and field tested strategies for using shared reading and read aloud as platforms for figuring out words and comprehending texts. She is a strong advocate of small group work-guided reading, word-study groups and teaching children one on one.
- Practice- In the Taberski framework, independent reading is used as a time for practice. Students play key roles in this practice and Sharon has a set of detailed and easily adaptable guidelines for matching children with books for independent reading. Her work includes booklists and ready to use information that is available for reproduction.
- Response- It's important for students to know that they are doing well and where they must focus their efforts to improve skills. Taberski explains how her students use writing and dialogue as tools for independent reading.

Vail, Priscilla

Noted for her research in the study of dyslexia and its myths, Vail has articulated ways in which children can develop their reading skills as they cope with this disorder and techniques parents and educators can use to support reading development. She has also worked on specific test taking skills for children coping with dyslexia and other special needs. Her strategies can be infused in the regular education program to enhance all students' reading achievement schools. She is a proponent of phonics instruction and skills within the context of an integrated whole language approach (once called integrated language arts).

Another focus of Vail's research is the link between language and thinking. She is concerned with how a child's receptive language, expressive language and metacognition can be fostered. She has developed assessment methods for each of these capacities and activities to help strengthen them in children grades k-4.

BIBLIOGRAPHY OF PRINT RESOURCES

PROFESSIONAL BOOKS:

Adams, M. (1990). *Beginning to read: Thinking and Learning about Print.* Cambridge, MA: MIT Press.

Anders, P., & Bos, C. (l986). Semantic Feature Analysis: An Interactive Strategy for Vocabulary Development and Reading Comprehension, *Journal of Reading*, 29, 610-616.

Blevins, W. (l997). *Phonemic Awareness Activities for Early Reading Success.* New York: Scholastic.

Boyd-Bastone, P. (2004). Focused Anecdotal Record Assessment (ARA): A Tool for Standards Based Authentic Assessment. *Reading Teacher, 58* (3), pp. 230-239.

Calkins, Lucy McCormick. (2001). *The Art of Teaching Reading.* New York: Longman.
   This is the woman who beautifully explains the reading workshop and its relationship to the writing workshop as she shares wonderful snapshots of mini lessons, conferring, conferencing, independent reading, guided reading, book talks, prompts, coaching, and classroom library use. Exceedingly readable and direct.

Campbell, Robin. (2004). *Reading and Writing for Real Purposes.* Portsmouth, NH: Heinemann.
   This work focuses on how children who deftly absorb and interconnect symbols and sounds of their universes can be supported in K-1 classes to extend this ability into phonics learning. Campbell demonstrates how immersion in a highly literate classroom filled with print and language stimuli allows kids to build accurate letter-sound relationships. The book provides a framework for teaching phonics using proven field-tested Campbell strategies.

   Among these strategies are: early mark making, read-alouds, playing with language in rhyme and song, writing and reading in a variety of genres, exploring environmental and classroom print, and using students' own names. Samples of student work are included.

Chancey, C. (l994). Language development, metalinguistic awareness, and emergent literacy skills of 3 year old children in relation to social class. *Applied Psycholinguistics*, 15, 371-394.

Clay, Marie M. (1993). *An Observation Survey of Early Literacy Achievement.* Portsmouth, NH: Heinemann.

Clay, Marie M. (1993). *Reading Recovery: A Guidebook for Teachers in Training.* Portsmouth, NH: Heinemann.

Cooper, J. David. (2004). *Literacy-Helping Children Construct Meaning.* Boston, MA: Houghton Mifflin. (5th Edition).

This book explains with numerous charts, tables, templates, and excerpts form actual texts, what the balanced literacy approach to the teaching of reading and writing is. It offers the new teacher: exact schedules, strategies, guidelines, assessment tools, bibliographies, research, and even scripts for conferring with children.

Cooper is a clear and crisp writer who does not overwhelm the reader, but rather engages the reader. Even veteran teachers would return again and again to this text for support and refreshing insights.

Cox, Carole. (2005). *Teaching Language Arts.* Boston, MA: Pearson.

A compendium of state of the art lesson plans, web resources, online case studies, teaching ideas and extensive templates. All of these materials are aligned to the balanced literacy reading and writing workshop model.

The book also includes teaching ideas for the ELL reader, children with learning disabilities, and speakers of non- standard dialects. The book also features snapshots of second language learners as well as bi-literacy web resources.

Cullinan, Bernice E. (1998). *Three Voices-An Invitation to Poetry Across the Curriculum.* New York: Stenhouse. K-6 and beyond.

Two classroom educators and a noted researcher in children's literature demonstrate how poetry can be used in the classroom to teach various aspects of reading and to nurture lifelong literacy. Thirty-three grade and age appropriate strategies are included which have been field tested in classrooms across the country.

Ezell, H. K., & Justice, L. M. (2000). Increasing the Print Focus of Adult -Child Shared Book Reading through Observational Learning. *American journal of Speech Pathology,* 9, 36-37.

Flesch, Rudolf. (1985). *Why Johnny Can't Read* New York: Harper and Row.

Fountas, Irene C., & Gay Su Pinnell. (2001). *Guiding Readers and Writers 3-6.* Portsmouth, NH: Heinemann.

This work includes 1000 leveled books with guidelines for using them as part of a reading and writing workshop. The book explains how to use various genres in the classroom and how to use visual graphic organizers for the teaching of reading and writing.

Fountas, Irene. C., & Gay Su Pinnell. (1999). *Matching Books to Readers Using Leveled Books in Guided Reading K-3*. Portsmouth, NH: Heinemann.
> This major contribution to the field has a list of 7, 500 grade and age appropriate books. In addition the authors include word counts to be used for keeping running records, text characteristics, guidelines for leveling of additional books and suggestions for developing classroom library collections.

> Other works by these researchers also published by Heinemann include:
>> *Voices on Word matters: Learning about Phonics and Spelling in the Literacy Classroom* (1999) and *Word Matters-Teaching Phonics and Spelling in the Reading/Writing Classroom* (1998).

Fry, Edward Bernard, Kress, Jacqueline, Fountakidis, Dona Lee. (2000). *The Reading Teacher's Book of Lists*. San Francisco, CA: Wiley Press.
> This book is an invaluable one for the working classroom educator. It includes ready to use lists that cover a multiplicity of teacher needs. Among them are: spelling demons, readability graphs, phonics, useful words, reading math, vowel lists, anagrams, portmanteaus (do you know what they are and how well they can work in word study?), web sites, classic children's literature, etc. Even a veteran teacher educator will find useful and new resources. Also wonderful for developing independent word study investigations and literature explorations.

Ganske, Kathy. (2000). *Word Journeys-Assessment-Guided Phonics, Spelling, and Vocabulary Instruction*. New York, NY: Guilford Press.
> This book offers a practical approach for assessing children's spelling. The author has created a DSA (Development Spelling Analysis) tool which teachers can use to evaluate individual children's spelling progress and to differentiate instruction. The book includes snapshots of children at different levels of spelling development.

Hall, Susan. (1994). *Using Picture Books to Teach Literary Devices*. Westport, CT: Oryx Press.

How to Help Every Child Become a Reader. Just Publishing. K-6 and beyond.
> This accessible text draws on materials developed by the US Department of Education to share research, resources, referrals and suggestions for supporting all children to become lifelong and engaged readers. It offers specific suggestions and resources for assisting struggling readers including those with special needs and those from ELL backgrounds.

Labov, L. (2003). When Ordinary Children Fail to Read. *Reading Research Quarterly*, 38, 128-31.

Macmillan, B. M. (2002). Rhyme and Reading. A Critical Review of the Research Methodology. *Journal of Research in Reading,* 25(1), 4-42.

Makor, Barbara. *Primary Phonics Readers.*
Short storybooks that K-2 can own and read independently.
   They feature phonetically controlled texts, sounds and spellings that are grade and age appropriate and high interest child-centered themes. As children progress through the series of twenty titles, they review and enhance their mastery of phonetic elements, sight words, and sequences at a more rapid pace. This material is compatible with the majority of phonics programs.

Munro, J. (I998). Phonological and Phonemic Awareness: Their Impact on Learning to Read Prose and Spell. *Australian Journal of Learning Disabilities*, 3, 2, 15-21.
   Paperback Nursery Rhyme Sampler-Whispering Coyote Press-Essential for a Prek-1 classroom and useful even in grades 1 and 2; these classic nursery rhymes promote phonemic and phonological awareness and children's ownership of their reading through song and movement.

Routman, Regie. (2000). *Conversations: Strategies for Teaching, Learning, and Evaluating.* Portsmouth, NH: Heinemann.

Routman, Regie. (I994). *Invitations: Changing as Teachers and Learners K-12.* Portsmouth, NH. Heinemann.

Routman, Regie. (I996). *Literacy at the Crossroads: Crucial Talk About Reading, Writing, and Other Teaching Dilemmas.* Portsmouth, NH: Heinemann.

Routman, Regie. (2002). *Reading Essentials.* Portsmouth, NH: Heinemann.

Statman, Ann. *Handprints-Leveled Storybooks for Early Readers Educators Publishing Service*-Grades K-2.
   These fifty titles which come with five teacher's guides were leveled using the Fountas and Pinnell Guided Reading Leveling System. The stories reflect real world situations and people young readers know. They include: sentence structure, pictures and cues that focus strategic reading. Print size, sentence positioning, and word spacing is appropriate for the level of the particular storybook. The titles build a strong sight vocabulary through the use of high frequency words. Language used within the series progresses from natural to formal book language.

Schumm, Heanne Shay. *The Reading Tutor's Handbook.* Free Spirit. K-6 and beyond.

> This guide offers step by step instructions, templates and handouts for providing children with differentiated reading support. It is not only helpful for teachers, but also can be shared with paraprofessionals, teachers, interns, and parents as a support framework for the classroom reading program.

Taberski, Sharon. (2000). *On Solid Ground: Creating a Literacy Environment in Your K-3 Classroom.* Portsmouth, NH: Heinemann.

Terban, Marvin. *Time to Rhyme-A Rhyming Dictionary.* Boyd Mills Press. Grades 1-3.

> This book is easily enough formatted so that it can be used to introduce children in the early elementary grades to the use of a rhyming dictionary as a reference tool. Its simple word groupings encourage writing which can also reinforce and reciprocally enhance reading skills through the reading and writing workshop.

Vail, Patricia. *Reading Comprehension-Students Needs and Teacher's Tools.* Educators Publishers Service K-6 and beyond.

> This is a compendium of explanations of specific instructional practices, terms, student projects, learning games and resources which are critical for successfully teaching reading.

ALPHABET BOOKS

A major genre of fiction and non-fiction for the teacher of reading is the alphabet book. These books' appeal, concepts, and efficiency as models for reading and writing merit them a special section in this bibliography. Even those whose text is simple enough for Prek-2, can serve as anchor books and models for writing workshop in grades 3-6.

Aigner-Clark, Julie. (2002). *Baby Einstein- The ABCs of Art.* Illustrations by Nadeen Zaidi. New York: Hyperion Books.

Beaton, Clare. *Zoe and Her Zebra.* Barefoot Books. Prek-1.

> This board book features a character young children can identify with named Zoe. Her adventures are told in a simple, repetitive text with a soft literally "touchy" felt art.

Bunting, Eve. *Girls A to Z.* Boyd Mills Press. PreK-1.

> This book uses the alphabetic format to promote the opportunity for girls to select various professions and careers ranging from astronaut to zookeeper. Bunting's text is breezy and rhymes.

Cheney, Lynne. (2002). *America- A Patriotic Primer*. New York: Simon and Schuster Books. Illustrated by Robin Priess Glasser.

Cheney, Lynne. *A Is For Abigail: An Almanac of Amazing American Women*. New York: Simon and Schuster Books. Ages 4-8.

Glaser, Milton. (2003). *The Alphazeds*. Miramax. Ages 4-8.

Grimes, Nikki. *C is for City*. Illustrated by: Pat Cummings. Boyd Mill Press. K-3.
  This alphabet rhyme book doubles as a guide to city activities. With its built in invitations to readers to search for alphabetical items, it is perfect for use as an informal assessment tool or an interactive/paired reading anchor text.

Inkpen, Mick. (2000). *Kipper's A to Z*. San Diego: Harcourt. Ages 3-7.

Isadora, Rachel. (1999). *ABC Pops! (Picture Books)*. Disney Press. Ages 4-8.

Johnson, Stephen. (1995). *Alphabet City*. Penguin Books. All ages.

Kelley, Marty. *Summer Stinks*. Zino Press. Prek-1.
  This work describes the summer season in terms of things which "stink" about it, including ants, bugs, and sweat. Fun to read and add to as the alphabet letters are learned and vocabulary is built up.

Martin, Mary Jane. *From Anne to Zach*. Boyd Mills Press.
  In this captivating book which can serve as a touchstone text for model collaborative authoring, children learn the letters of the alphabet through other children's names.

Melmed, Laura Krauss and Frane Lesser. (2003) *Capital! Washington DC from A to Z*. New York: Harper Collins.

Musgrove, Margaret. (1976). Illustrated by Leo and Diane Dillon. *Ashanti to Zulu. African Traditions*. New York: Dial Books for Young Readers.
  This is a Caldecott-winning book which uses the alphabetic format for a richly detailed and researched study of 26 African Peoples. It includes a map and pronunciation guide and illustrations that were researched in the Schomberg Center and the American Museum of Natural History. Even the frame design for each illustration reflects the African Kano knot which signifies endless searching.

Paratore, Colleen. *26 Big Things Hands Do*. Minneapolis, MN: Free Spirit.
  What is delightful about this alphabet book is that it presents the alphabet letters as positive actions children can perform with their own small hands to help others. These actions include: applauding, giving gifts, planting, and volunteering. Of course, alphabet study can continue with adding other "helping actions" to the word wall or substituting them in the text.

Pelham, David, (1991). *A is for Animals*. New York: Simon and Schuster

Seeley, Lorna. *The Book of Shadow Boxes*. Peachtree.
Within the shadow of each letter's shadow box lies a hidden treasure for the young reader to find. The book is intricately and exquisitely designed and conceptualized by Ms. Seeley. Its visual fascination extends well beyond the elementary grades as it of course fosters not only the alphabetic principle, but also reading comprehension and literacy response.

Sneed, Brad. (2002). *Picture a Letter*. New York: Penguin Books.

Seuss. *ABC*. Random House. Ages 2-up.

Thornhill, Jim. *The Wildlife ABC and 123: A Nature Alphabet and Counting Book*. Maple Tree Press. K-1 with additional nature notes on the species for the teacher/parent.
In addition to fostering the alphabetic principle, the book nicely mixes geographic, multicultural, and scientific knowledge into a beautifully designed text. It uses children's fascination with nature to foster reading and math literacy.

Zschock, Martha and Heather. (2002). *Journey Around New York from A to Z*. *Beverly*. Mass: Commonwealth Editions
Zschock, Martha. (2001). *Journey Around Boston from A to Z*. Beverly Mass: Commonwealth Editions.

TRADE BOOKS

These books foster particular aspects of reading skills, fluencies and competencies.

Blackstone, Stella. *Where's the Cat?* Barefoot Books. Prek-k.
This book which focuses its primary school readers on searching for a lost cat provides excellent use of repetitive language and encourages interactive reading.

Campbell, Bebe Moore. (2003). Sometimes *My Mommy Gets Angry. New York, New York: G. P. Putnam's Sons*.
This is a moving story about a young girl whose mother suffers from mental illness. It is told in a way that is easy to read, along with beautiful illustrations. The main character is Annie. Sometimes her mother is very happy and other times very angry and sad. Annie has learned what to do when her mom is having a bad episode. She has books to read, a special stuffed animal and some secret snacks. Annie also has a strong support system in place with friends, neighbors, her teacher and grandmother.

This book is a good introduction to the issue of mental illness. It is especially important in that students see how this young girl is able to cope with this difficult part of her life. "Sometimes by mommy has a dark cloud inside of her. I can't stop the rain from falling, but I can find sunshine in my mind."

Teachers can introduce students to this issue with this poignant book. Students can brainstorm different scenarios and discuss how they can be resolved. They can discuss who their support network includes and what it takes for a person to be strong enough to weather such a storm.

The book is a much needed resource for children in times where Annie's situation is far more common than is generally known. Annie's capacity to make effective, affirming social decisions makes the work an inspirational touchstone for other peers who need to confront their parents' emotional crises. Children might be inspired to author poetry or create deliberately fictionalized narrative accounts about how they have confronted various crises.

In offering an upper elementary grade and age appropriate narrative of a peer dealing with an emotionally ill parent, this book provides readers confronting similar family and caregiver issues with an opening for discussion and for hopeful outreach. Just reading this account may well be the first step necessary to assist a youngster in acknowledging a "hidden problem" and getting crucial adult assistance in dealing with the crisis.

Garza, Carmen Lomas. (1990). *Family Pictures Cuadros de familia*. Children's Book Press.

This book tells the story of the author's childhood growing up in a Hispanic community in Texas. The book is written in both Spanish and English, accompanied by the author's most incredible paintings. The paintings are unique, somewhat folksy, colorful, and totally entrancing. They bring you into Carmen's world. Once inside it, you don't want to leave.

There is so much to explore in this book; it works well with the study of "myself and family", community, communities around the world, Mexico, family traditions and customs. It emphasizes social and emotional learning and how a young girl can find her way in the world. The traditions followed by her community and family were not necessarily accepted or understood by white America. Yet these values gave her the strength to be her own person and to rely on both her relationships and rich inner life to express herself.

There are so many activities that this book inspires. Children can study the origins of the piñata, and make one. They can make a cookbook of recipes from Mexico or from their own homes. Children can also be encouraged to design their own book of family pictures. They can emphasize special occasions that they celebrate or focus on family traditions which reflect their cultural backgrounds. The richness and lushness of the paintings invites the readers to construct meaning and to create their own narratives, procedural accounts, poetry, and dialogues inspired by one or more of the paintings.

Picture walk through the illustrations. Given the Spanish/English text, this strategy can be an engaging spatial entry point for descriptive and narrative spoken and written presentations. The lushly detailed illustrations of family rites and celebrations can be springboards for children's literary and artistic renditions of equivalent family pictures and events which are prompted by Carmen's selections.

Use of dual language text for the book validates children's and family member's responses in languages other than English. Obviously, this book and its format are inspirational for ELL/Bilingual learners and for special needs learners who can be captivated by the paintings.

The power of this book lies in its accessing and modeling the magic of family rites and rituals for a broad spectrum of linguistics, intrapersonal, spatial, and kinesthetic learners from monolingual, bilingual and special needs backgrounds. Common to all of its audience members are the social and emotionally celebratory components of Family Pictures.

Glaser, Shirley, & Glaser, Milton. (2003). *The Alphazeds Words*. Hyperion Books. This book is incredible in so many ways! It is an alphabet book that can be read by or to little ones and not so little ones. It starts with an empty room. One by one, each letter of the alphabet enters the room, each with its own distinct look, fantastic illustrations and typography by the designer Milton Glaser. Each of these letters also has its own distinct personality. A is angry, B is bashful, J is jealous, and so on. The room gets quite crowded. How do all of these different personalities manage to get along and coexist? Not too well apparently, as there is shouting, pushing, hitting and kicking. In the midst of all the chaos, the light in the room goes out and there is silence.

> "When the light came back on, something
> extraordinary had happened. Four letters
> had gotten together to comfort one another.
> Together they had managed to create something
> larger and more important than themselves.
> *"They had made the first word."*

This is a great lesson on how each of us can be an individual, yet when we work together, something wonderful can happen. This book illustrates an incredible lesson in social and emotional maturity, and helps the child realize that it isn't just about "me."

There are many different activities that a teacher can use with this book. The children can work in groups to make their own alphabet book of emotions. They can then present the book as a group, discussing the roles each of them played, and how they each used their unique talents to make the book.

Older children grades 3 and up, can research and present as a group some important discoveries that were made more special because they involved people working together. They can also work on a project about cooperative learning, perhaps surveying class and schoolmates on how they feel they learn the best.

Hest, Amy. (1985). *The Purple Coat*. New York: Macmillan Publishing Co.
In the autumn of every year, Gabrielle travels with her mother to New York City to visit her Grandpa who owns a tailor shop. Once there, he always makes her a new coat, but this year Gabrielle decides the usual navy blue coat won't do. The Purple Coat follows Gabrielle in her attempt to establish her own identity.

Lionni, Leo. (1980). *Inch by Inch*. Astor-Honor Publishing Co. Inc.
In *Inch by Inch*, an inchworm (which is a caterpillar, or larval stage, of the fall cankerworm, which becomes a moth) keeps itself from being eaten by various birds by proving its worth as a measuring device.

Lupton, Hugh. *The Story Tree- Tales to Read Aloud*. Barefoot Books. K-3
These seven multicultural stories are accessible enough to children to encourage their eventually taking over the read aloud sharing on their own. This book is also a good one for family literacy sessions and for parent volunteers to read aloud in the classroom.

Martin Jr., Bill, & John Archambault. (1966). *Knots on a Counting Rope*. New York, New York: Henry Holt and Company.
This beautifully illustrated book reaches out in so many different directions, and we can all learn so much from it. Knots on a Counting Rope is the story of a Native-American boy who is blind and is learning from his grandfather how to survive in this world. Boy-Strength-of-Blue-Horses insists on hearing the story of his birth over and over again.

Every time his grandfather retells the story of the boy's birth, he adds a knot to his counting rope. Each time he hears the story, Boy-Strength-of-Blue-Horses gains more confidence in himself. The story emphasizes the Native-American tradition of storytelling, and there are numerous art, math and social studies lessons that offshoot from this book.

Of course, the telling and retelling of the story celebrate the young blind hero's strengths and weaknesses and ability to set goals with optimism. Stories of one's birth related by others are powerful demonstrations of social skills of the highest order.

This book also deals extensively with social and emotional learning. Children learn that those with disabilities need to be treated with sensitivity while learning to find their place in the world. One way in which children's social and emotional learning is strengthened is by understanding themselves and those around them. In order to facilitate this, each child will interview at least one family member about when he/she was born. The accounts collected with appropriate photos or memorabilia can then be shared in class and perhaps even authored into a *Knots on a Counting Rope* style book format.

Children can also retell the story of the boy using the counting system of cultures other than Native American. This literary response will incorporate cultural study, respect and empathy into ongoing reading and writing workshop efforts.

McCully, Emily Arnold. (1992). *Mirette on the High Wire*. G.P. Putnam's & Sons.
Mirette helps her mother run a boardinghouse for acrobats, jugglers, actors and mimes. Her life changes when she discovers a boarder crossing the courtyard on air. She begs him to teach her how he does it. He refuses to teach her, but she begins practicing on her own. As she improves, he begins to help her. In the end she helps him overcome his fear of the high wire.

Rabe, Bernice. (1981). *The Balancing Girl*. E.P. Dutton.
Margaret, a girl in a wheel chair is excellent at balancing all kinds of objects. Margaret shows her friend Tommy how good she is at balancing at the school carnival.

Ringgold, Faith. (1991). *Tar Beach*. New York, New York: Crown Publishers.
This book is one of my favorites, and it is moving in its words, art, and the beautiful story it tells. This is an effective book to use for younger grades to connect with myself, my family and my community. It can also be used in connection with a mapmaking unit. The children can be encouraged to make a map of their neighborhood from an aerial view.

A starting point for a discussion would be why the author portrayed New York from such a vantage point. In this beautiful book, the narrator, Cassie Louise Lightfoot, lets her dreams and ambitions take her to places in New York City that she ordinarily would not be able to be part of because of her circumstances. As a result of her self-motivation and self-awareness, Cassie is able to go as far as her dreams will let her. In this book Cassie also shows strengths in the areas of emotional sensitivity, as well as inter and intra-personal relationships.

Children can author their own Tar Beach equivalent night fantasies and then share them with one another through an exhibit or big books. Although Cassie's family is obviously poor since they have to picnic on their roof, Cassie's dreamlike lushly illustrated flight over Harlem validates the beauty of their family life and of the city landscape which is accessible to all. This is an invaluable lesson in the importance of the wealth inherent in the appreciation of family connections and the beauty of nature and public architectural designs! A song of family and of the city!

Schories, Pat. *Breakfast for Jack/Jack and the Missing Piece*. Front Street.
These wordless stories help pre-literate children, ELL learners new to this country and special needs children explore the basic elements of story-character, setting and plot. The lack of words allows the children to "construct their own meaning," and create their own different stories which "fit" the illustrations.

Steinberg, Laya. *Thesaurus Rex*. Barefoot Books.
This book introduces a dinosaur with an interest in words whose story is told through a wonderful rhyming text which can be used for fostering phonemic awareness and for choral readings.

Uhlberg, Myron. *The Printer*. Peachtree.
This story celebrates the conventions of print in that the boy narrator's father is a deaf man who speaks with his hands and as a job chooses to turn lead type letters into words and sentences. An excellent book to support family literacy and an appreciation for the conventions of print.

Van Allsburg, Chris. (1988). *Two Bad Ants*. Houghton Mifflin Co.
In *Two Baxd Ants*, news comes to the ant world of a great discovery in a far away place. A delicious crystal has been found. A group of ants set out to bring back this crystal to their queen. Two ants are overwhelmed by the treasure and stay behind in this dangerous alien world. It is a tale of choices, consequences and the discovery of life's real treasures.

Walter, Mildred Pitts. (2004). Illustrated by Larry Johnson. *Alec's primer.*
Lebanon, NH: University Press of New England.

> This is the true account of a Virginian slave who was taught to read by his owner's daughter. He later fought in the Civil War on the Union side and became a landowner himself in Vermont. The beautifully written narrative is complemented by the vibrant paintings of Larry Johnson which include authentic period details.

Webliography

Reading Online
http://www.readingonline.org
This online web resource which is sponsored by the International Reading Association is full of specific reading teaching ideas, lessons and new research. It includes summaries of conference presentations and even tips on how to use technology to teach reading.

Balanced Literacy
http://www.thekcrew.net/balancedliteracy.html
Established in 1996, this site is organized according to the components of the balanced literacy approach. It also has an excellent listing of professional books that can assist with various aspects of teaching reading.

Carol Hurst
http://www.carolhurst.com/index.html
This is a terrific resource for exploring the children's literature works which are at the crux of author and genre study. It can be used for material to supplement period studies and discussions of authors' lives. Older children will be able to explore it on their own.

Read, Write, Think
http://www.readwritethink.org/lessons/
This resource maintained by the NCTE, National Council of Teachers of English, has a growing database of age and grade specific literacy lesson plans. It also includes all the graphic organizers cited in this book and many more, ready to download.

Inspiration Software
http://www.inspiration.com
http://www.inspiration.com/freetrial/index.cfm
This is the home site for the Inspiration and Kidspiration mind mapping software. These online templates and capacities assist the reading teacher with customizing the various graphic organizers discussed throughout the book, and with gaining the ability to design customized graphic organizers for a particular theme, study or student group. A free trial version of this resource which is child friendly can be downloaded.

Visual Thesaurus
http://www.visualthesaurus.com/online/
This is really both an online dictionary and a thesaurus.

Resources for Read Aloud, Shared Reading, and Independent Reading available on the Internet include the following:

http:// www.mightybook.com/library_4to6.htm.
This is a library of books read aloud by the computer. Children can listen to these books or practice reading with a buddy as the computer broadcasts the text. Of course, this type of read aloud would only be used IN ADDITION to the vibrant read-aloud of the teacher.

http://www.enchantedlearning.com/Rhymes.html
These are online nursery rhymes ready for reading to the children and posting throughout for room or for literacy center display.

SEDL-RCI Framework of Reading
http://www.sedl.org/reading/framework/assessment.html
This is an excellent resource for readings in the theories and methods of foundations. There are topic aligned links to specific theorists which can be included at the close of your lesson planning and may be reviewed before certification tests.

TOOLS TO HELP YOU TEACH THE FOUNDATIONS OF READING AND SUCCEEDING IN CONSTRUCTED RESPONSE CERTIFICATION EXAMINATIONS

Appendix 1- The Record of Reading Behavior- A close up look at a key assessment tool.

Often in the constructed response question on a foundations of education certification test or on a general elementary certification test; the educator is asked to analyze a record of reading behavior or to construct an appropriate one from data given in an anecdote. Furthermore with the current climate of accountability, it is a good idea for new teachers and for career changers to examine closely the basic elements of recording reading behavior.

While there are various acceptable formats for emergent literacy assessment used throughout the country, the one selected for use here is based on the work of Marie Clay and Kenneth Goodman. These two are key researchers in the close observation and documentations of children's early reading miscues (reading mistakes).

It is important to emphasize that the teacher should not just "take the Record of Reading Behavior " and begin filling it out as the child reads from a random book prior to beginning of the observation. There are specific steps for taking the record and analyzing its results.

1. Select a text
If you want to see if the child is reading on instructional level, choose a book that the child has already read. If the purpose of the test is to see whether the child is ready to advance to the next level, choose a book from that level which the child has not yet seen.

2. Introduce the text
If the book is one that has been read, you do not need to introduce the text, other than by saying the title. But if the book is new to the child, you should briefly share the title and tell the child a bit about the plot and style of the book.

3. Take the record
Generally with emergent readers' grades 1-2, there are only 100-150 words in a passage used to take a record. Make certain that the child is seated beside you, so that you can see the text as the child reads it.

If desired, you may want to photocopy the text in advance for yourself, so you can make direct notations on your text while the child reads from the book. After you introduce the text make certain that the child has the chance to read the text independently. Be certain that you do not "teach" or help the child with the text, other than to supply an unknown word that the child requests you supply. The purpose of the record is to see what the child does on his or her own.

As the child reads the text, you must be certain to record the reading behaviors the child exhibits using the following notations.

In taking the record, keep in mind the following: Allow enough time for the child to work independently on a problem before telling or supplying the word. If you wait too long, you could run the risk of having the child lose the meaning and his/her interest in the story as he or she tries to identify the unknown word.

It is recommended that when a child is way off track, you tell him or her to "Try that again" (TTA). If a whole phrase is troubling, put it into square brackets and score it as only one error.

The notation for filling out the Record of Reading behavior involves noting the child's response on the top with the actual text below it.

Comprehension Check

This can and should be done by inviting the child to retell the story. This retelling can then be used to ask further questions about characters, plot, setting and purpose which allow you to observe and to record the child's level of comprehension.

Calculating the Reading Level and the Self-correction Rate

Calculating the reading level lets you know if the book is at the level on which the child can read it independently or comfortably with guidance or if the book is at a level where reading it frustrates the child.

Generally, an accuracy score of 95-100% suggests that the child can read the text and other books or texts on the same level.

An accuracy score of 90-94% indicates that the text and texts likely will present challenges to the child, but with guidance from you, a tutor or parent, the child will be able to master these texts and enjoy them. This is instructional level.

However, an accuracy score of less than 89% tells you that the material you have selected for the child is too hard for the child to control alone. Such material needs to be shared with the child in a shared reading situation or read to the child.

KEEPING SCORE ON THE RECORD

Insertions, omissions, substitutions, and teacher told responses, all count as errors. Repetitions are not scored as errors. Corrected responses are scored as self corrections.

No penalty is given for a child's attempts at self correction that results in a finally incorrect response but the attempts should be noted. Multiple unsuccessful attempts at a word score as one error only.

The lowest score for any page is zero.
If a child omits a line or lines, each word omitted is counted as an error. If the child omits a page, deduct the number of words omitted from the total number of words which you have used for the record.

Calculating the Reading Level

Note the number of errors made on each line on the Record of Reading Behavior in the column marked E (for Error).

Total the number of errors in the text and divide this number into the number of words that the child has read. This will give you the error rate.

If a child read a passage of 100 words and made 10 errors, the error rate would be 1 in 10. Convert this to an accuracy percentage, or 90%.

Calculating the Self Correction Rate

Total all the self-corrections.
Next, add the number of errors to the number of self-corrections and divide by the number of self-corrections.

A self correction rate of 1 in 3 to 1 in 5 is considered good. This rate indicates that the child is able to help himself or herself as problems are encountered in reading.

Analyzing the record

This record should assist the educator in developing a detailed date specific picture of the child's progress in reading behavior. It should be used to help the educator individualize instruction for the specific child.

As the errors are reviewed, consider whether the child made the error because of semantics (cues from meaning), syntactic (language structure), or visual information difficulties.

As self-corrections are analyzed, consider what led the child to make that self-correction. Check out and consider what cues the child does use effectively and which the child does not use well.

Consider the ways in which the child tackles a word which is unknown. Characterize that behavior and consider how the teacher can assist the child with this issue.

If a child can retell at least three quarters of a story, this is considered adequate for retelling.

Analysis of reading behavior records can and should support the educator in designing appropriate mini lessons and strategies to help the child with his or her recorded errors and miscues.

Sample Test

1) **The major difference between phonemic and phonological awareness is:**

A) One deals with a series of discrete sounds and the other with sound-spelling relationships.

B) One is involved with teaching and learning alliteration and rhymes.

C) Phonemic awareness is a specific type of phonological awareness that deals with separate phonemes within a given word.

D) Phonological awareness is associated with printed words.

2) **The theorist in early reading (emergent reading) who has identified five tasks for phonemic awareness is:**

A) John Munro

B) Brian Cambourne

C) Marilyn Jager Adams

D) Lucy Calkins

3) **An oddity task is one in which children:**

A) Identify the odd number in a mathematical series and talk about how they did it.

B) Perform a creative exercise designed for differentiated learning styles.

C) Recognize which sound is odd in a series of like sounds.

D) Design a different activity for themselves.

4) **All of the following are true about phonological awareness EXCEPT:**

A) It may involve print.

B) It is a prerequisite for spelling and phonics.

C) Activities can be done by the children with their eyes closed.

D) It starts before letter recognition is taught.

5) Ms. James is seated with a child by her side. The child is reading aloud from an open book. Ms. James is teaching in a school that has embraced the Balanced Literacy Approach. Therefore it is most likely that Ms. James is writing and recording:

A) The child's use of expression in reading aloud.

B) The child's errors and miscues.

C) Her observations of the child's attitude toward reading.

D) The child's feelings about the particular passage being read.

6) Most of the children in first-year teacher Ms. James's class are really doing well in their phonemic awareness assessments. However, Ms. James is very concerned about three children who do not seem to be able to distinguish between spoken words that "sound alike," but are different. Since she is a first year teacher, she feels her inexperience may be to blame. In truth, the reason these three children have not yet demonstrated phonemic awareness is most likely that:

A) They are not capable of becoming good readers.

B) They are bored in class.

C) They may be from an ELL background.

D) Ms. James does not pronounce the different phonemes clearly enough.

7) **Ms. Ramsey has forgotten her credit cards and has limited cash in her wallet. She is buying supplies for her reading classroom that she wants to have annotated with the children's names by the first day of school. She should buy all of the following with her cash except:**

A) Folders.

B) Markers.

C) Rulers.

D) Index cards.

8) **Ms. Rivers is preparing for a parent teacher conference. She does all of the following EXCEPT:**

A) Collects individual child running records.

B) Puts away all the book bags and leveled pots so the classroom will be more spacious.

C) Puts out by each child's seat the child's weekly log and spelling folder.

D) Sets up work samples by each child's place.

9) **In terms of a balanced literacy classroom, a "leveled bin" indicates:**

A) A plant set at child's eye level for descriptive writing purposes.

B) A bin with books the child has selected.

C) A bin with books leveled by the teacher.

D) A bin with all kinds of reading materials including magazines and packaging on a child's level.

10) **Mark Garner has been told that he will have to support some special needs readers in his classroom in addition to the rest of the students. He can expect to have:**

A) Gifted children who are accelerated in reading skills for their grade and age.

B) Children who have disabilities and will need special support in accessing the content and methods he uses with the rest of the class.

C) Children who come from native language backgrounds other than English.

D) Children who display the capacities and needs detailed in a and b.

11) Julia has been hired to work in a school that serves a local public housing project. She is working with kindergarten children and has been asked to focus on shared reading. She selects:

A) Chapter books.

B) Riddle books.

C) Alphabet books.

D) Wordless picture books.

12) It is 4 PM, yet Francine is still in her classroom. The seats in her classroom are filled with adults of various ages who are holding books. They are seated two by two with both holding copies of the same book. Francine probably is:

A) Explaining to parents how she will teach a particular story.

B) Demonstrating shared reading with a buddy for volunteer parents.

C) Hosting a parents organization meeting for her grade level.

D) Distributing old books from the class library to parents.

13) The work of Chard and Osborn (1999) in establishing guidelines for children with reading disabilities has shown that it is essential for them to:

A) Read wordless picture books.

B) Learn at least 10 sight words.

C) Work intensely on the alphabetic principle.

D) Focus on using syntactic clues.

14) A key theorist whose work has helped teacher's document children's oral reading progress throughout the school year is:

A) Jerome Bruner.

B) Daniel J. Chard.

C) J. David Cooper.

D) Marie Clay.

15) The first grade class is on a neighborhood walk. As the children approach the neighborhood Kentucky Fried Chicken chain, Danny reads from the store window "Kentucky Fried Chicken Hot and Crunchy." Danny has never read or been taught to read this before. The most likely explanation for Danny's being able to read this is that he is:

A) An advanced reader who is self improving.

B) His parents have taught him to read the signs and materials at the Kentucky Fried Chicken store.

C) He is in the logographic phrase of phonics learning.

D) This was just a lucky guess on his part.

16) An observer enters Julia's first grade classroom. Children are working with oaktag strips and placing the word letters on these strips on a sentence strip holder. Then they seem to be involved in some kind of counting. The observer is confused. This activity is taking place during the reading block. Julia explains:

A) The children are counting letters.

B) This is word sorting and the children are grouping words by length, common letters and sound.

C) The children are combining mathematics counting and word study.

D) The children are doing a strategy sheet based on a particular word family.

17) As he walks up and down the hallway, Mr. Adams, the new Assistant Principal, continually hears Ms. Brown telling her children to go to the wall.Mr. Adams looks briefly at the literacy block schedule and continues on his walk through the building. He realizes that Ms. Brown's children are at work on:

A) A new hall display.

B) Taking down an old display and then redoing it for a new theme.

C) Adding words to their spelling word wall.

D) Measuring the height of plants for a mathematics lesson.

18) Randy is proud of how many new vocabulary words he has learned. He enjoys playing with a device his teacher has, since it helps him to show all the words he can create from various letters. The device is a:

A) Word strip.

B) Letter holder for making words.

C) Word mask.

D) None of the above.

19) Ability grouping means:

A) Grouping of children according to the results of an IQ test.

B) Grouping of children with similar test results for instructional purposes.

C) Grouping of children according to their oral reading accuracy rate.

D) Grouping of children wit similar needs for instructional purposes.

20) Tim is not in the same ability group as his best friend Alex. He starts to cry even though he is a second grader. The teacher comforts him by telling him the truth that:

A) He is just as smart as Alex.

B) He can play with Alex during recess.

C) Ability groups change as the children's needs in them change during the year.

D) Tim is smarter than his best friend Alex.

21) "Beautiful Beth is the Best Girl in the Bradley Bay area." This sentence could be used to help children learn about:

  A) Assonance.

  B) Alliteration.

  C) Rhyming pairs.

  D) None of the above.

22) Greg Ball went to an author signing where Faith Ringgold gave a talk about one of her many books. He was so inspired by her presence and by his reading of her book *TAR BEACH,* that he used the book for his reading and writing workshop activities. His supervisor wrote in his plan book, that he was pleased that Greg had used the book as an/a _____ book.

  A) Basic book.

  B) Feature book.

  C) Anchor book.

  D) Focus book.

23) A delegation from the United Kingdom has come to the United States and since they are considering adapting the balanced literacy approach, they are very interested in seeing the small group demonstrated. Mr. Adams knows that he should bring them into Greg's room when Greg is doing which activity?

  A) A mini lesson.

  B) A conference with individual students.

  C) A time when children are divided into small and independent study groups.

  D) A read-aloud.

24) As the visitors from the United Kingdom tour the school, they are pleased to hear a sing-song chant "Don't fall asleep at the page, don't forget the _____ " Mr. Adams explains to them that the first graders are learning about pointing at words and moving from the left to the right, this is called:

  A) Directionality

  B) Return sweep

  C) Top to bottom

  D) Line for line reading

25) Andrew is just starting school, but it looks like he will be successful in reading because:

    A) He comes from a family which cares about his progress.

    B) He is phonemically aware and knows his alphabet.

    C) He has been in pre-school.

    D) He is well behaved.

26) Gracie seems to be struggling with her reading, even in first grade, although her mother works at a publishing firm and her dad is an editor. Her speech is also full of mispronunciations, although her parents were born in the school neighborhood. Gracie should be checked by:

    A) A reading specialist.

    B) A speech therapist or an audiologist

    C) A pediatrician.

    D) A psychologist.

27) Ronald's parents are hearing impaired. He probably will need:

    A) Extensive work with the use of picture cues

    B) Work with songs, rhymes and read alouds to promote phonemic awareness.

    C) No extra work or support.

    D) None of the above.

28) Maria was an outstanding student in her elementary school in Brazil. Now she is nervous about starting fourth grade in the US, although she learned English as a second language in Brazil. She and her parents should be relieved to know that:

    A) She will get extra help in the United States with her English.

    B) There is a positive and strong correlation between a child's native language and his/her learning of English.

    C) Her classmates will help her.

    D) She will have a few months to study for the reading test.

29) Paul is a new teacher. He has just started his logs and assessments for his children's phonemic awareness. He asks a reading teacher to look over his log, but the log is returned to him:

    A) Paul gave the log to the wrong colleague.

    B) The colleague would not help him out by reviewing it.

    C) The log did not have the dates the child's behavior was observed and had no stated performance standards.

    D) The log didn't have a cover letter from Paul.

30) The term graphophenemic awareness refers to:

    A) Handwriting skills.

    B) Letter to sound recognition.

    C) Alphabetic principle.

    D) Phonemic awareness.

31) A stationery store owner in the neighborhood of the school is amused by the fact that the children on a school walk, are rushing up to various store signs and street signs. The children are probably exploring:

    A) The alphabetic principle.

    B) The principle that print carries meaning.

    C) Letter sound recognition.

    D) Phonemic awareness.

32) As Ms. Maxwell enters a first grade class, the teacher is busily writing down what the children are saying. The teacher is probably doing this to:

    A) Demonstrate how to copy down speech.

    B) Make a connection and promote awareness of the relationship between spoken and written language.

    C) Authenticate the children's comments.

    D) Raise the children's self esteem.

33) A district observer notes that fifth graders are showing younger peers in the third grade how to hold a book and walk around with it, they assume:

A) That the fifth graders are particularly theatrical.

B) That the fifth graders are proud of how they read stories aloud.

C) That the fifth graders are training the younger children in book holding.

D) That this has nothing to do with instruction.

34) Environmental print is available at all of the following except:

A) Within a newspaper.

B) On the page of a library book.

C) On a supermarket circular.

D) In a commercial flyer.

35) Book handling skills include ALL of the following except:

A) Putting a cellophane or plastic cover on a book.

B) Identifying the back cover of the book.

C) Reading the book jacket.

D) Reading dedication page and the title page of the book.

36) The best way for a primary grade teacher to model directionality and one to one word matching would be:

A) Using a regular library or classroom text book.

B) Using her own person reading book.

C) Using a big book.

D) Using a book dummy.

37) As far as the balanced literacy movement is concerned the "WHOLE" is:

A) All the reading themes to be covered that day.

B) The whole class meeting for the mini lesson.

C) The complete unit to be covered over the month.

D) All of the reading and writing work to be done in connection with one book.

38) The "TO, WITH, BY" continuum means:

A) The teacher works with the children.

B) The children work Independently.

C) Everything is led by the teacher and taught to the children.

D) The teacher first teachers to the children, then works with them and ultimately the children learn by themselves.

39) Factual book features children should learn include:

A) Captions.

B) Glossaries.

C) Diagrams.

D) All of the above.

40) When they are in 6th grade, children should be able to independently go through an unfamiliar collection and:

A) Use only the table of contents.

B) Use the first line indices, and find a poem by author and subject.

C) Use only the glossary.

D) None of the above.

41) At a faculty meeting Ms. Riley found out that she might have crisscrossers in her class and that Mr. Brown had them and he was happy about it:

A) Crisscrossers are students who have skipped a grade.

B) Crisscrossers are students with excellent skills in reading and in Math.

C) Crisscrossers are second language learners who have a positive attitude toward first and second language learning.

D) Crisscrossers are second language learners who are only positive about English Language Learning.

42) Cues in reading are:

A) Vowel sounds.

B) Digraphs.

C) Sources of information used by readers to help them construct meaning.

D) None of the above.

43) As part of a study for a unit on the history of Massachusetts, Mr. Gentry is using the early childhood book *26 Letters and 99 Cents* by Tina Hoban. He wants his readers to study it and create a more detailed guide to their state using its concept. This is a technique frequently used in:

A) Reading and writing workshop.

B) Writing process instruction.

C) Readers workshop.

D) Technical writing.

44) A key theorist who supports a phonics centered approach is:

A) Marie Clay.

B) Sharon Taberski.

C) Shelley Harwayne.

D) Rudolf Flesch.

45) To decode is to:

A) Construct meaning.

B) Sound out a printed sequence of letters.

C) Use a special code to decipher a message.

D) None of the above.

46) To encode means that you:

A) Decode a second time.

B) Construct meaning from a code.

C) Tell someone a message.

D) None of the above.

47) There are two basic types of text structure:

A) Fiction and non-fiction.

B) Primary and pre-k.

C) Expository and narrative.

D) Wordless and text rich.

48) While the supervisor is pleased overall with Barbara's first year of teaching, he feels that given the fact that two of her students are transfers from Mexico and one student has a hearing impairment, she has to plan for:

A) Extra homework for all of them.

B) Extra time for the hearing impaired child.

C) A buddy to work with the two students from Mexico.

D) Differentiated instruction to meet these students varied special needs.

49) The district is emphasizing that all students in grades 3-6 must focus this month on the reading of functional documents. Ms. Ramirez just smiles and scoops up a handful of free newspapers which she gets on subscription. This is Wednesday and there is a food section. She plans to use:

    A) The main news stories.

    B) The sports pages.

    C) The recipe pages.

    D) The comics.

50) Ms. Ramirez also wants the children to share their functional reading skills with their families, so she asks that they take the newspapers home to focus on the:

    A) Advice columns.

    B) Fill in coupons.

    C) Metropolitan news briefs.

    D) Weather section.

51) Mr. Adams was pleased with Ms. Ramirez's reading lesson, but he realized that she would have visually represented the comparisons she was trying to get the children to make better, if she had used:

    A) a big book.

    B) More expressive language.

    C) A better literary example.

    D) A graphic organizer.

52) Margaret is the winning Ps 123 orator. She loves reciting poetry by Shel Silverstein. Who would guess that she is also a poet in her first language? Margaret's first language is definitely:

    A) English.

    B) French.

    C) Spanish.

    D) NOT English.

53) A teacher is asking children to look at the beginning letters of words. She then asks the child to connect the beginning letter to the text and story and to think about what word would make sense there. This is an example of:

A) A balanced literacy approach.

B) A phonemic approach.

C) A phonic approach.

D) AN ELL differentiated approach.

54) The teacher is watching the children go from oral speech into writing. The teacher says, "Great job:"

A) A good decoding.

B) A good recoding.

C) A good encoding.

D) All of the above.

55) By November the first graders have a vocabulary of words which they can correctly pronounce and read aloud. These words are their:

A) Sight vocabulary.

B) Recognition vocabulary.

C) Personal vocabulary.

D) Working vocabulary.

56) As the child is reading and has made an incorrect attempt, the teacher prompts:

A) That is a mistake, do it again.

B) No, you are stupid. .. why can't you get it?

C) Does that make sense to you?

D) Forget it, this is too hard for you.

57) Asking a child if what he or she has read makes sense to him or her, is prompting the child to use:

A) Phonics cues.

B) Syntactic cues.

C) Semantic cues.

D) Prior knowledge.

58) When you ask a child, if what he or she has just read "sounds right" to him or her, you are trying to get that child to use:

A) Phonics cues.

B) Syntactic cues.

C) Semantic cues.

D) Prior knowledge.

59) By definition, which children in a classroom will have trouble with syntactic cues?

   A) Those from families who do not have household libraries.

   B) Those not in a top reading group.

   C) Those from ELL backgrounds.

   D) All of the above.

60) "Self correct" in reading means:

   A) The teacher corrects on the record the errors the child makes.

   B) The child goes back and corrects errors made in a running record.

   C) The reading specialist teaches this to the child.

   D) a and b.

61) A natural role for a highly proficient reader would be:

   A) To assist the teacher with cleaning the classroom and organizing the student folders.

   B) To develop charts for the teacher by copying needed poems for full class study.

   C) Tutor and support struggling readers.

   D) Work on his/her own interests while the teacher works with the rest of the class.

62) A theorist who believes that there is a finite body of approved literature children should be taught on various grade levels and has produced books about what everyone needs to know to be literate on various grade levels is:

   A) Rudolf Flesch

   B) J. David Cooper

   C) John Dewey

   D) E. D. Hirsch

63) Children "own" words when all of the following happen except:

A) They find these words on their own.

B) The teacher provides a mandated word list.

C) They use the words in their own writings.

D) The words appear in literature that interests them.

64) A discussion circle can convene:

A) After the children have finished reading a text as a group.

B) Before the children read a text as a group.

C) While the reading of the text is going on.

D) All of the above.

65) To promote word study, children can:

A) Be required to go to the dictionary at least once or twice a day.

B) Collect and share words of interest they find in their readings.

C) Do vocabulary work sheets from a basal reader or commercial vocabulary book.

D) Do all of the above.

66) In order to get children to compile specialized vocabulary, they can use:

A) Newspapers.

B) Internet resources and approved web-sites that focus on the special interest.

C) Experts they can interview.

D) All of the above.

67) If children are engaged in creating a museum within classroom project to exhibit their work, they are:

   A) Not doing any reading or writing.

   B) Doing many authentic reading, writing, and researching tasks.

   C) Not likely to visit a real museum.

   D) All of the above.

68) Teachers should select at least ___words for pre-reading vocabulary discussion:

   A) 12.

   B) 15.

   C) 2-3.

   D) 8-10.

69) The teacher should choose words for pre-story discussion and exploration based on:

   A) The teacher's interest.

   B) Whether the teacher feels the children have prior knowledge of or experience with the words.

   C) A pre-existing grade level required vocabulary list.

   D) Words that will impress his or her supervisor.

70) Two steps a teacher might take before selecting words for study are:

   A) Reading the story and story mapping.

   B) Asking advice from a veteran teacher and the grade leader.

   C) Looking in a teacher's guide and copying out the words listed there.

   D) All of the above are correct

71) A teacher discovers after considering his class's prior knowledge of the story material that he would need to teach 12 words at least before he starts teaching the story to the whole group. This indicates:

   A) The children will need a read-aloud.

   B) The children will need independent reading.

   C) The children will need guided reading.

   D) The children will need shared reading.

72) The teacher is very concerned about identifying a book that is "just right" for Jay to read independently. This means that Jay should be able to read this book with:

A) Below 92% accuracy

B) 100% accuracy

C) 95-100% accuracy

D) 92-97% accuracy

73) Jay really wants to read a book that he can only read with 94% accuracy. He could get to read this book as:

A) An independent reading.

B) A guided reading.

C) A shared reading.

D) All of the above.

74) When taking a child's running record, the kinds of self corrections the child makes:

A) Are not important, but the percentage of accuracy is important.

B) May show something about which cueing systems the child relies on.

C) Can be meaningful if analyzed over several records.

D) Both b and c

75) A "decodable text" is:

A) A text that a child can read aloud with correct pronunciations.

B) A text that a child can answer comprehension questions about with a high percentage of accuracy.

C) Text written to match the sequence of letter-sound relationships that have been taught.

D) None of the above.

76) Once a teacher has carefully recorded and documented a running record:

A) There is nothing further to do as long as the teacher keeps the running record for conferences and documentation of grades.

B) The teacher should review the running record and other subsequent ones taken for growth over time.

C) The teacher should differentiate instruction for that particular student as indicated by growth over time and evidence of other needs.

D) Both b and c

77) **The reliability of a test is measured by:**

   A) The number of children who can pass it.

   B) The number of children who fail it.

   C) The degree to which it measures what it is supposed to measure over time.

   D) None of the above

78) **A quartile on a test is:**

   A) A quarter of the grades grouped.

   B) The division of the percentiles into four segments each of which is called a quartile.

   C) 25 of the tests scored.

   D) b and c

79) **Validity in assessment means:**

   A) The test went off without any previewing of the questions or leaks on its contents.

   B) The majority of test takers passed.

   C) The correct time was allowed for the children to complete the test.

   D) The test assessed what it was supposed to assess and measure.

80) **Vocabulary should be introduced after reading if:**

   A) The children have identified words from their reading which were difficult and which they need explained.

   B) The text is appropriate for vocabulary building.

   C) The teacher would like to teach vocabulary after the reading.

   D) a and b

81) **The teacher is working on a life science unit in grade five and using many print and electronic sources for information. Some of these words have a linear and some of them a hierarchical relationship to one another. The teacher has spent much time explaining how the words connect with one another. At this point, it would be a good idea to:**

   A) Use a root family diagram or tree.

   B) Work with the base words.

   C) Use hierarchical and linear arrays.

   D) Start semantic mapping for a particular concept.

82) **Direct teaching of a concept or strategy means:**

A) The teacher teaches the concept or strategy as part of a genre lesson.

B) The teacher teaches the concept as part of the writing workshop.

C) The teacher explicitly announces to the class that this strategy will be taught.

D) The teacher teaches the strategy to a small group of children or to an individual child.

83) **The word "bat" is a ___word for "batter-up":**

A) Suffix.

B) Prefix.

C) Root word.

D) Inflectional ending.

84) **"Ballgame" is a _____word. Its meaning is derived from the combination of "Ball" and "Game":**

A) Contraction.

B) Compound.

C) Portmanteau.

D) Palindrome.

85) **In a balanced literacy classroom, new vocabulary would most likely appear on:**

A) An experiential chart.

B) A class newspaper.

C) The word wall.

D) Outside the room on a bulletin board.

86) **An effective way to build vocabulary and to make connections with mandated science and mathematics material is to teach Greek and Latin roots using:**

A) Semantic maps.

B) Hierarchical arrays.

C) Linear arrays.

D) Word webs.

87) **As a parent walked through the first grade floor of her school, she kept hearing repeated clapping. Most likely the children were:**

A) Clapping to show respect for one another.

B) Rehearsing for how they would clap at a play.

C) Clapping out syllables of multi-syllabic words.

D) All of the above.

88) As part of study about the agricultural products of their state, children have identified 22 different types of apples produced in the state. They can use a _____ to compare and contrast these different types of apples:

A) Word web.

B) Semantic map.

C) Semantic features analysis grid.

D) All of the above.

89) Based on individual conferences with many children, the teacher realizes that although they are all self-improving readers, they need help in better use of the context to define words. The teacher decided to try the use of:

A) A dictionary to look up words.

B) A thesaurus to use with the dictionary.

C) Contextual redefinition training.

D) Instruction in how to effectively use a dictionary.

90) The parents of Ramon, a child who has grown up in Puerto Rico and studied English there as a second language, ask that the teacher provide him with individual support in context redefinition. Ramon is scoring above grade level in reading. His mother, who is also a teacher of reading, argues that:

A) He should get extra help because he has just transferred from another country.

B) Being walked through the process of using contexts is helpful for an ELL student.

C) He needs to work with a peer on this skill.

D) None of the above.

91) A bound morpheme is:

A) A prefix.

B) A contraction.

C) An inflectional ending that can be added to a base word to change its case, gender, number, tense or form.

D) A root word.

92) A second grader is writing his first book review. He has conferred with his teacher several times while he was writing the book review. Now he is rehearsing it with the teacher before he reads it aloud to the class. The child's learning of how to compose and deliver a book review has been:

A) Done independently.

B) Assisted by family support.

C) Done in a cooperative group setting.

D) Scaffolded by the teacher.

93) One of the many ways in which a child can demonstrate comprehension of a story is by:

A) Filling in a strategy sheet.

B) Retelling the story orally.

C) Retelling the story in writing.

D) All of the above.

94) A strategy is:

A) A practice or routine the teacher can continually refer to.

B) A practice or routine a child can continually refer to or use.

C) A sheet or template for a practice the child can continually fill out.

D) All of the above.

95) The Stop and Think Strategy means that the child reader will:

A) Read through until the end of the story or text.

B) Ask himself or herself if what he or she has read makes sense to him or her.

C) Stop after reading some text and write down his/her concerns.

D) All of the above.

96) Taking responsibility for a child's own learning, will usually involve the child in:

A) Reading and writing on his/her own.

B) Developing a personal literacy project which will later be shared with the teacher and peers and family.

C) Putting away books and materials when directed.

D) a and b.

97) "Sounds right" can sound wrong to:

A) Any reader who is not a fluent or early reader.

B) AN ELL reader.

C) A struggling reader.

D) None of the above.

98) "Bias" in testing occurs when:

A) The assessment instrument is not an objective, fair and impartial one for a given cultural, ethnic, or special needs participant.

B) The testing administrator is biased.

C) The same test is given with no time considerations or provisions for those in need of more time or those who have handicapping conditions.

D) All of the above.

99) Norm-referenced tests:

A) Give information only about the local samples results.

B) Provide information about the local test takers did compared to a representative sampling of national test takers.

C) Make no comparisons to national test takers.

D) None of the above.

100) If you get your raw score on a test, you will get:

A) The actual number of points you scored on the test.

B) The percentage score of the number of questions you answered correctly.

C) A letter grade for your work on the test.

D) An aggregated score for your performance on the text.

101) The data coordinator of the district who is concerned with federal funding for reading will probably want to start aggregating scores immediately because:

A) It is interesting to crunch more data.

B) By aggregating, the individual scores can be combined to view performance trends across groups.

C) This will help the district determine which groups need more remedial instruction.

D) b and c

102) A standardized test will be:

A) Given out with the same predetermined questions and format to all.

B) Not be given to certain children.

C) If given out in exactly the same format with the same content, may be taken over a lengthier test period (i.e. 4 hours instead of three or two).

D) All of the above.

103) Mr. Mandrake is subbing for Ms. Matley. He sees by the schedule that he is supposed to start the day after the morning meeting with a Read-Aloud. He notes a large picture on the easel and grabs the book just two minutes before the Read-Aloud is to start. He shouldn't heave a sigh of relief because:

A) He needs to be familiar with the book so that he can plan the read-aloud.

B) He does not know if the class has already heard this book.

C) He has not planned vocabulary, themes, or activities to go with the book.

D) All of the above.

104) The science fair is coming up and Ms. Gardner is trying to find time in her busy schedule to work on her class's earth worm diary project. With all of the mandated tests and assemblies, she has not found time to start her students on their earth worm research. Within the context of reading instruction, she can:

A) Begin a thematic study unit.

B) Start with a read aloud of the *Diary of an Earth Worm* by Doreen Cronin.

C) Scaffold the research process by going online with her children using an approved search engine to find matches for earthworm sites.

D) All of the above.

105) Annie's mother has been invited to class to serve as a guest reader. She scoops up her favorite books from her family bookshelf and rushes off to school. When she gets to Annie's classroom, she is greeted and ushered into a rocking chair and given a special hat to wear. The explanation is:

A) The children are excited to have a volunteer and are bored with their teacher day in and day out.

B) This is a class designated author's chair and an author's hat has been worked on by the whole class for anyone who comes to read to them or who reads his/her own writings.

C) Both a and b

D) None of the above.

106) Four of Ms. Wolmark's students have lived in other countries. She is particularly pleased to be studying Sumerian proverbs with them as part of the sixth grade unit in analyzing the sayings of other cultures because:

A) This gives her a break from teaching and the children can share sayings from other cultures they and their families have experienced.

B) This validates the experiences and expertise of ELL learners in her classroom.

C) This provides her children from the US with a lens on other cultural values.

D) All of the above.

107) As Ms. Wolmark looks at the mandated vocabulary curriculum for the 6th grade, she notes that she can opt to teach foreign words and abbreviations which have become part of the English language. She decides:

A) To forego that since she is not a teacher of foreign language.

B) To teach only foreign words from the native language of her four ELL students.

C) To use the ELL students' native languages as a start for an extensive study of foreign language words.

D) To teach 2-3 foreign l language words that are now in English and let it go at that.

108) As Mr. Adams exits his school building, he notices that Mr. Mark, a new teacher, is leading a group of happy looking fifth graders back into the building. They are carrying all kinds of free pamphlets and circulars from a local coffee house. Mr. Adams immediately asks Mr. Mark why the class went to that coffee house during the lunch break. When he hears Mr. Mark's answer, he is delighted:

A) Mr. Mark says they went looking for environmental print and words with a café and latte root.

B) Mr. Mark says they didn't spend any money and got free hot chocolate.

C) The children will have to summarize a pamphlet as homework.

D) All of the above.

109) Mr. Adams has complained to Mr. Mark that there are too many newspapers piled up in his classroom. Mr. Mark has responded that he does not want to throw away these piled up newspapers because:

A) They can be used for letter–sound correspondence.

B) They represent environmental print.

C) They can be used to create print-meaning signs.

D) All of the above.

110) In Ms. Francine's class, dictionary use is a punishment. Mr. Adams is:

A) Pleased with the way that Ms. Francine approaches dictionary use

B) Unconcerned with this approach to the use of the dictionary

C) Convinced that the teacher should model her own fascination and pleasure in using the dictionary for the children.

D) Delighted by the fact that children are being forced to use the dictionary.

111) Dictionary study:

    A) can begin in grades 1 or 2.

    B) can begin in pre-K using the lush picture dictionaries.

    C) should start on grade three level.

    D) a and b.

112) An excellent research project that can combine dictionary study with science research would be:

    A) A student authored dictionary terms and phrases about earthworms.

    B) A teacher developed specialized dictionary of words and phrases about. earthworms.

    C) A collection of articles on earthworms put together by the school librarian.

    D) b and c.

113) A veteran teacher waited for her adult daughter outside of her daughter's first class in the Teaching of Reading. As she and her daughter talked about the first session of the course, the teacher never heard an explicit mention of the teaching of reading. All she heard about was:

    A) Learning about narratives.

    B) Dealing with text structures.

    C) Constructing meaning.

    D) All of the above.

114) Making inferences from the text means that the reader:

    A) Is making informed judgments based on available evidence.

    B) Is making a guess based on prior experiences.

    C) Is making a guess based on what the reader would like to be true of the text.

    D) All of the above.

115) Sometimes children can be asked to demonstrate their understanding of a text in a non-written format. This might include all of the following except:

A) A story map.

B) A Venn diagram.

C) Storyboarding a part of the story with dialogue bubbles.

D) Retelling or paraphrasing.

116) A very bright child in a grade one class came from a family which did not a have a strong oral story telling or story reading tradition in its native language. This child would need support in developing:

A) Letter-sound correspondence skills.

B) Schemata for generic concepts most children have in their memories and experiences based on family oral traditions and read a loud.

C) Oral expressiveness.

D) b and c.

117) The concerned parent whose child had a visual impairment wanted as much help for him as the teacher and the school district could give her. She begged: "Please, he didn't attend pre-school, he has no prior knowledge." Strictly speaking this is:

A) Correct, since he didn't get pre-school experiences.

B) Incorrect, since prior knowledge covers everyone's experiences.

C) Incorrect, since he did have prior knowledge experiences but these didn't match those of many of his peers, so he would need to enhance his prior knowledge.

D) b and c

118) **Mr. Mark is a brand new teacher who is not from the neighborhood where his school is located. He is a bit nervous as this is his first teaching assignment. He does not yet know how to relax enough to get his students to activate prior experience. He should:**

A) Try a free recall question: Tell us what you know about...

B) Try an unstructured Question: Let's talk About...

C) Use word association: What do you associate X with?

D) All of the above.

119) **Among the literary strategies that teachers can use to activate prior knowledge are:**

A) Predicting and previewing a story.

B) Story mapping.

C) Venn diagramming.

D) Linear arrays.

120) **Ms. Angel has to be certain that her fourth graders know the characteristics of the historical fiction genre. She can best support them in becoming comfortable with this genre by:**

A) Providing sequel and prequel writing opportunities using that genre.

B) Reading them many different works from that genre.

C) a and b.

D) Having them look up the definition of that genre in a literary encyclopedia.

121) **Author's viewpoint questions stump Gary. His teacher can help him by asking him during their reading conferences:**

A) If Gary feels the book he is reading, is it just right for him.

B) What the author would say about what the character is doing in the story.

C) How the story can be changed to another genre.

D) If Gary wants to read more books by this author.

122) Ms. Clark-is seen by outside observers from her district, seated in front of her class of sixth graders with a notebook in her lap and an easel. She reads aloud from a book and then writes down a series of questions. As she reads along, she sometimes writes down the answers to her own questions. This is most likely:

A) A sign that Ms. Clark is uncertain of her own comprehension capacity.

B) She is modeling self questioning for the children.

C) She is aware that she is being watched and wants to make a good impression.

D) All of the above.

123) Bill has been called up to the teacher for an individual conference. She asks him to retell one of the books he has listed on his weekly log. He begins and is still talking 7 minutes later. Most probably, Bill:

A) Told the entire story with all its details and minor characters.

B) May or may not have really gotten the main points and perspectives of the story.

C) May have really liked the Story.

D) None of the above.

124) Ms. Ancess used to take time to have her children memorize major poems and even had an assembly for parents and school staff where the children dramatically recited various poems. Now that she is worried about the children's reading scores, she doesn't want to waste time with this memorization. Actually if she still includes this high interest, child-centered experience:

A) The children can use their oral fluency and her modeling as a bridge for enhanced comprehension.

B) The children can get a sense of "ownership" of the words.

C) Children and parents will have a "break" from worrying about the test.

D) None of the above.

125) To help children with "main idea" questions, the teacher should:

A) Give out a strategy sheet on the main idea for children to place in their reader's notebooks.

B) Model responding to such a question as part of guided reading.

C) Have children create "main idea questions" to go with their writings.

D) All of the above.

Answer Key

1. C	46. B	91. C
2. C	47. C	92. D
3. C	48. D	93. D
4. A	49. C	94. D
5. B	50. B	95. B
6. C	51. A	96. D
7. B	52. D	97. B
8. B	53. C	98. D
9. C	54. B	99. B
10. D	55. B	100. A
11. D	56. C	101. D
12. B	57. C	102. D
13. C	58. B	103. D
14. D	59. C	104. D
15. C	60. B	105. B
16. B	61. C	106. D
17. C	62. D	107. C
18. B	63. B	108. D
19. D	64. A	109. D
20. C	65. D	110. C
21. B	66. D	111. D
22. C	67. B	112. A
23. C	68. C	113. C
24. B	69. B	114. A
25. B	70. D	115. D
26. B	71. C	116. B
27. B	72. D	117. D
28. B	73. A	118. D
29. C	74. D	119. A
30. C	75. A	120. C
31. B	76. C	121. B
32. B	77. C	122. B
33. C	78. B	123. A
34. B	79. D	124. A
35. A	80. D	125. D
36. C	81. C	
37. B	82. C	
38. D	83. C	
39. D	84. B	
40. B	85. C	
41. C	86. D	
42. C	87. C	
43. A	88. D	
44. D	89. C	
45. B	90. B	

Rationales for Sample Questions

1. This is a sheer memorization question. By definition, phonemic awareness falls under the phonological awareness umbrella. All of the other choices do not deal with the DIFFERENCE between the two types of awareness.

2. Another memorization question which can only be answered by either knowing Adams's theory or by knowing that the other theorists listed did not present that theory. Anywhere from 10-15% of the questions on the certification tests are based on knowledge of the theorists and key terms associated with their theories.

3. This question involves the test taker's knowing that in reading the term "oddity task" involves identification of an odd sound within a series of like sounds. Choice A dealing with mathematics plays on that discipline's definition of odd which would not be tested on a foundations of reading exam. The other choices are "common sense definitions" of oddity which are not appropriate answers for a test in reading.

4. The key word here is EXCEPT which will be highlighted in upper case on the test as well. All of the options are correct aspects of phonological awareness except the first one, A, because phonological awareness DOES NOT involve print.

5. This question requires knowledge of running records and familiarity with error recording and miscues. The test taker has to know that this is the standard format for a running record of reading behaviors and that choices "C" and "D" deal with attitudes and feelings which are not part of the running records used as part of the balanced literacy approach.

6. Choice A is not correct. All children are capable of becoming good readers and the other choices, given Ms. James's dedication, are not the most likely reason these three children (a minority of the class) are struggling.

7. The answer is "B" because all of the other options are essential for record keeping. The key word here is "EXCEPT."

8. The answer is "B" because the teacher does not want the room to appear more spacious, but wants parents to have a feel for the book bags which indicate the primacy of reading.

9. The answer is "C" and this is a memorization question.

10. All the answers are correct.

11. Given the fact this is a kindergarten in a public housing project, she will be most successful with wordless picture books, since there is no guarantee the children have had prior exposure to the other types of books listed. The answer "D" will allow them to construct a story from the pictures.

12. The answer is "B" because the question details that the adults are seated two by two holding copies of the same book. This is the buddy reading style.

13. The answer is "C" and this is a memorization question.

14. The answer is "D", Marie Clay, and this is a name you "have to know" from this guide or your courses.

15. This is a classic manifestation of "C", the logographic phrase of phonics learning.

16. The answer is "B", and again this answer would grow out of teaching experience and familiarity with manipulatives or reading this guide.

17. The answer is "C" because in today's balanced literacy classroom, a wall is a word wall.

18. The answer is "B" and this is a familiar device in today's reading classroom.

19. The answer is "D" and this is a key definition which should be memorized.

20. The answer is "C" by definition; also a teacher would never get into the other personal comments which are offered as choices with a second grader.

21. This is a question that any English literature or Reading major can answer. The answer is "B."

22. This is another question using current terminology. While all the other choices make sense, "C" is correct because a book that is used to teach reading and writing is called an Anchor book.

23. "C" is the only correct answer choice because small refers to group size.

24. The answer is "B" and this term is in the Glossary.

25. This IS a deliberately tricky question. Each of the choices has merit. The best choice is "B" because that one is confirmed by current research.

26. This one is "B" because Gracie is a neighborhood child and shouldn't be having these difficulties with pronunciation.

27. This is one you can work out. The answer is "B" because obviously Ronald's parents will not be singing with him and doing lots of read alouds.

28. All of these choices have an element of truth in them, but go with "B" which reflects research results.

29. The answer is "C" because all logs need to have dates and standards.

30. The answer is "C" and it is a definition question.
If you missed it, re-read through the Glossary.

31. The behavior described here only matches one reading activity, "B."

32. This is another deliberately tricky question. All of the answers may appeal to you, but, choice "B" is the theoretical way to describe what the teacher is doing when he or she writes down what the children are saying.

33. This is a standard part of "book holding", so that the answer is "C."

34. The key word here is "EXCEPT" and environmental print is not defined as print in a library book, so choice "B" is the right one.

35. Ironically "A" is correct because book handling as defined in reading, does not include putting covers on books.

36. Key word in this question is "best" and the answer is "C" because this type of a book is best for teaching and display.

37. This is another deliberately tricky question, since all of the answers make sense, but only "B" is correct because that is the definition of "WHOLE" in balanced literacy.

38. The answer is "D" and is another definition question.

39. The answer is "D." All of the above is the correct answer because captions, glossaries and diagrams are but three of the text features that students need to be able to identify in a text. Other text features include headings, charts, maps, indexes, and tables

40. This is a question, you can reason out. The most complex task described here is "B.".

41. This is a definition question and the answer is "C."

42. This too is a definition question and the answer is "C."

43. The answer is "A." The fact that Mr. Gentry wants his class to use this for both reading and writing , should help you pick the right choice even if you don't know the answer.

44. The answer is "D." Flesch was a proponent of the phonics approach to reading in his book "Why Johnny Can't Read" which was essentially a critique of the American educational system. Neither of the other three choices propose explicit teaching of phonics to help children master reading.

45. The answer is "B" and a definition question.

46. The answer is "B" and is a definition question. If you are missing many definitions, perhaps make flash cards of the Glossary words and study them intensively.

47. The answer is "C," Expository and Narrative. Fiction and non-fiction are genres, Primary and pre-K are grade levels, and Wordless and text rich are types of books for young children.

48. This is a tricky question because all of the choices have an element of truth in them. But the best choice is "D" because it includes the special approaches Barbara will have to take with her ELL and special needs students.

49. Functional literacy refers to knowing things that students have to do on a day to day basis. Reading a recipe is classified as functional literacy because students learn how to read directions to perform a task. The answer is "C."

50. Coupons, like want ads are functional the families can fill in or act on. The answer is "B."

51. The answer is "A" because the BIG BOOK is a good visual display tool, ' .

52. This is a deliberately misleading question; all the test taker can know for certain is that Margaret's first language is NOT English. You know she is an ELL student because the question talks about her "first language." The answer is "D."
53. The focus on letters and sounds is "C" a phonics approach.

54. This is another definition question; read the definition section carefully before the exam. The answer has to be "B."

55. The term is "B" recognition vocabulary. This is a definition you have to know.

56. Obviously, "B" can not be right. Generally, a caring teacher would not say "D," but "C" is the preferred wording in use now in reading classrooms.

57. Semantic cues are the hints that students can discern from the reading to help them make sense of the text. In some cases, the message of the text depends on the other words around them, so students learn how to determine the meaning from context clues. The answer must be "C."

58. This is another one of those answers using the language of linguistics in reading. The answer has to be "B," syntactic clues.

59. This question can actually only have a single correct answer. It is "C" because by definition a child from an ELL background does not have a strong accurate sense of what "sounds right" in English.

60. There is only one correct answer here and it is "B." This is a key principle of the running record.

61. While all of the choices are possibilities, the concept of the highly proficient reader tutoring leads to answer "C."

62. The answer is "D" and this has to be memorized and known.

63. Again the test taker has to find the choice which is incorrect and it is choice "B" when the teacher puts up a mandated word list.

64. By definition, a discussion group can convene only "A" after the children have read a work.

65. All of the answers will promote vocabulary, so the answer is "D."

66. The answer is "D" because all of the responses are correct.

67. There is only one correct answer here and it is logical, "B."

68. The correct answer is "C," 2-3 words. Teachers should select a small number of words for pre-teaching to allow the students time to comprehend the text and achieve the objectives related to the reading. For example, in a non-fiction text, these words could be key terms related to the main topic. Even students with an extensive oral vocabulary may not be able to recognize words in print because they are not words that they normally encounter in their reading. The activities the teacher plans in relation to the words will help the students internalize the strategies more readily when only a few words are selected each time.

69. This is another one where the correct answer is "B" and only "D" is an unlikely choice.

70. This is one you can reason through and choose "D" easily.

71. This is one you can reason through, if you know that generally during READ ALOUD you do not stop to explain many words. You would not want to give material for independent or shared reading where so many words had to be explained. Hence the correct choice is "C," guided reading.

72. The answer is "D" because those are the "just right percentages."
73. The answer by definition is "A" because if "just right." is synonymous with the independent reading level.

74. The answer is "D" and related to taking a child's running record.

75. This is choice "A" which is the definition of decodable.

76. Students learn at different rates, therefore students in any class will be at varying levels of learning. By differentiating instruction and incorporating assessment **for** learning rather than assessment **of** learning, teachers can help students succeed. When teachers assess student growth over time and monitor the areas in which they are experiencing difficulty, they can alter the instruction and the activities to match student needs. The answer is "C."

77. This is a definition question and the answer is "C."

78. While this is also a definition question, choice "B" is one that a linguist would choose.

79. "D" is the answer here and it also makes good sense to the test taker.

80. This is a question the literate test taker should be able to "reason" through. Vocabulary introduced by children and a good text with opportunities to expand vocabulary are needed. Answer "D" which includes both "A" and "B" is the right choice.

81. The astute test taker should get this right whether he or she actually knows these materials or not. "Hierarchical" appears in both the question and in the correct choice "C."

82. The answer is "C" and this is a definition question.

83. The answer is "C."

84. Answer "B."

85. The answer can only be "C" and should be part of the test taker's theoretical background.

86. The answer is "D" and historically these have been used to teach Greek and Latin roots.

87. This is related to phonics and the answer is "C."

88. The answer here is "D" and all of these graphic organizers would work with the topic of apples.

89. The answer is "C" and the trick is to notice the "better use of context" in the question and match it up with "C," contextual redefinition training.

90. The answer is "B" and it is one that is confirmed in theory and is referenced in this guide.

91. The answer is "C," a definition question.

92. This is easy to see that it is "D", scaffolded by the teacher. The child has been assisted by the teacher as he prepared the book review.

93. The answer is "D" since all the options are good ones.

94. The answer is again "D" since all the options work.

95. This is a tricky question and requires that the test taker know the very specific definition of the STOP and THINK strategy to know that the only correct answer is "B."

96. Again this has to do with the way "responsibility for your own learning" is now defined and the answer is "D."

97. This is a truism of ELL education and the answer is "B."

98. This is one where the correct answer of "D" is also the commonsense response that a literate test taker would select.

99. There is only a correct answer here by definition and "B" is it.

100. Again these are all definitions which the test taker should memorize before the test (see the Glossary in this guide). The correct answer is "A."

101. Again this is a definition answer and the correct choice is "D."

102. This is all about what a standardized test means and answer is "D."

103. The answer is "d," but this is a question anyone who has gotten through the coursework or taught, should have no problem with.

104. This is a question someone who has taught or gone through course work should ace to get "D." Remember going online with children and using approved search engines is fine.

105. The best answer is "B" and involves knowing about the "author's chair" concept.

106. This a question where the correct answer "D" makes good common and educational sense.

107. This is a question where you can reason your way to the correct answer, "C." "A" sounds chauvinistic and unrealistic and "B" is limiting and teaching only 2-3 words is not a good use of instructional time.

108. This is a question where the correct choice is "D" and makes good teaching and learning sense.

109. This is a question where choice "D" makes good sense to a teacher who knows the value of having newspapers for class projects.

110. The word "punishment" in the question should alert the test taker to the answer that the only choice "C" can be right.

111. This is a question that any literate test taker who has been in a children's book section recently can answer. Choice "D" is correct.

112. This question is tricky in that only choice "A", which deals with a student product, is correct. The others are all adult centered.

113. The only answer here is "C" which emphasizes "constructing meaning," the current phrase for "reading."

114. This is a definition question that a literate test taker can answer based on the general definition of inferences. The answer is "A."

115. Answer "D" is correct. Retelling and paraphrasing can be in oral form whereas the other choices all involve writing or the use of pencil and paper. By asking students to retell a story, the teacher can determine the level of comprehension. Of course, this has to be modeled for the student, especially paraphrasing, so that the student relates the important facts or events and does not include any information that is not necessary.

116. Although the question appears to be a very technical one, it actually can be easily and correctly answered by seeing how choice "B" echoes the fact that most children would have schemata based on family oral traditions.

117. This is a question which a caring and literate test taker could correctly answer and get "D" as a response. Everyone has prior knowledge of some sort.

118. Again this is a common sense question and "D" is the correct choice.

119. This is a question that a literate test taker could answer and the best choice is "A" because in their predictions, children evidence prior knowledge.

120. The answer is "C. "Online encyclopedias meet the information technology outcomes that align with language arts outcomes. When students are taught to avail of the online encyclopedias, it can save enormous amounts of space in the classroom as well as trips to the library. Students can complete all their work on the computer without having to stop and thumb through a regular encyclopedia to find the information they need.

121. This is a question where the correct choice "B" is the only one that mentions an author.

122. The only answer here is "B" because this is a technique children are taught and Ms. Clark is modeling it. "C" is insulting to Ms. Clark and "A" is insulting as well.

123. The only obvious choice after 7 minutes of talk is "A."

124. Choice "A" is the best theory answer here.

125. This is one where all the options are right. The answer is "D."

Constructed Response Questions

Constructed Response Question One

Jean is a first year teacher who is taking over the classroom of a thirty-year veteran teacher who is retiring. Jean goes in to meet with the teacher. The teacher, Ms. Banks, talks about the importance of teaching the young first graders the concepts of print.

She gives Jean a list of these concepts and suggests that Jean create some assessment format so that she can be certain that all of her first graders learn these concepts. She also tells Jean that she will be volunteering her time in a neighborhood preschool program close to her home and so she will be taking her private books and materials with her. She suggests that Jean go over the list of concepts of print and consider the needs of her class as she prepares for teaching this crucial set of skills. Before Jean leaves the classroom, Ms. Banks tells her that the kindergarten teacher has let her know that three children who will be in her class next year are from ELL backgrounds where their families are not involved in oral story telling or reading from native language texts.

Ms. Banks' concepts of print list:

- STARTS ON LEFT

- GOES FROM LEFT TO RIGHT

- RETURN SWEEP

- MATCHES WORDS BY POINTING

- POINTS TO JUST ONE WORD

- POINTS TO FIRST AND LAST WORD

- POINTS TO 1 LETTER

- POINTS TO FIRST AND LAST LETTER

- PARTS of the BOOK: Cover, Title Page, Dedication page, Author and Illustrator

Jean thanks Ms. Banks for all of this help and asks if she can send Ms. Banks some of her teaching ideas for Concepts of Print and the ways she plans to differentiate instruction for her ELL students before the end of the year. Ms. Banks smiles and says she feels good to know that her classroom will be taken over by Jean. She promises to review Jean's response.

Constructed Response Answer One

First, as far as assessment for the key skills of concepts of print, I have decided that it is very important that I have a record of when and how well each of my students masters these concepts. After much thought, I realized that I will be keeping assessment notebooks for all of my students as part of my general reading and teaching. Therefore, I plan to print out all the key concepts of print on an 8" x 11" piece of paper in a grid format. This sheet will be included with other assessment grids for each individual child.

After conferencing with the child and I determine the child has demonstrated mastery of a particular concept, I will check it off on the grid and date that mastery. If I have other comments to make about the child's level of mastery or fluency, I will make an anecdotal notation about the child as well. I think that this will guarantee that I have a detailed checklist record and anecdotal record of all my children's individual progress on concepts of print.

I plan to use big books and many of the latest picture books, including Caldecott award winners in demonstrating and sharing with children many of the concepts of print. I will do much of my instruction mini-lessons. In fact I intend to use some of my own favorite alphabet books to introduce these conventions. With a book like Clare Beaton's, *Zoe and her Zebra*, I can easily and naturally cover the title page, cover, illustrator, and also manage to engage the children in the use of repetitive language.

Once I have shared that delightful book with the children as a read-aloud, we will be able to return to it again and use the repetitive language of it in its big book format to demonstrate for the children how they can point under each word as if there is a button to push. I can also demonstrate for the children how they should start at the top of the text and move from left to right. I will model going back to the left and under the previous line in a return weep.

After modeling this as part of the mini-lesson, the children can be divided in small groups or pairs and take other big book and practice the "point under each word" and the "return sweep" as part of "shared reading" or buddy reading. I should be able to identify some highly proficient readers who will be happy to serve as 'buddy' reader/tutors for the ELL children. I will ask that these "buddies" take time in small groups to work on another book from the alphabet book collection to share with the class as a whole. The use of the alphabet books also helps me to get some time in on the alphabetic principle.

I will also do a classroom writing workshop using the original alphabet book I use for the read-aloud, say *Zoe and Her Zebra* as a model for creating our own story. Perhaps we will call it *Barry and his Boxer*. In this way we will have a concrete literary product that demonstrates the children's mastery of and fluency in the concepts of print as they create an "in style of" story about a peer using illustrations, title page, dedication page, numbering of pages, back and front cover and other concepts of print.

I think that using individualized assessments, a group/class collaborative writing project, and an anchor alphabet book will help me successfully teach the concepts of print and address the needs of my ELL learners as well.

Constructed Response Question Two

Marianne has been selected as one of a team of teachers who will start teaching in a brand new school building that has been under construction for several years. While Marianne, a grade three teacher , is thrilled to be moving into new facilities, she is a bit overwhelmed to have to "set up her room" all over again at the new site. Her administrator, Mr. Adams, tells her that there are five new teachers with no previous experience teaching primary school age children who will be on staff. He tells her that these educators could really use help setting up their classrooms.

Marianne smiles and decides that she would very much like to use her set-up of her own grade three classroom as a workshop and demonstration for setting up a literacy teaching environment for these new staff members. Mr. Adams thinks that is a great idea and asks Marianne for an agenda and for a general description of what she will cover in her three hour workshop so that he can give it to the district office.

Marianne is happy to comply because she realizes that she will be assisting new colleagues and getting ten helping hands to help her set up all the materials she has accumulated over a twenty-year career.

Constructed Response Answer Two

The concept of sharing with new colleagues how to set up a classroom is very exciting to me. I know, based on my experiences, how crucial a well-planned and conceptualized space is for young learners' literacy learning. Therefore this is an agenda for what I will cover in my three hour in service session for my new colleagues.

First, I will discuss how whatever the size of the classroom space, it must be sectioned off into the following areas: a meeting area, with a sofa or "soft" setting; a chair, easel and basket to store book bags; a conference table; children's tables; and bin/basket main area for trade books; and another space for computers.
I may even give out a diagram of my classroom from my old school and some pictures. We will discuss collaboratively how I will set up my own new space as well as how they will want to set up their own spaces to allow for different uses of space within their own classrooms.

I will get into the issue of whether or not they want to have a traditional desk or use smaller tables for everyone. I think that they will need time to consider their own teaching styles in this regard. All teachers need to set up a space where they can easily confer with children and have access to individual assessment notebooks, reading folders (plus poetry/spelling, reading response, and handwriting notebooks) for all their students. I intend to show them how to prepare these folders for each child and how to store them so they can get to them when they need to make additional annotations for each child. Given the fact that I am working with new colleagues, I suspect that this will take at least an hour and a half of our time. I am also going to model for them a weekly reading log.

Most important of all, I am going to spend the major amount of time talking to them about the book bins as I place mine around the classroom. I will show them how to label the books using the Fountas and Pinnell levels and how to arrange the book bins with the spines out so that the children can see the books. Together we will examine how the bookcases should be close to the walls and the expository books should be separated from the narrative texts. I will also get together my audio-cassettes and book sets so that they can see how I set up my read-along center for all my children. I will share some dual language tapes I use with ELL students as well. I have some extra "author's hats" and author's chair slipcovers I will share with them.

I also intend to show them how to select big books for the easel display and anchor books to be shown there as well. By the way, I will also coach them how to write away for supplies and how to store supplies in common areas so that some children are not missing necessary materials for class activities.

Even though we are focusing on literacy, I am going to show them where to store mathematics materials, other texts, and art supplies.   I will end the session by making sure that they know where to place their chart wall and the word wall. If I have time, I will sit down with each of them and start them on the word wall and some key charts for their first day. They will leave my room with an actual experience of setting up a literacy environment, plus viable teaching and reading suggestions for the first day. Most importantly, I will be available for an in-school classroom consultation, if necessary.

Tips and Reflections for tackling the Constructed Response Questions:

- Use as many phrases and words from the question as possible in your response.

- Be specific. Mention specific books, authors, theorists, and strategies you have studied. Even though this is a test about the teaching of reading, make specific use of children's trade books and literature if appropriate.

- Use as many details as you are given in the question to make your response. Write no more than 5-7 moderately brief paragraphs. The more you write, the larger the margin for error. Check your spelling, grammar and check to see that you answered everything that was asked, but no more than what was asked. Be positive and proactive about your ability to respond to whichever situation is presented.

- Stick with strategies, teaching ideas, and methods that are tried and true.

- Reread your writing at least twice for spelling and grammatical errors.

Additional Professional Citations

Block, Cathy Collins. (2002). *Comprehension Instruction: Research Based Practices.* New York: The Guilford Press.

Calkins, Lucy McCormick. (2001). *The Art of Teaching Reading.* New York: Longman.

Cambourne, Briane. (2002). "Conditions for Literacy Learning." *The Reading Teacher*, 55, (8): 758-62.

Cambourne, Briane. (1993). *The Whole Story: Natural Learning and the Acquisition of Literacy in the Classroom.* Auckland, NZ: Ashton, Scholastic.

Cunningham, Patricia M. (2000). *Phonics They Use: Words for Reading and Writing.* 3rd Edition. New York: Addison Wesley Longman.

Evidence Based Reading Instruction. (2002) Articles from International Reading Association. Newark, Delaware: *International Reading Association.*

Hoyt, Linda. (2002). *Make it Real-Strategies for Success with Informational Texts.* Portsmouth, NH: Heinemann.

Kimball-Lopez, Kimberley. (1999). *Connecting with Traditional Literature.* Boston: Allyn and Bacon.

Moustafa, Margaret. (1997). *Beyond Traditional Phonics.* Portsmouth, NH: Heinemann.

Owocki, Gretchen. (2003). *Strategic Instructions for K-3 Students.* Portsmouth, NH: Heinemann.

Owacki, G, and Y. Goodman. (2002*). Kidwatching-Documenting Children's Literacy Development.* Portsmouth, NH: Heinemann.

Quindlen, Anna. (1998). *How Reading Changed My Life.* New York: Ballantine Books, 1998.

Routman, Regie. (2000). *Conversations.* Portsmouth, NH: Heinemann.

Schultz, C. (2000). *How Partner Reading Fosters Literacy Development in First Grade Students.* Action Research project, Saginaw Valley State University, University Center, Michigan.

Short, K., J. Harste and C. Burke. (1996). *Creating Classrooms for Authors and Inquirers.* Portsmouth, NH: Heinemann.

Trelease, Jim. (2001). *The Read-Aloud Handbook.* 4th Ed. New York: Penguin.

Wilde, Sandra. (2000). *Miscue Analysis Made Easy: Building on Student Strengths.* Portsmouth, NH: Heinemann.

Wilde, Sandra. (2000). *Reading Made Easy.* Portsmouth, NH: Heinemann.

XAMonline, INC. 21 Orient Ave. Melrose, MA 02176

Toll Free number 800-509-4128

TO ORDER Fax 781-662-9268 OR www.XAMonline.com

ILLINOIS TEACHER CERTIFICATION SYSTEM - ICTS - 2006

P0#   Store/School:

Address 1:

Address 2 (Ship to other):

City, State Zip

Credit card number_____-_____-_____-_____   expiration_____

EMAIL _____

PHONE   FAX

13# ISBN 2007	TITLE	Qty	Retail	Total
978-1-58197-977-0	ICTS Assessment of Professional Teaching Tests 101-104			
978-1-58197-976-3	ICTS Basic Skills 096			
978-1-58197-996-1	ICTS Elementary-Middle Grades 110			
978-1-58197-997-8	ICTS Elementary-Middle Grades 110 Sample Questions			
978-1-58197-981-7	ICTS English Language Arts 111			
978-1-58197-991-6	ICTS Family and Consumer Sciences 172			
978-1-58197-987-9	ICTS Foreign Language- French Sample Test 127			
978-1-58197-988-6	ICTS Foreign Language- Spanish 135			
978-1-58197-992-3	ICTS Library Information Specialist 175			
978-1-58197-983-1	ICTS Mathematics 115			
978-1-58197-989-3	ICTS Physical Education 144			
978-1-58197-995-4	ICTS Principal 186			
978-1-58197-993-0	ICTS Reading Teacher 177			
978-1-58197-994-7	ICTS School Counselor 181			
978-1-58197-978-7	ICTS Science- Biology 105			
978-1-58197-979-4	ICTS Science- Chemistry 106			
978-1-58197-980-0	ICTS Science- Earth and Space Science 108			
978-1-58197-984-8	ICTS Science: Physics 116			
978-1-58197-982-4	ICTS Social Science- History 114			
978-1-58197-985-5	ICTS Social Science- Political Science 117			
978-1-58197-986-2	ICTS Social Science- Psychology 118			
978-1-58197-975-6	ICTS Special Education Learning Behavior Specialist I 155			
978-1-58197-990-9	ICTS Visual Arts Sample Test 145			

	SUBTOTAL	
FOR PRODUCT PRICES GO TO WWW.XAMONLINE.COM	Ship	$8.25
	TOTAL	

Printed in the United States
148419LV00001B/134/A